D0852221

E

The World & All That Is in It

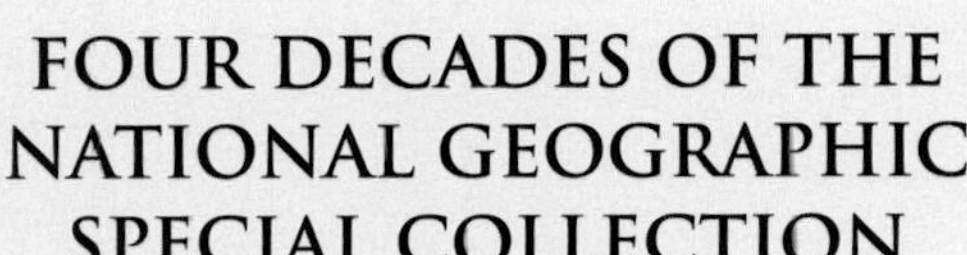

FOUR DECADES OF THE NATIONAL GEOGRAPHIC SPECIAL COLLECTION

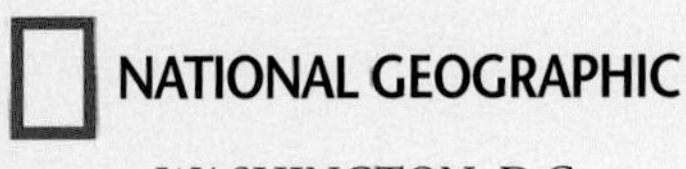

NATIONAL GEOGRAPHIC

WASHINGTON, D.C.

CONTENTS

Opposite: *Haloed by wirelike feathers, the crowned crane is one of the more elegant species along the Nile River.*

E

FOREWORD

THE WORLD & ALL THAT IS IN IT

By Gilbert M. Grosvenor
Chairman of the Board, National Geographic Society

How often is one given the opportunity to participate in a spectacularly successful publishing venture that produces and sells 1,800,000 books from a single promotion? Once in a lifetime, if you're lucky. I got lucky.

Those fortunate stars were surely aligning in 1954, when I started working at *National Geographic* magazine, because soon afterward the Society began diversifying its offerings to members. We embraced television, produced atlases and globes, and began publishing large, handsome, lavishly illustrated books.

Yet the Special Collection—or Special Publications, as the series was originally called—was born under a different, if somewhat exalted, set of circumstances. For one thing, their midwife was First Lady Jacqueline Kennedy. In 1961, Mrs. Kennedy asked for our help in compiling an illustrated guidebook to the White House, which we agreed to do as a public service to the nation. *Living White House: An Historic Guide* was so successful that we ended up providing more books: on the Capitol, the Washington Monument, and the Supreme Court. All were produced by five hard-working *National Geographic* editors who, on top of their regular magazine duties, frequently pulled all-nighters to meet these additional deadlines.

Robert L. Breeden, a brilliant picture editor, was in charge, and inspired by his experience with these public service books he conceived the idea of Special Publications, distinct from our regular book program and consisting of an annual offering of four smaller, tighter, more focused volumes driven by a single promotion. I realized that this proposed project might change the nature of publishing at the Geographic, for a key element of the plan was having Society members help select in advance the books we would produce.

I had majored in statistical psychology in college, but whenever I had floated the idea of title-testing at the Geographic, I had met resistance. Here was an opportunity to prove my contention that inexpensive title-testing might help us predict a book's popularity and would help us better serve our members.

I wanted to be part of this exciting venture. The timing couldn't have been more perfect, but my father,

In the best of National Geographic tradition, the books in the Special Collection have featured exotic images from far-flung places. The caption on this Bushman matron from Vanishing Peoples of the Earth *(1968) noted that her music expressed the life of her people, "sometimes gay, sometimes sad."*

"AS RICH IN INTEREST AND VARIED IN SCOPE AS THE SOCIETY'S MAGAZINE ITSELF," WROTE MELVILLE BELL GROSVENOR IN MARCH 1966, INTRODUCING THE NEW BOOK SERIES.

Melville Bell Grosvenor, the Society's President and Editor of the magazine, was only lukewarm. He loved his atlases and those big, handsome, illustrated volumes we published. But at age 63 and absorbed in the challenge of dramatically modernizing *National Geographic* magazine, he was reluctant to take on four more books a year. Then one day on the golf course I urged him to embrace Breeden's proposal. This distracted him so much that he shanked several shots. That did it. He turned to me and blurted out: "OK, OK—if you young turks want to take this thing on, I'll support it—but it's your baby!"

Breeden and staff were in business. Youth had prevailed, and we had an opportunity to shine. I was to play a minor role as executive editor, and working with Bob Breeden, Don Crump, Mary Ann Harrell, Phil Silcott, and Will Gray was not only an instructive experience for me: It was a fun one as well.

Our first series of four Special Publications was released in 1966, and as we predicted, they proved immensely popular. We were off and running, and each year a new series would be released, the subjects ranging from anthropology to zoology. Whether a sailing adventure, a profile of Jane Goodall or Jacques Cousteau, a portrait of Australia, or a voyage down the Nile, each volume would combine sparkling text with sumptuous illustrations. I suspect thousands of hikers followed in our authors' footsteps after reading *The Appalachian Trail* or *The Pacific Crest Trail.* My own favorites were the volumes on hidden wilderness areas or special interest titles like *Nature's Healing Arts, American Craftsmen,* or *Those Inventive Americans.*

Year in and year out, such books—more than 56 million volumes to date—were devoured by our members. As gratifying as this was, it was equally satisfying to me to see title-testing and membership surveys vindicated. These techniques soon spread throughout the Society, and as a result we were better able to answer our members' needs. And talk about membership loyalty—our records show that 60 percent of those people now receiving and enjoying Special Publications have been doing so for 20 years or more. It is gratifying to see that our efforts still have good results. We continue to evolve in concert with our members' needs, as we have for 120 years.

The Society's second President, Alexander Graham Bell, described the Geographic's sphere of interest as being quite literally "the world and all that is in it." So when we began compiling this volume—just a sampling of the remarkable range of writing and photography that has appeared in 43 years of Special Publications—no other title was seriously considered. This anthology, created to honor a long and splendid line of titles, is not just a celebration of marvelous books and the talented people who made them, but it is above all a reflection of that entangled, enchanting, and ever fascinating world they sought to portray.

THIS BOOK PRESENTS *selections from 24 of the 185 extraordinary volumes published between 1966 and 2009. To make the selection, we consulted many who know these books from over the decades—and still it was a task. Many great titles remain unmentioned, yet we hope that the selection represents the breadth and depth of the entire series, for so long a mainstay, enrichment, and delight for the National Geographic Society membership. In excerpting these passages, we chose not to alter the style of individual writers, even when it may differ from style today.* — *The Editor*

CHAPTER ONE

THE FIRST FOUR VOLUMES

Introduction by Robert L. Breeden

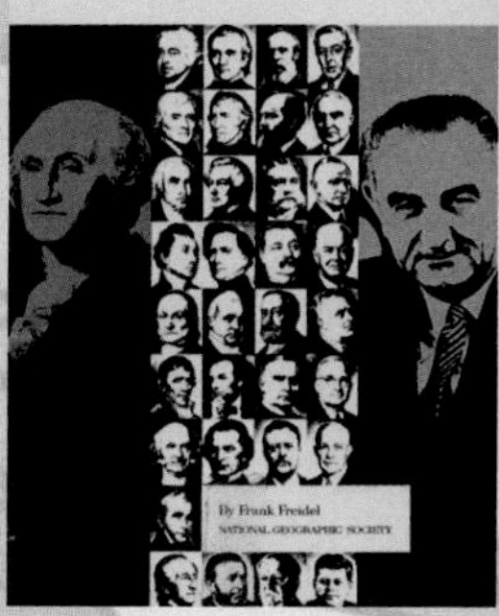

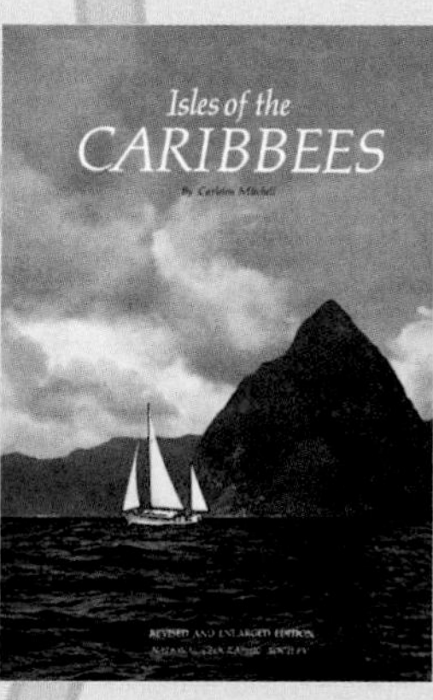

The four titles published in the program's first year, shown above, established the range of interests to be covered by the Special Collection: American history, world cultures, travel and adventure, and science and natural history.

Robert L. Breeden led the Special Publications division of the National Geographic Society for 25 years, as editor from its inception in 1965 until 1980 and as senior vice president until his retirement in 1990. Here he recalls the division's origin and the challenges of publishing its first four books in 1966-67.

If Jacqueline Kennedy had never been First Lady, this book would never have been written. She could never have imagined that a White House guidebook she initiated in 1961 would ultimately lead to a series of National Geographic books published over the next four decades.

Near the end of her first year as First Lady, Mrs. Kennedy requested that the newly formed White House Historical Association publish the first official guidebook of the White House in its 162-year history. She wanted to offer the thousands of visitors who toured the Executive Mansion an inexpensive, educational publication to help them recall their visit and learn more about the White House and its first families. Proceeds would go toward purchasing rare furnishings and works of art for a major restoration to reflect the history of the White House and the Presidency.

The Association turned to the National Geographic Society for help in publishing the book. The Society responded generously, offering all photography, editing, and production supervision as a public service. Because I had been an editor on a *National Geographic* White House article published earlier in the year, Dr. Melville Bell Grosvenor, then President and Editor, assigned me to produce the book with a handful of magazine staff members. On a crash schedule, we finished it in record time, and *The White House: An Historic Guide* went on sale on July 4, 1962, for one dollar a copy. The first edition of 250,000 copies sold out in less than 90 days, just as the next of many revisions went to press. Its immense success quickly inspired similar books on the Capitol and the Supreme Court.

The books were so overwhelmingly popular that I urged Dr. Grosvenor to consider forming a small department to produce them, and to publish a few small, highly illustrated books for our members. After studying the proposal with other Society officers, he agreed, and on July 1, 1965, the Special Publications division was created, with a staff of five.

WE FACED THE DAUNTING CHALLENGE OF continuing the public-service work and also producing four 200-page books in the following year—and in the years ahead. Our first task: to select the subjects for that initial series. Dr. Grosvenor had asked that we consider devoting each four-book series to a single subject, beginning with a set of biographies. We would start with a book on U.S. Presidents, followed by individual volumes on George Washington and Abraham Lincoln, with a fourth to be determined.

Shortly afterward, Dr. Grosvenor became fascinated with a magazine article and National Geographic television special then under way about Jane Goodall and her study of wild chimpanzees. "She's got to do a book for us!" he nearly shouted. "We'll make it the fourth one in your series." I watched his enthusiasm melt as I slowly recited the four subjects in sequence: Presidents, George Washington, Abraham Lincoln—and chimps. Confronted with that unhappy incongruity, we agreed to abandon the idea of limiting each series to just one

WE PRINTED AN UNPRETENTIOUS QUESTIONNAIRE THAT BEGAN SIMPLY, "MAY WE HAVE THE BENEFIT OF YOUR OPINIONS?" IT WENT TO 5,000 MEMBERS, AND AN INCREDIBLE 60 PERCENT RESPONDED.

subject. Instead we would do books with a wide range of titles, following the mantra of the magazine set down by Alexander Graham Bell, second President of the Society: to cover "the world and all that is in it."

Fortuitously, our members provided us with our first Special Publication, published in May 1966. *National Geographic* magazine had published a four-part series on the U.S. Presidents by Harvard historian Frank Freidel that brought hundreds of letters from readers asking us to combine the articles in a separate volume. Demand for the resulting book, *Our Country's Presidents,* sent it into nine editions.

In our second book, *The River Nile,* staff writer Bruce Brander captured the sense of adventure evoked by *National Geographic* articles about the Nile as far back as 1910. His arduous journey took him from the river's source to its delta 4,415 miles away.

A far different adventure unfolded in our third Special Publication, *Isles of the Caribbees,* written by veteran seaman Carleton Mitchell, whose sailing stories often appeared in the magazine. Aboard his yawl *Finisterre,* Mitchell cruised from Grenada to the Virgin Islands.

And, as Melville Grosvenor had insisted, Jane Goodall's aptly titled *My Friends the Wild Chimpanzees* rounded out the series.

LONG BEFORE WE BEGAN WORK ON JANE'S book, we had to start planning the next four subjects. As I studied the staff's list of some 20 suggestions, I wondered, "Why not involve our members in selecting books? Send them a questionnaire. Get their opinions." Since it was a new concept, I went over it the next day with Gilbert M. Grosvenor, our newly named editorial director, who later became Editor of the magazine and Chairman of the Society. He shared my enthusiasm, and together we selected the ten subjects we believed the Society should publish. The staff then wrote short descriptions of them, and we printed an unpretentious questionnaire that began simply, "May we have the benefit of your opinion?" It went to 5,000 randomly selected members; an incredible 60 percent responded!

The top four favorites became our second series: *Exploring Canada From Sea to Sea, World Beneath the Sea, The Revolutionary War,* and *Isles of the South Pacific.* Meanwhile, our questionnaires kept going out, and over time, the Society began using adaptations of them for other products.

We learned early that our books could unexpectedly bring humorous, sometimes hilarious moments—and also times of crisis. During work on Jane Goodall's chimp book, we found we lacked enough human-interest pictures, the hallmark of Geographic publications. We had plenty of photographs of chimpanzees, Jane, and the terrain, but few of Jane's crew or anyone else. Time was short. I cabled photographer Baron Hugo Van Lawick to telephone me at once.

His call came at 3 a.m. and was relayed from Nairobi through London to Washington—before the days of satellites, cell phones, or e-mail. The connection was terrible. I shouted to Hugo, "We need more pictures of people!" Silence. The London operator came on; could he assist by relaying the message? I declined his offer and shouted to Hugo again—and again—without success. The London operator now insisted on relaying. Exasperated, I relented and told him, "Please tell the baron to shoot more people!"

A startled "I beg your pardon?"—then silence. No doubt the London operator sensed a revolutionary plot was afoot.

IN *THE APPALACHIAN TRAIL,* PUBLISHED IN 1972, author Ron Fisher complained of nearly collapsing from exhaustion at the end of his first day of climbing. His two companions, he wrote, "mercifully lifted my thousand-pound pack from my back." His hyperbole was completely lost on a disbelieving member, who chided, "I doubt that your pack weighed a thousand pounds. My dining room table weighs 200 pounds, and I can hardly budge it."

There were darker, critical times, too. We were well along with *World Beneath the Sea,* our sixth book, when we found that the quality of author Jim Dugan's writing was falling below the level of his earlier work for the Society. Critique sessions and encouragement didn't help. In fear of missing our deadline, I cautiously suggested to Jim that we send other writers to cover and produce the remaining chapters for him, with the understanding that his name would appear as author and that he could freely edit and revise their work. Fortunately, he agreed. While Jim went off to work on an incomplete chapter, other writers fanned out to finish the book.

On June 1, 1966, a beautiful spring afternoon was shattered by the news that Jim Dugan had died of a heart attack after he emerged from a dive aboard a small submersible. Still stunned by the sudden death of a longtime friend of the Geographic, the writers assigned to complete the book wrote the remaining chapters under their own names.

The swiftness of a talented staff member averted another disaster. Coming off the Nile book, Bruce Brander undertook the challenge of writing *Australia,* our ninth Special Publication. After covering much of the continent's coast and outback, he delved into research, preparing for a return trip to finish his work. Without warning—and with our press date only weeks away—Bruce resigned, leaving half the book yet to be done.

I quickly called on Mary Ann Harrell, one of our original five staff members, to prepare immediately to fly to Sydney, where she started coverage of Australia's most populous area and Tasmania. In just six weeks, she handed in her manuscript—only days before we went to press.

Mary Ann had started as a researcher on that fledgling staff; she soon became a writer, and then one of our finest editors. Others followed much the same path. For me, one of my most gratifying experiences in Special Publications was witnessing an indefatigable staff take the opportunities offered by a fast-growing division.

A former intern, Don Crump began as a member of the core group and went on to lead the division. Serving briefly as a production manager, Ron Fisher evolved into the most prolific writer, author of 10 books and contributor to 19 more. Bill Allen, a young picture editor, became Editor of the magazine. At least three secretaries worked their way up to become editors, and researchers regularly took on writing assignments and often moved into editing. Those multitalented people, together with the many who followed, all contributed to the growth of a division that produced nearly 200 titles in its 43-year history—something the five of us on that original staff never dreamed would happen.

Modern and historical paintings illustrate key moments in the lives of the nation's chief executives. Here, George Washington gives the first Inaugural Address in New York City, April 30, 1789. The war hero was so nervous that his voice was sometimes inaudible; he apologized for being "unpracticed in ... civil administration."

Our Country's Presidents (1966)

by Frank Freidel

John Adams

SECOND PRESIDENT 1797-1801

JOHN ADAMS is known as the President who saved the United States from fighting a needless war. He once suggested for his epitaph, "Here lies John Adams, who took upon himself the responsibility of the peace with France, in the year 1800."

This was Adams's crowning achievement, but he was also one of the leading patriots in the long struggle for colonial rights, a prime mover for the Declaration of Independence, a valued diplomat, the first Vice President, and the second President.

Adams was a learned and thoughtful man, master of the classics and the law, and more remarkable as a political philosopher than as a politician. "People and nations are forged in the fires of adversity," he once asserted, doubtless thinking of his own as well as the American experience.

For several generations his forebears had farmed stony fields at Braintree in Massachusetts Bay Colony. There, in 1735, Adams was born. The house still stands, the oldest original Presidential birthplace. It and the smaller house next door, where his son John Quincy was born, are preserved as historic sites in what is now Quincy.

Though early identified with the patriot cause, John Adams, a Harvard-educated lawyer, undertook the unpopular task of defending the British officer who he felt was unjustly charged with responsibility for the Boston Massacre. The officer was acquitted.

Adams was distrustful of mobs, yet considered the Boston Tea Party, which dumped cargoes of taxed tea into the harbor, "the grandest event which has ever yet happened since the controversy with Britain opened."

He became one of the most vigorous delegates to the First and Second Continental Congresses. By the summer of 1776 he was a leader in the movement for independence.

Adams spent most of the remainder of the Revolutionary War on diplomatic missions, serving in France and Holland and helping negotiate the Treaty of Peace. From 1785 to 1788 he was Minister to the Court of St. James's, returning in time to be elected Vice President under George Washington. Adams's two terms as Vice President were frustrating experiences for a man of his vigor, intellect, and vanity. When he suggested an elaborate title for the President, his reward was to be himself mocked as "His Rotundity."

Like Washington, Adams seldom tried to act as a party leader; he left the organization of the Federalists to Hamilton. In his political thinking, Adams was more moderate than

Wife of one President, mother of another, Abigail Adams managed the Adams farm in Massachusetts during the Revolution. Experience in Paris and London as a diplomat's wife made her an astute First Lady. Adams's reliance on her good sense gave her the bitter nickname "Mrs. President." First mistress of the White House, she hung washing in the unfinished East Room to dry.

Burning with patriotic fire, strong-minded John Adams put oratory and law training to good use in the Revolutionary struggle. In the Continental Congress he led the floor fight for the Declaration of Independence.

24

PAINTING BY GILBERT STUART, NATIONAL GALLERY OF ART, GIFT OF MRS. ROBERT HOMANS

Painting by Edgar Parker, White House Collectio

Portraits of the Presidents and their wives bring history to life in Our Country's Presidents.

A series of *National Geographic* articles led to the one of the most popular books of the Special Collection, *Our Country's Presidents.* The author was Harvard professor and Franklin D. Roosevelt biographer Frank Freidel. Editor in Chief Melville Bell Grosvenor wrote the foreword, setting a personal, friendly tone for the book with reminiscences about meeting several Presidents, starting when he was a child, encounters Grosvenor likened to "shaking hands with history." The volume of mini-biographies similarly gives insight into the workings of these national leaders, as well as background on the problems they faced.

Freidel and editor Gilbert Grosvenor chose for the most part to present the Presidents in a straightforward, uncritical way. Understanding that administrations come in and out of favor from decade to decade, they gave us portraits that are still useful and informative.

About Hoover, Freidel writes, "Congress criticized him unfairly, making him the scapegoat for the depression." About Buchanan: "In a calmer age," he "might have been a successful President." For Pierce, Buchanan's successor, Freidel has only mild criticism: "Too much blame should not be assessed against [him], even though his amiability was more striking than his judgment." For the more recent Presidents he adopts a hands-off attitude, letting history be the judge. The resulting book is a paean to the office of the Presidency.

Carry a Big Stick

From Frank Freidel's portrait of the 26th President

Theodore Roosevelt brought excitement and strength to the Presidency. He led vigorously toward progressive reforms and a strong foreign policy, taking the view that he was a steward of the people, limited only by specific constitutional restrictions. In the popular eye he was the "buster of trusts" and wielder of a "big stick." "I did not usurp power," he later wrote, "but I did greatly broaden the use of executive power."

Roosevelt's youth differed sharply from that of the log-cabin Presidents. He was born to a well-to-do family in New York City in 1858; his brownstone home on East 20th Street is a national historic shrine. But Roosevelt, too, had to struggle—against

In 1914 former President Theodore Roosevelt, age 56, explored Brazil's River of Doubt. Three men died; Roosevelt got an abscess and jungle fever but recalled, "I had to go. It was my last chance to be a boy."

RUDYARD KIPLING RECALLED LISTENING TO ROOSEVELT IN THE EARLY 1890S. "I CURLED UP ON THE SEAT OPPOSITE AND LISTENED AND WONDERED, UNTIL THE UNIVERSE SEEMED TO BE SPINNING ROUND—AND THEODORE WAS THE SPINNER."

ill health. When his father told him he had the mind but not the body to sustain a worthwhile career, he replied, "I'll make my body."

From early childhood Roosevelt was a naturalist, and he learned to ride, hunt, and thrive in the wilderness. He eventually did build a strong body and became a lifelong advocate of physical and moral excellence....

In all his adventures, both in his youth and as a man, he showed utter fearlessness. "There were all kinds of things of which I was afraid at first," he said, "ranging from grizzly bears to 'mean' horses and gunfights; but by acting as if I was not afraid I gradually ceased to be afraid. Most men can have the same experience if they choose."...

When war came, Roosevelt became lieutenant colonel of the Rough Rider Regiment. Advanced to colonel, he got the Rough Riders into the thick of the fight in Cuba. Flamboyantly brave and devoted to his men, he was the favorite of the war correspondents.

In the path of heavy fire from the Spanish on the San Juan ridge, Roosevelt, on horseback, paraded conspicuously before his troops as he marshaled them and gave the order to charge. Up Kettle Hill they went, "cheering and running forward between shots." In a few minutes the Rough Riders were at the top, and Roosevelt became one of the most popular heroes of the war. A monument on San Juan Hill near Santiago was erected in memory of the valiant charge.

Boss Tom Platt, needing a hero to draw attention away from scandals in New York State, accepted Roosevelt as the Republican candidate for governor in the fall of 1898. Roosevelt won, "played fair" with Platt, as he had promised, yet brought distinction to his administration. In 1900, Platt, with the aid of other bosses, managed to push Roosevelt out of New York and into the Vice Presidency, despite the protests of President McKinley's manager, Mark Hanna.

With the assassination of McKinley, Roosevelt, at 42, became the youngest President in the Nation's history. "Now look," moaned Hanna, "that damned cowboy is President of the United States."...

ROOSEVELT'S IDEAL WAS TO USE THE government as the arbiter among conflicting economic forces, especially between capital and labor. He shared American pride in the enormous productivity of factories, with consequent high living standards, but he realized that the abuses growing out of the new industrial combinations—the trusts—must be curbed. He insisted that moderate reform was the only conservative way to prevent drastic upheaval. Roosevelt fought for legislation to investigate large interstate corporations and to impose supervision on them; in 1903 Congress established a Department of Commerce and Labor which contained a Bureau of Corporations to investigate trusts. Roosevelt also initiated numerous antitrust suits....

Some of Roosevelt's highest achievements were in conservation. He believed in both the scientific development of national resources and the preservation of wilderness areas.... In foreign policy, Roosevelt steered the United States toward more

Reissued in nine editions over the course of 17 years, Frank Freidel's Our Country's Presidents *became a mainstay of the Special Collection. Some illustrations gazed back in history, such as the Evart Augustus Duyckinck painting of Lincoln reading his Emancipation Proclamation to his Cabinet (top). Others brought the book to the present day, such as the photographs of the 1960 presidential campaign (middle) and the historic swearing-in ceremony of Lyndon B. Johnson alongside newly widowed Jacqueline Kennedy on November 22, 1963.*

active participation in world politics. He liked to quote what he called a West African proverb, "Speak softly and carry a big stick, you will go far." The "big stick" was the new American Navy, which he prodded Congress to build up to a strength equaling that of other world powers.

To enable the fleet to move readily between the Atlantic and Pacific Oceans, Roosevelt took drastic measures (keenly resented in Latin America) to begin construction of a canal across the Isthmus of Panama. And to forestall the intervention of European creditors and the establishment of unfriendly foreign bases in the Caribbean, he sent an American official to police the finances of the Dominican Republic.

At the request of Japan, in 1905 he mediated the Russo-Japanese War, winning the Nobel Peace Prize—and the ill will of the Japanese, who did not gain as much as they had hoped....

"Teddy" brought a new vibrancy to the Presidency. His high-pitched, earnest voice, jutting jaw, and pounding fist captivated audiences. And he was a brilliant conversationalist of almost limitless range. Rudyard Kipling recalled listening to Roosevelt in the early 1890s at Washington's Cosmos Club: "I curled up on the seat opposite," Kipling said, "and listened and wondered, until the universe seemed to be spinning round—and Theodore was the spinner."

Cargo-laden naggars, *or feluccas, capture the wind of the Nile Delta in their capacious sails. In his extensive journeys, this book's author traveled partly by felucca, vessels that have served for centuries; the journey ended in the fertile delta, where the world's longest river slides into the Mediterranean Sea.*

THE RIVER NILE (1966)

by Bruce Brander

ROGER WOOD STUDIOS

Grasping the rod of majesty and the flail of power, Tutankhamun rides a black panther in this statuette, one of four similar carvings found in his tomb. He wears the White Crown of Upper Egypt, adorned with the royal serpent.

162

Other priests, however, despising such blasphemy, frantically hustled mummies from one hiding place to another. Rameses III was entombed four times, and an unfinished tomb at Deir el Bahri became the final ancient resting place for 35 bodies.

Right up to the present, western Thebes has provided all the thrills of a desert treasure island. Mr. Ramadan told me, "I think some of the villagers, living in huts built against ancient tombs, still hope to find antiquities. They use the tombs for storage or bedrooms. They work their fields in the daytime. At night they go home and dig.

"We inspect the tombs at intervals to make sure relics we know about haven't been tampered with. The last big tomb robbery in western Thebes happened in 1941. People got into 16 tombs and took plaster inscriptions to sell, but all of them were caught. Now we have many policemen to stop illegal trading in such things."

"Is there any chance of major new discoveries?" I asked.

"In the past ten years," he said, "we've identified about ten new sites, some temples but most of them tombs."

"Do you think you might find something more spectacular," I persisted, "like King Tutankhamun's tomb?"

"Possibly, yes," he answered. "Queen Hatshepsut has never been found. Some of the other Pharaohs are still missing. And no one has excavated thoroughly in an area we call the Western Valley, a second valley of kings. Yes, there's always the possibility of anything here."

In the Valley of the Kings, archeologists have found more than 60 tombs, all but Tutankhamun's despoiled. They recovered mummies of important kings, and valuable objects that early robbers had left behind. But by 1922, no one in modern times had seen a royal crypt with more than a fraction of its treasure intact.

Howard Carter had no reason to expect a bonanza on November 4 of that year, when he uncovered a rubble-strewn step below the tomb of Ramesses VI. But the 49-year-old archeologist considered even a new step a triumph. His colleagues had been tearing up the area for more than a century; only ten years before, one of them

Emblem of Hathor, a cow's head shows exacting workmanship; black glass outlines eyes of limestone and obsidian. Anubis (below), the canine "lord of the necropolis," keeps an alert vigil over the king he must lead to the other world.

The River Nile details both the current struggles and the rich past of dwellers along the 4,145-mile waterway.

Writer Bruce Brander explored the Nile and its basin by camel, truck, river-launch, and felucca. Blending geography, archaeology, anthropology, history, and travel journalism, his book took readers from the source of the Nile in Tanzania north to its delta on the Mediterranean Sea. "I scuffed into a spiderweb of lanes," he wrote of the adventure. "As long as even the local wise man could remember, no foreigner had walked here before."

The excerpt here comes near the beginning of his journey. Brander's descriptions of the Tutsi and their dances are wonderfully vivid. They allow the reader to see what he saw, to feel the excitement he felt. In setting up the Hutu-Tutsi conflict, he starts with a reference to Mark Twain, a perennial favorite among *National Geographic* writers. He then neatly outlines the history of the bitter struggle between the two tribes, taking sides with the "proud, shrewd" Tutsi aristocrats. Though he mentions the 10,000 killed in 1963-64, he probably did not know that only a few years earlier some 150,000 had died.

Hindsight gives us a clearer vision of Rwanda's volatile situation at that time. Brander's visit was during a relatively peaceful year; the recent atrocities he reported were only a prelude to the early 1990s, in which hundreds of thousands, mostly Tutsi, were killed, and during which about two million, mostly Hutu, fled as refugees, many dying of disease and starvation along the way.

Water for a Giant

From Bruce Brander's travelogue up the Nile en route to Egypt

Just as cattle might be used in trade to buy a hut or a secondhand car today, they once bought much of the Nile's sourceland. About the time Europeans were migrating to colonies in America, tall herdsmen of the Hamitic race were driving their four-legged wealth along a southwest arc across Africa. The lean nomads originated in Ethiopia, most authorities believe. Their cattle represented an ancient strain, resembling the long-horned bulls that stride in stone across some Egyptian ruins.

Some of these nomads stopped in the southern Sudan and Uganda. Others pushed onto the cool green slopes of Rwanda and Burundi. Here Hutu tribesmen, part of the great Bantu family, were already farming the hills. Instead of arguing over the land, it appears that the two peoples came to an agreement, a strange social arrangement that reminds me of Tom Sawyer's fence-painting deal.

The Hutu admired the tall newcomers and their animals; they would labor for the herdsmen if

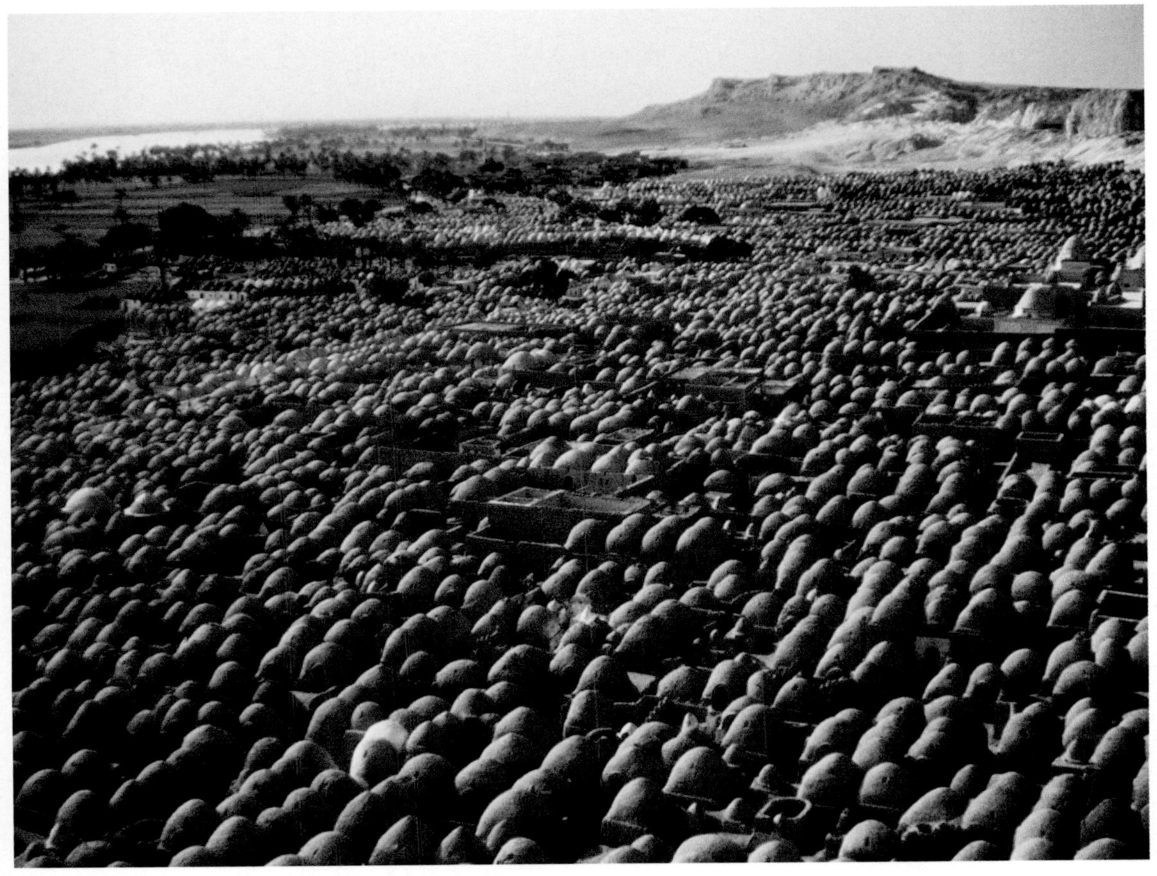

City of the dead: Domed tombs stretch along the Nile beneath stark cliffs at Egypt's Zâwyet el Amwât. A contemporary Islamic burial ground, it adjoins one dating from the days of the earliest dynasties.

At a wedding reception in Omdurman, opposite Khartoum, turbaned members of the Mahdi sect of Islam celebrate outside the beehive-shaped tomb of sect founder Muhammed Ahmed.

only the herdsmen would let them take care of the splendid cattle. This put the cattle-rich nomads on the royal road to dominance. A feudal system called *ubuhake* spread over the land and solidified. The Hutu became serfs, caring for cattle and performing most manual chores; the herd owners, known by the tribal name of Tutsi, became overlords.

At the turn of the century, the two countries formed part of German East Africa, but local ways changed little. In 1923, a League of Nations mandate left the region in Belgian hands, and Belgium governed it as a single colony. Ruanda-Urundi. Still, each section kept its Tutsi *mwami,* or king, and the cattle-owning Tutsi chiefs continued to dominate the Hutu.

The rulers, better known abroad as the Watusi, have fascinated foreigners. They are among the giants of the continent, rod-straight and aristocratic. Not all Tutsi stand as tall as foreigners expect; they average five feet nine inches. But men rising seven feet six are not uncommon.... I could often recognize the Tutsi at a glance. Their faces are lean and triangular, their great eyes round and wistful. They look frail; they carry themselves with the grace of ballet dancers, gliding rather than walking, moving like wisps of dark smoke....

Anyone who sees a Tutsi dance puts it away with the unforgettable sights of life. Great drums, each half the height of a man, blast like cannonfire—slowly at first, faster to raise the gooseflesh, deeper to a steady hypnotic rumble. Drummers squeeze their eyes shut and leap in a swirl of red and white cloth. Lean dancers in leopard skins and ankle bells prance and writhe, swishing long staffs in front of them. Their leaps are phenomenal, and flopping headdresses of white colobus monkey fur make them seem higher still....

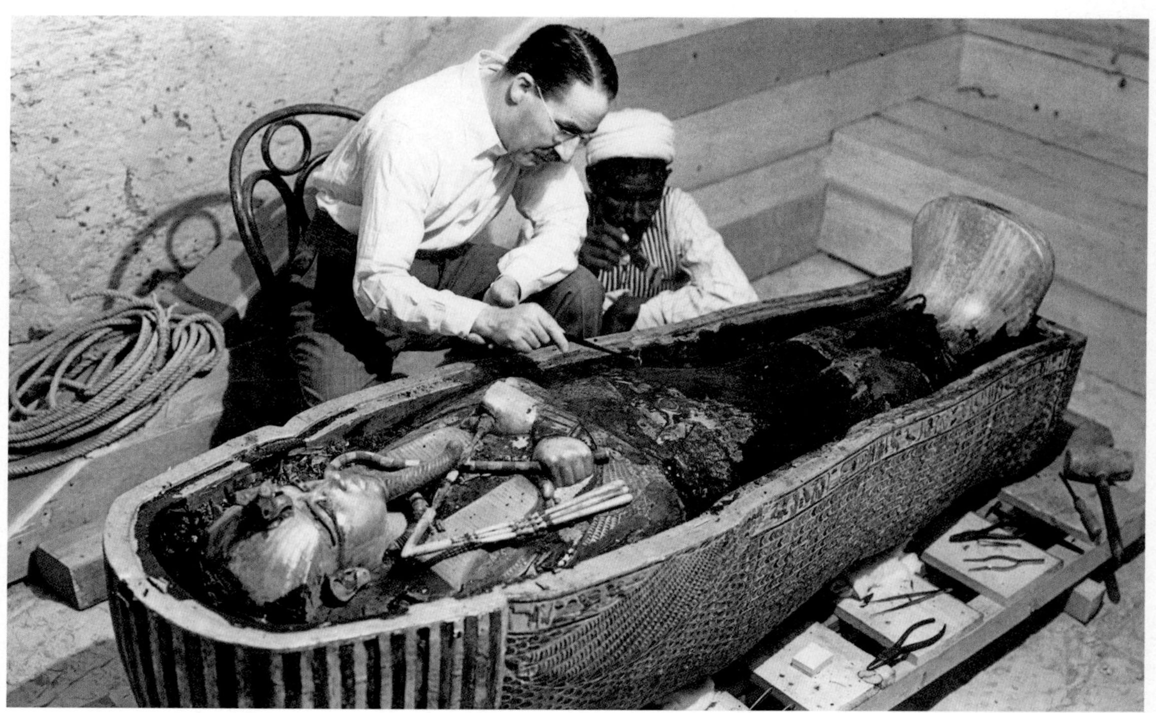

Archaeologist Howard Carter chips at solidified sacred oils on the coffin of Tutankhamun (circa 1370-52 B.C.). Carter discovered the pharaoh's crypt in 1922 in Egypt's Valley of the Kings, the Nile's most fertile area of antiquities.

Modern culture with a strong connection to the past was a central theme of The River Nile. *Here Tutsi warriors in Rwanda keep tradition alive in the spirited national dance; their headplumes are made of colobus monkey fur.*

CAN FEUDALISM SURVIVE IN A TIME OF worldwide social revolution? In 1954, Belgian administrators in Ruanda-Urundi decided it was dangerous, at best.... That year, they issued a decree requiring chiefs to give two-thirds of their cattle to serfs who tended the herds.... But the Tutsi resented the new order, just as the Hutu had come to resent the old. A turning point for half the region came in 1959, when Ruanda's mwami died. Before the new king came to power, the Hutu rebelled. They outnumbered their Tutsi overlords six to one, and soon overpowered the aristocrats. July, 1962, brought independence to both countries. Ruanda became the Republic of Rwanda. While its Hutu ministers went about their duties in economy cars and patched clothing, thousands of its Tutsi citizens smouldered in exile. Urundi added a B to its name: it remained a kingdom (until a republic was proclaimed late in 1966)—and a sanctuary for refugees....

The Nile runs everywhere through these two lands, in streams that furrow the hills with bright fresh water. But some sources are more significant than others. Rwanda's Lukarara River, for example, is the longest headwater. From its tip in the nation's far west, map-makers begin to measure the Nile's 4,145-mile length. Eventually, all these streams meet, mix, and pour into the huge basin of Lake Victoria. There ends one of the Nile's great source systems. Not far away, another one begins.

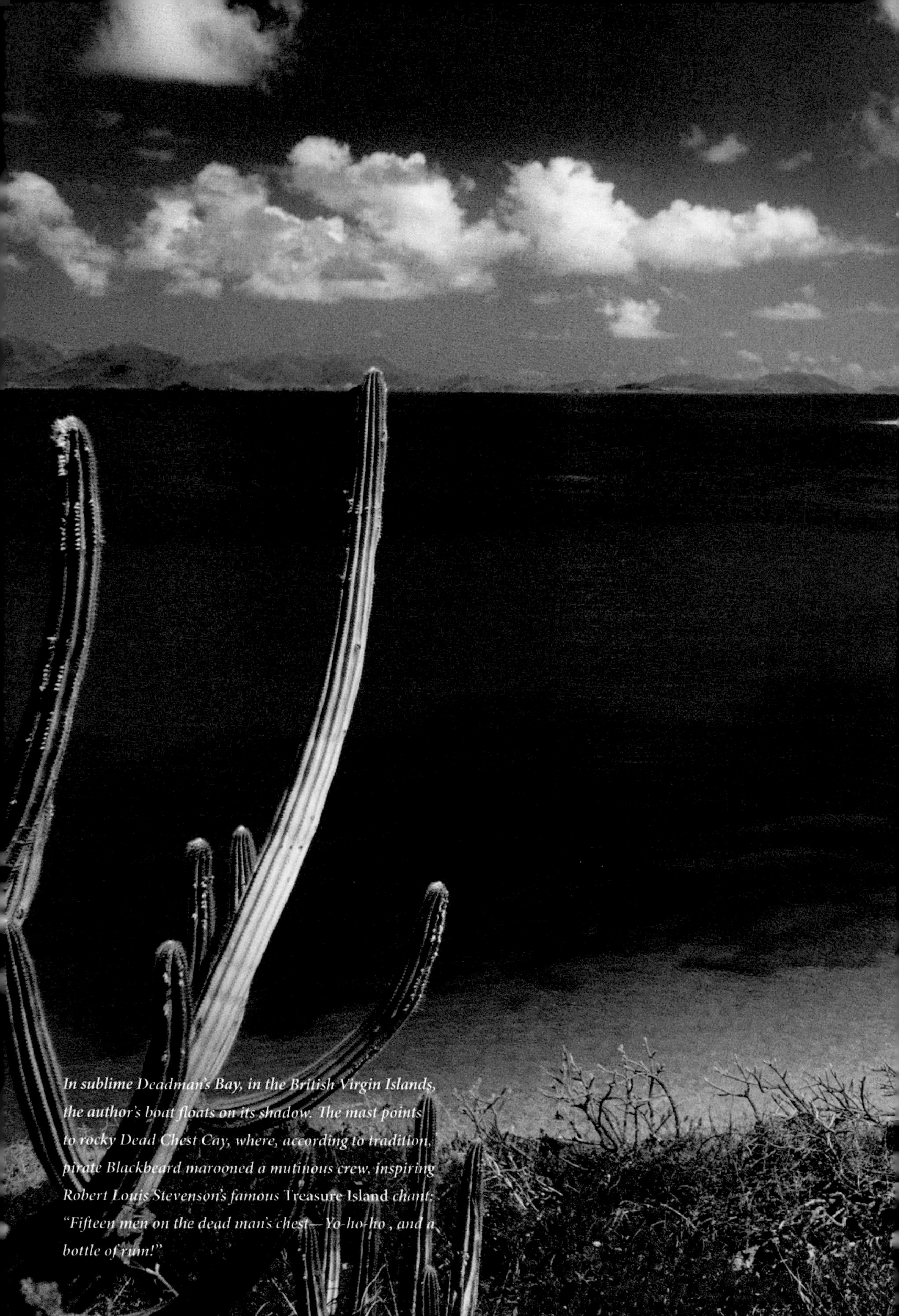

In sublime Deadman's Bay, in the British Virgin Islands, the author's boat floats on its shadow. The mast points to rocky Dead Chest Cay, where, according to tradition, pirate Blackbeard marooned a mutinous crew, inspiring Robert Louis Stevenson's famous Treasure Island *chant: "Fifteen men on the dead man's chest—Yo-ho-ho , and a bottle of rum!"*

ISLES OF THE CARIBBEES (1966)

by Carleton Mitchell

and built her dream house, Island Fancy. Her adventures inspired a book, *Grandma Raised the Roof*, which she dedicated to her seventh grandchild.

As we relaxed on the veranda, Grandma showed me a tile inscribed with her philosophy of life: "How beautiful it is to do nothing, and after doing nothing, to rest." Although this might not be a fitting motto for St. Croix and bustling St. Thomas, it is apt for St. John. And, happily enough, St. John is likely to remain much as it is today, largely because of the foresight and generosity of one individual.

In 1952 Laurance S. Rockefeller arrived for a visit, and quickly decided the island was too lovely to be transformed by civilization. Through Jackson Hole Preserve, Inc., a conservation organization, his representatives bought land, until in 1956 he was able to offer more than 5,000 acres to the people of the United States. The resulting Virgin Islands National Park has since tripled in size, and now includes three-fourths of the island and much of its offshore waters.

"In 1962 we extended our boundaries to take in 5,650 acres of ocean floor," William Bromberg, the park superintendent, told me. "Off the coasts we have ranger-patrolled areas up to a mile out. Spearfishing and the taking of marine specimens are not allowed. It is equally important to preserve unspoiled a part of St. John's underwater heritage."

St. John is as rich in history as in the charms of nature. When the Danes arrived in the mid-17th century, looking for farmland, they found St. Thomas and St. John uninhabited. Shortly after establishing a colony on St. Thomas, some settlers moved to St. John, but the British on Tortola drove them off. In 1716 the Danes tried again, and were allowed to remain.

By 1733, St. John had 109 estates planted in cotton and cane, and 1,295 inhabitants, with slaves outnumbering the planters more than five to one. The future seemed bright. But then came a summer of drought,

Carnival reaches high tide in Charlotte Amalie with a Saturday parade for adults, near the end of a spirited week. A pre-Lenten festival elsewhere, Carnival falls late in April in the Virgin Islands; originally it followed the cane harvest.

NATIONAL GEOGRAPHIC PHOTOGRAPHER JAMES L. STANFIELD

202

Inside views of the lives of islanders make Isles of the Caribbees *more than a passing glance at the West Indies.*

Sailing legend Carleton Mitchell wrote *Isles of the Caribbees* at the age of 54, several years after winning the famous 635-mile Newport-to-Bermuda race three times in a row (1956, 1958, and 1960). Earlier in life he had worked as a stevedore and a U.S. Navy combat photographer during World War II. First sailing the Caribbean in 1948, he wrote of his experiences in *Islands to Windward,* a book that National Geographic Society President Melville Bell Grosvenor called "a classic among lovers of the West Indies."

Isles of the Caribbees was born during a sailing trip Grosvenor took aboard Mitchell's 38-foot yawl, *Finisterre.* Mitchell was telling yarns about pirates, sea battles, memorable fishing trips, and wild storms, and Grosvenor asked him to write a book about it all. The result is a fun-loving adventure, both armchair travel book and informal guide for anyone eyeing Caribbean destinations.

The journey started in Grenada and continued north to the Virgin Islands. Grosvenor noted that Mitchell "writes as he sails—intensely, with great order and flair. We would cruise all night, Mitch navigating, standing his watch, and skippering to boot. Then at dawn he would go ashore to spend the day interviewing people, collecting notes."

Carleton Mitchell died in 2007 in Key Biscayne, Florida, at the age of 96. "Somehow the detached life on the sea gives me the ability to think," he wrote. "It's a life of action, yet contemplation."

Of Sailors and the Sea

From Carleton Mitchell's chapter on the Grenadines

Suddenly, as we cleared Grenada, a mighty gust struck us and *Finisterre* lay over on her side as though pushed down by a giant invisible hand. Off went the motor. Whitecaps began to march; as *Finisterre* came alive, spray flew aft like salted rain, drenching us in the cockpit. Even in cruising trim, *Finisterre* retains her feel of liveliness and power. This was what she had been built for, to slash through ocean swells with never a worry to her crew. Size is not a deciding factor in seaworthiness; lifeboats survive after the steamer has foundered. Rhythmically her sharp bow sliced each oncoming wave, while astern plumed a long lane of foaming wake. Blue water below, blue sky above, and green islands beckoning ahead—none of us would have traded places with any man. Soon over the jib appeared Kick 'em Jenny, a rocky islet in the Grenadines. "Nobody knows where the name comes from," said Laddie McIntyre. "Maybe it's a corruption of the French, *cay que gene,* 'the troublesome cay,' because the currents around it gave the old sailing ships such a hard time. Some say it's Kick 'em Jenny because it kicks like a mule; others claim you can see a donkey in the shape of the rock."

We tacked in close. Around the base of the desolate islet, water creamed white, while seabirds rose from crevices and screamed at us. But no donkey in the rocks, no kick of watery heels for *Finisterre.* A cloud drifted above, the breeze dropped, and we swept past without breaking stride.

Perhaps the least known but among the loveliest of the Windward Islands, the Grenadines have no airports, no easy means of access—only roving yachts, and a waddling diesel mailboat, whose passengers share the deck with produce and livestock. More than 100 islands and rocks scattered along a submerged ridge extend 50 miles between Grenada and St. Vincent. The southern islands come under the jurisdiction of Grenada, the northern under St. Vincent, with the dividing line slicing across the northern tip of Carriacou.

So simple is the view of the world held by many of the isolated residents of Carriacou that they often refer to nearby Grenada as "the mainland."

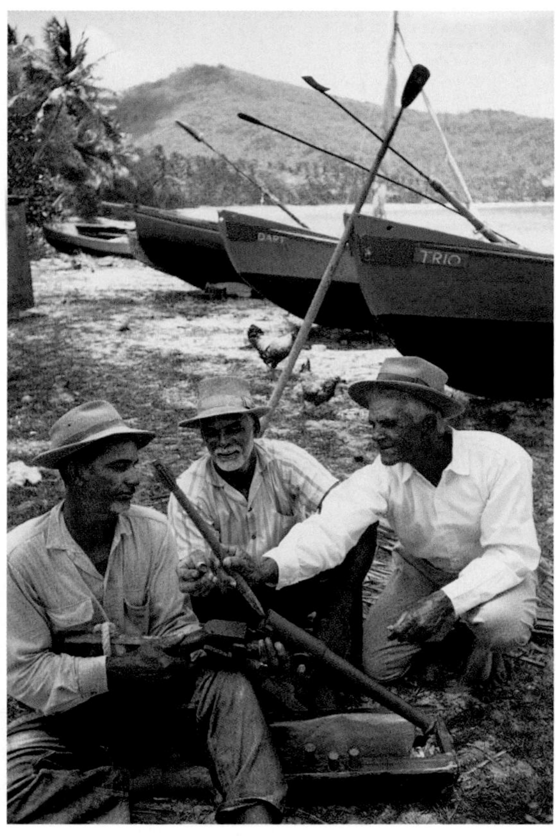

On the island of Bequia, whalers load a harpoon gun. In 1966, when this book was written, most locals still preferred to "dart the iron" by hand.

AT MIDNIGHT ALL THE WOMEN GATHERED.
HALF SANG IN PATOIS, "WHO IS THIS FOOD FOR?" AND THE OTHER HALF CHANTED,
"FOR GOOD PEOPLE WHO ARE NO LONGER HERE ON EARTH."

Yet Hillsborough, with electric lights, taxis, and a small hospital, is a relatively sophisticated metropolis, and I had selected its lovely bay as our destination for the night. But as *Finisterre* rounded the final point we had a sudden warning of things to come.

Swells curled into the anchorage. Where normally the water off the beach lay smooth, breakers ran hissing across the sand to wash the base of the palms. Hillsborough is an open roadstead—not a landlocked harbor but a crescent-shaped bay exposed to swells from the north. When trade winds are light and seas small, open roadsteads can be pleasant anchorages. But after a spell of fresh winds, boats roll uncomfortably in the swells. We backtracked around the point to drop anchor in Tyrrel Bay, near a cove known as the Carenage. Stemming from the term "to careen"—to heave down a sailing ship to work on her bottom—a carenage is a sheltered pocket where a helpless vessel will not be at the mercy of the weather.

No sooner had *Finisterre* dropped her hook than a boat put off from shore, an old friend waving from the stern. He was J. Linton Rigg, former yacht broker, ex-member of the War Shipping Administration, and one of the all-time greats of ocean racing. Linton had retired on Carriacou after exploring the Caribbean. The island had no place for visitors, so he opened a six-room hotel, the Mermaid Tavern, on the Hillsborough waterfront, then built his home, Tranquillity, high on a windward slope.

The next day, as I entered Tranquillity, I closed behind me a gate bearing a quotation from *A Midsummer Night's Dream:* "Weaving Spiders Come Not Here." We gazed over waving palms to green and blue shallows as brilliant as stained glass. Two small cays, Little Martinique and Little St. Vincent, lay at the edge of soundings, and beyond stretched the open Atlantic, dappled by drifting trade wind clouds. There was no sound except the sigh of the breeze. As we lunched on the terrace, Linton talked of his neighbors, the fisher-folk and farmers of Windward, the village hidden under the palms below.

"When I had my housewarming party, the whole village of Windward attended. We started with Big Drum dances, sometimes called 'nation' dances, because they originated with tribes, or 'nations,' in Africa. Indoors, the older women prepared a feast. They asked me what my mother and father—both had been dead for some time—would like to eat and drink. I thought a minute and said maybe a cup of tea for my mother and a glass of rum for my father, then some soup and roast fowl.

"Later, I went in and found a table set for two, with exactly the things I had specified. They told me it was the 'parents' plate,' which couldn't be touched until daylight, and an old woman called a *gan-gan* was set to watch. At midnight all the women gathered. Half sang in patois, 'Who is this food for?' and the other half chanted, 'For good people who are no longer here on earth.'"...

In 1656 a visitor to the Grenadines wrote, "The most beautiful of all the little isles is *Kayryoüacou,*" and for me that is still true. Above Hillsborough Bay, palms overhang a double curve of white sand, almost as perfect as though inscribed by two sweeps of a compass, and the water shades through tones of blue into the azure of the Caribbean....

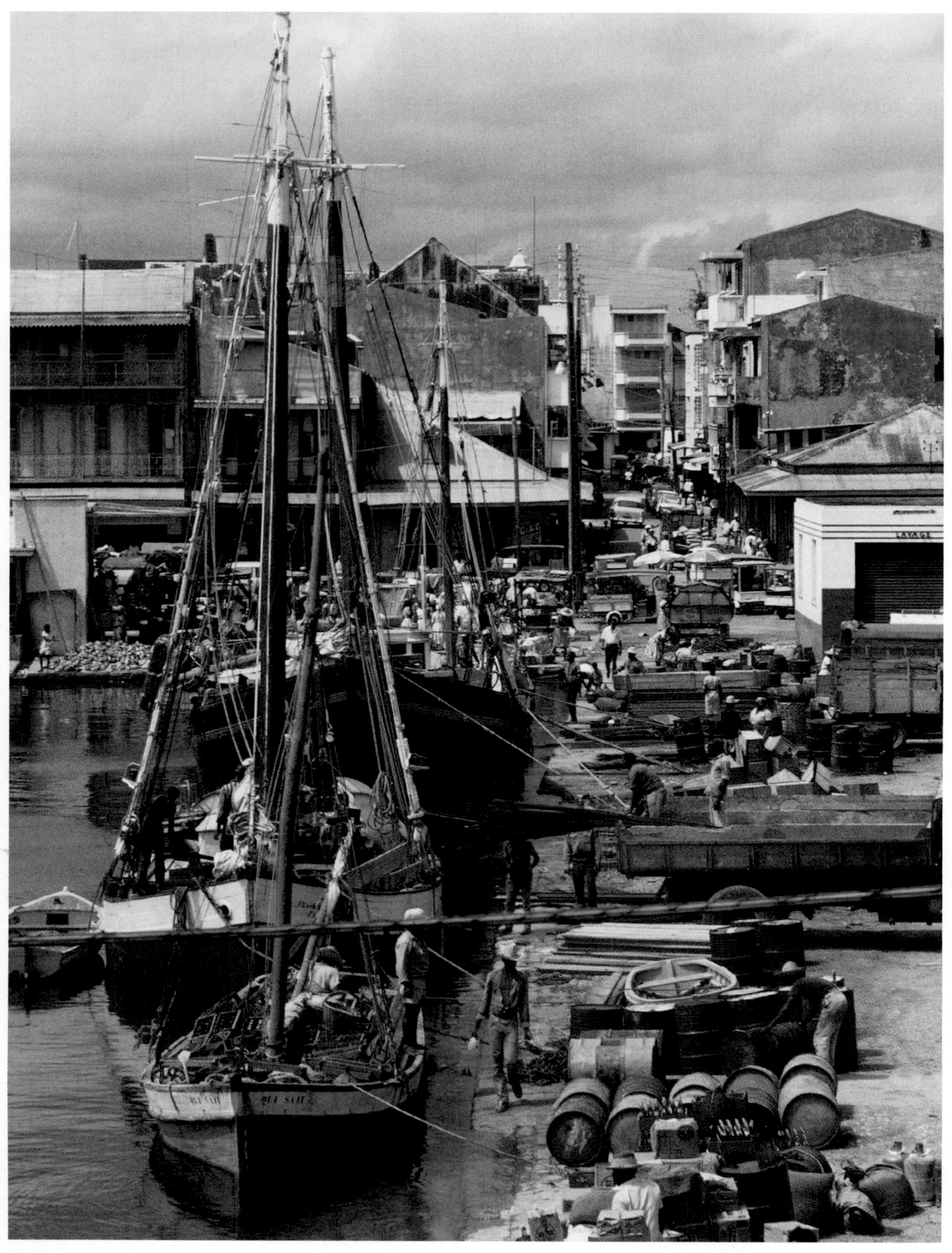

Dockside hubbub greets sailing vessels at Pointe-à-Pitre, the commercial center of Guadeloupe. The adjoining Citée Transit *neighborhood is full of locals waiting for their slums to be rebuilt.*

155

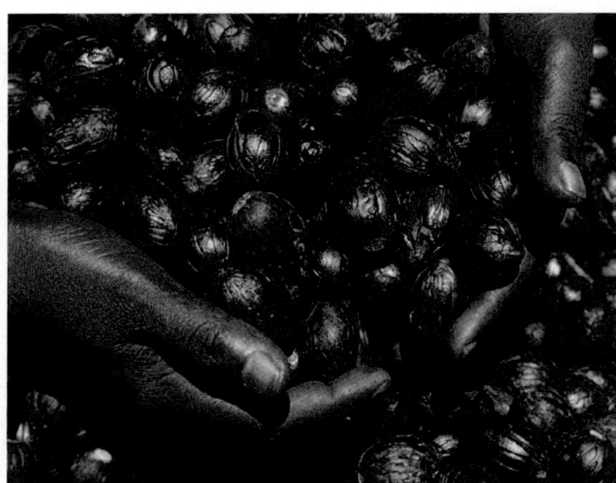

In a jump rope race (top), Montserrat girls dash to the finish line. Spectators cheer and jeer fighting cocks in Marigot, capital of Saint Martin (bottom left). A worker displays the bounty at a Charlotte Town plant on Grenada (center right). Two in one: Mace comes from the ruby-colored coating that stripes the fibrous brown hulls of ripe nutmeg. Using tough linen thread (bottom right), a Bequia islander reinforces the edge of a canvas sail.

OUR NEXT GOAL WAS THE TOBAGO CAYS, a few miles to the north and east of Carriacou, a cluster of uninhabited cays lying in a semicircular lagoon formed by a barrier reef. As we entered, I ignored the chart to con *Finisterre* from the bow by the color of the water ahead. Coral patches showed up as purple-brown smears, and channels as dark blue lanes, paling into green nearer shore. Off the beaches the water was so transparent that I found it hard to tell where dry sand began.... Although the Tobago Cays sometimes provide shelter for a cluster of cruising boats, we were alone....

Bequia is a true island of sailors and the sea; not of the mechanized vessels of today, but of the past, when sail was the only way to transport people and cargo. Ashore I met sailmakers on benches in the shade of almond trees, plying palm and needle on canvas and tarred manila, not synthetic fabrics. Nearby, shipwrights swinging adzes faired timbers, putting a vessel together on the beach. In the shallows, a crew was careening a schooner by block and tackle attached to her mast; they shouted in unison as they hove on the lines, exposing one side all the way to the keel for caulking and repainting.

At Friendship Bay on the southeastern coast, I stepped into a living mariners' museum. On the beach whaleboats balanced on bones of their prey, lovely double-ended craft straight from the golden age of Nantucket, with the old-time cutout in the bow thwart to steady the harpooner's knee. Bequia remains one of the few places where men still pursue and capture whales by hand. Harold Corea, member of a whaling family, tended a vat of boiling pitch. In a long house roofed by palm thatch were stacked oars, harpoons, and neatly coiled line. "Whales begin to come through in February," Harold told me. "Starting in March and running until summer, four boats will go out every day, six men to a boat. Last year wasn't so good, bu the year before we took a humpbacked cow, very big, maybe 65 to 70 feet long, and also her calf."

As *Finisterre* tacked toward Port Elizabeth, I saw a natural stone arch, without noticing that anything lay beneath it. But when we returned in the Whaler for a closer look, I found that the rock arch was probably the world's largest picture window.

"Moonhole just happened," its designer and owner, Thomas G. Johnston, told me. After 25 years as an advertising executive, he "suddenly awakened on a Monday morning—in spring—fed up with existing simply for a better job and bigger bank account." He and his wife, Gladys, came to St. Vincent, gravitated to Bequia, and discovered the natural bridge that became part of their home.

Moonhole rambles along the slopes as though it were an outcropping of the rock. In the guest room a tree sprouts from the floor, and one of Tom's proudest moments was when a hummingbird felt so at home that she built a nest and raised two babies. "Moonhole is the local name for the formation because in some lights the round opening in the hillside glows like a full moon," Tom said. We sat on the terrace, protected from a shower by the stone arch overhead; it formed not only a roof but also a spectacular frame for Admiralty Bay and the blue Caribbean beyond.

Bowing to Jou Jou, Jane Goodall accepts the touch of a chimpanzee she had never seen before. Caged alone in the Brazzaville Zoo in the Republic of the Congo for years, the chimp was desperate for contact with other beings. A simple touch became a transcendent moment.

My Friends the Wild Chimpanzees (1967)

by Baroness Jane van Lawick-Goodall

By walkie-talkie, Jane tells her camp staff that she intends to stay overnight in the mountains, observing chimps in their nests.

Chimpanzees, like people, exchange greetings when they meet after being apart for any length of time. When this occurs, an observer can usually determine the relationship of one chimp to the other. They may meet as two friends and show pleasure in their reunion, or one may make submissive gestures, acknowledging the other's higher rank.

When Mike arrives in any group the other chimps invariably hurry to pay their respects, touching him with outstretched hands or bowing, just as courtiers once bowed before their king. And, just as the king chose either to acknowledge a courtier or to ignore him, so Mike may take notice of his inferiors, touching them briefly, or he may do nothing. Depending on his mood, he may even threaten or strike those who hasten to greet him.

Many of the apes' forms of greeting startlingly resemble our own. They often kiss. Rodolf in particular frequently touches the face of a subordinate with his lips, or presses his open mouth onto the neck or shoulder of another adult male. Pepe and Figan, to mention but two, often press their mouths to the lips of other individuals. Hand-holding, as a gesture of greeting, is not common in the chimpanzee community at the reserve, but it does occur. Melissa for one, when first arriving in a group, occasionally holds her hand toward a dominant male until he reaches out and reassures her with a touch.

One of the most memorable reunions took place between old Mr. Worzle and timid Olly. As she approached him, panting nervously, he raised both arms as though pronouncing a blessing. Encouraged, Olly crept closer, crouching and holding her hand toward him. Mr. Worzle took her hand in his and drew her close, placing his other hand gently on her head. Then each flung both arms around the other and exchanged kisses on the neck. Finally, to complete the picture, Olly's daughter Gilka ran up and Mr. Worzle reached out and drew her into his embrace.

The similarity of many chimpanzee gestures and postures to those of man is to Hugo and me one of the most exciting aspects of our study. It thrills us quite as much as the discovery that wild apes make and use crude tools. For either the gestures used by both man and ape have evolved along closely parallel lines, or they have a common origin in some remote ancestor of both man and ape.

140

Illustrations by National Geographic artists and photos by Baron van Lawick evoke Goodall's bold lifestyle.

In 1960 26-year-old Jane Goodall came to the shores of Lake Tanganyika in East Africa, beginning the groundbreaking work that would become a lifelong effort and make her one of the most renowned field scientists in the world. The young Englishwoman had worked as a secretary for anthropologist Louis S. B. Leakey, and when he realized her serious intentions, he encouraged her to embark on a project new to science—an extended study of chimpanzees in the wild.

In this excerpt, Goodall relates the thrill of discovering that man is not the only maker of tools. During that first outing, her mother accompanied her, because local authorities would not allow her to travel alone in the bush. After a few months, her mother went home, and Goodall remained in the remote Gombe Stream Game Reserve for ten months with her African helpers.

By the mid-1960s she had earned a Ph.D. from Cambridge University and married wildlife photographer Baron Hugo van Lawick. (They divorced in 1974.) She had also received a research grant from the National Geographic Society.

The honors soon began stacking up for this slight woman who over the decades has proved herself a courageous giant. In 1977 she founded the Jane Goodall Institute for Wildlife Research, Education and Conservation, to protect chimpanzees and their habitats and to promote education and leadership for environmental causes.

At Long Last I Belong

From Jane Goodall's chronicles of life among the African primates

At the start of the rainy season in 1960, after four long, difficult months in the field, I made my first really exciting observation: I saw a chimp fashion and use crude tools!

That morning I felt rather despondent, for I had trudged the mountains for hours and had seen no chimpanzees at all. Then, as I headed for the Peak, I spotted a black shape beside the red-earth mound of a termite nest.

Quickly I sat down (even today the chimps seem more at ease if we observe them from their own level) and peered through my binoculars. I saw David Greybeard, and as I watched him I could hardly believe my eyes. He was carefully trimming the edges from a wide blade of sword grass!

I gazed, scarcely daring to breathe, as he pushed the modified stem into the nest. He left it for a moment, then pulled it out and picked off something with his lips. The chimp continued probing with the stem until it bent double. He then discarded it and reached out to pick a length of vine. With a sweeping movement of one hand, he stripped the leaves from the vine, bit a piece from one end, and set to work again with his newly prepared tool.

By naming the animals, detailing their family relationships, and developing lasting bonds with individuals, Goodall established friendships across the species barrier and expanded our definition of the family of man.

Clever David Greybeard rips a hole in the thatched roof of a "chimp-proof" storeroom (top) and helps himself to bananas. A curious bushbuck noses in for a close look at the young scientist.

For an hour I watched. From time to time David changed position, opening up new holes in the termite mound by scratching at the soil with his index finger. Finally, after again trying each of the holes in turn, he dropped the piece of vine and wandered away.

I hurried to the place and found a horde of worker termites busily sealing the holes David had opened. Each moistened bits of clay with saliva and pressed the minute pellets into place. Poking a blade of grass down one hole, I felt the insects bite it. When I pulled the stem out, four workers and a couple of the larger soldiers clung to it. I tasted one, for I make it a point to try almost everything the chimps eat, but it seemed rather flavorless to me. At that time my mother had not yet left the reserve, and I was so excited I could hardly wait for sunset to hurry down and tell her what I had seen.

"You see," I told her, "some wild animals can use objects as tools. There's the sea otter for one. It gets a flat stone from the floor of the sea, floats on its back with the stone lying on its chest, and bangs shellfish against it to open them. And wild chimps have been seen using tools. In West Africa an observer saw one poke a stick into honey in an underground bees' nest. A chimpanzee in Liberia hammered with a rock at a dried palm nut. But David didn't simply use tools—he actually made them!"

"Can you really say that he was truly making tools?" my mother asked.

I described how David had stripped leaves from the section of vine and trimmed the edges off the blade of grass.

"He didn't just make use of any old bit of material lying around," I explained. "He actually modified stems and grasses and made them suitable for his purpose."

"Then that means man isn't the only toolmaker after all!" my mother exclaimed.

Goodall confers with Tanzanian boys at her lakeshore camp. It was here that she first encountered a wild chimpanzee, when David Greybeard wandered in; eventually he took food from her hand.

Anthropologists, other social scientists, and theologians have defined man in a variety of ways. Until recently one widely accepted element of the anthropologists' definition was that "man starts at that stage of primate evolution when the creature begins to make tools to a regular and set pattern." The grasses and twigs used by the chimps for termite fishing do not, perhaps, comply entirely with this specification. Nonetheless, Dr. Leakey, on learning of my findings and referring to the description above, wrote, "I feel that scientists holding to this definition are faced with three choices: They must accept chimpanzees as man, by definition; they must redefine man; or they must redefine tools."

It is of great satisfaction to me to know that my work at the Gombe Stream Game Reserve is being taken into consideration by many scientists in their continuing efforts to redefine man in a manner far more complex and detailed than ever before attempted....

Many times since that first thrilling day I have watched chimpanzees fishing for termites. Usually they work about an hour. But if the insects refuse to bite, the chimps try one fishing tool after another in quick succession (as though they feel the tools are to blame), then wander away, often to try their luck at another nest.

Some authorities suggest that only when an implement is kept for future use is the toolmaker

A downpour brings out the wildness in the apes. This sequence shows a hooting chimp dashing down a slope, climbing a tree, and breaking off a limb.

"CHIMPS AREN'T REALLY ANIMALS, AND THEY AREN'T MEN, OF COURSE," SAID HUGO. "JUST STRANGE AND VERY WONDERFUL IN-BETWEEN CREATURES."

showing forethought; for this reason people often ask whether the chimps ever save the tools for reuse. This would have little point, since most of the objects would shrivel and become useless if kept. And, anyway, grass stems and twigs abound near the termite nests.

The chimpanzees do, however, select stems beforehand and carry them to termite nests quite out of sight, as far away as 100 yards. Such behavior seems to indicate a certain forethought. A mature male once picked a grass tool that he carried for half a mile while he carefully inspected eight nests. When none of them proved right for working, he gave up and dropped the stem....

I vividly recall the day deep in the forest when Hugo and I saw young Evered reach out, strip the leaves from a small branch, and stuff them into his mouth. "Whatever is he doing?" asked Hugo as Evered took the leaves out of his mouth after chewing them slightly. Soon we had the answer.

Holding them between his index and middle fingers, he dipped them into a little hollow in the trunk of a fallen tree. He lifted out the slightly mashed greenery, and we saw the gleam of water. Evered sucked the liquid from his homemade "sponge," and continued to dip and drink until he emptied the bowl....

IT WILL BE A SAD DAY TOO WHEN MY FIRST chimpanzee acquaintance, David Greybeard, is no more. To me, he is not just a chimpanzee—he is, quite truly, a friend....

It is David, alone of all the chimps, who has reached out to me across the barriers of species and language that separate ape from man. And he acted of his own free will. I thought back to that incident. I was alone with David that day, deep in the forest. I held out a palm nut to him and, although he did not want it, he accepted my offering. For a full ten seconds, he held my hand gently and firmly in his. Finally, with a last glance at the nut, he let it fall to the ground.

In that brief, exalted moment I had felt a thrill of communication with a wild chimpanzee—not by a scientific interpretation of his behavior, but rather by an instinctive understanding of his gesture. He had reached out to reassure me by the pressure of his fingers. Although he rejected my gift, he gave me one of his own: a primitive communion based on touch, so distinct from the sophisticated communion based on intellect.

I turned to Hugo.

"Doesn't it seem strange," I said, "that on the emotional level chimps are so nearly human, yet culturally and intellectually we are so widely separated?"

"Yes," Hugo replied, "but chimps aren't really animals, and they aren't men, of course. Just strange and very wonderful in-between creatures."

We gazed at David Greybeard and Goliath, at Flo and her family, resting so peacefully, so blissfully unaware of their own mystery, of the challenge their mere existence hurls at the scientist, at the philosopher. At that moment David awakened. As we contemplated this marvelous creature, he sat up and grunted. It was time to climb into the branches overhead for another stomachful of figs.

Goodall's 35 years studying wild chimpanzees gave her great empathy with captive animals such as this Congolese zoo chimp (above). A mother cuddles twins (below), a rarity among chimpanzees.

CHAPTER TWO

American History

Introduction by Mary Ann Harrell

Books in the Special Collection told key stories from American history—chronicling the American Revolution or the Massacre at Wounded Knee—and revealed untold tales, such as those of distinguished American inventors or cowboys in the wide-open Southwest.

Mary Ann Harrell joined the National Geographic Society staff in 1958 and soon became an editorial researcher on the magazine. She was one of the original members of the Special Publications division, working at times as researcher, editor, managing editor, ghost-writer, and bylined writer on a number of books in the series. She retired from the Society in 1994 and lives in Bethesda, Maryland. With an avid interest in and deep knowledge of American history, she here reflects on the titles in that category, backbone of the series.

Letters from readers played a significant part in the development of Special Publications from the first. The biographies in *Our Country's Presidents* prompted happy comments from parents whose children read them "and got an A for homework." American history has kept such strong appeal that specific eras inspired several books: the Civil War, in 1969, and the Revolutionary War, chronicled twice in the series, first in 1967 by Bart McDowell of the Geographic staff and then in 2004 by freelance writer John Thompson. Both studies of the earlier war trace the battles in the 13 rebellious Colonies—or states, depending on time and points of view—but they differ in detail.

Bart adopted a pattern favored for magazine articles: family exploration. He compared the interests of seventh-grader Kelly, who admired the self-made artillerist Henry Knox; Tina, already a young horsewoman; Josh, fascinated by drummer boys; and Robert, "our toddler and only illiterate." (I sympathized with Josh; I grew up hearing about an ancestor, age 17, who stood up, drumsticks in hand, to confront General Lord Cornwallis at Guilford Courthouse in 1781.)

John Thompson took more of a journalist's approach to the subject. Rarely, if ever, did his prose include the first person, and yet he retold familiar stories with a vivid sense of detail, as if he and the reader were there on the spot.

I was working as a researcher for the Special Publications division when Bart McDowell was writing his *Revolutionary War.* Research for this book was often fun. I remember asking a specialist at the Vermont Historical Society about Ethan Allen's challenge to the commander of Fort Ticonderoga: to surrender "in the name of the great Jehovah and the Continental Congress."

"We accept it as a valid tradition," she said, "but there's also the tradition that he said, 'Come out, you damned old rat!'" She added quietly, "He was capable of both."

STARS AND LESSER LIGHTS OF THE REBELLION grew brighter as we worked, and yet seemed far away. The British war effort of the 1770s and '80s in London seemed only too close to life in Washington, D.C., during the Vietnam era of the 1960s.

As the distinguished British historian Piers Mackesy described it in his own book, *The War for America, 1775-1783,* here was a great kingdom in trouble. Britain had a good army, the world's dominant navy, a settled government complete with red tape—and the nation was struggling in a distant conflict poorly understood. One British general thought his mission was "to assist the good Americans to subdue the bad." One British admiral compared the movement of his land forces to "the passage of a ship through the sea, whose track is soon lost."

OUR SUBJECTS ARE LARGE, INTRICATE, AS SUBTLE AS ANY LIFE;
THEY HUMBLE US.

At best, a ship with news from America might reach England in a month. A ship with orders from London might need two months, or four, to reach New York. After France (and its ally, Spain) joined the war against Britain, the arena expanded: the West Indies, the Mediterranean, and the Indian Ocean. News was always late, an order often untimely, the result a nightmare of stalled emergencies. By 1780, noted Dr. Mackesy, "the misdirection of a single ship might mean disaster." And the only allies of King George III were Indians on the frontier.

At least the American rebels had one advantage: their communications ran over land. When Cornwallis surrendered on October 19, 1781, the new nation learned of it quickly. But perhaps no news of the era spread so quickly as that of the Declaration of Independence in 1776—or was so happily remembered.

For years, neighbors of mine in Maryland gave a poolside party on the Glorious Fourth. It always featured a round of rum cocktails, New England–style, and the reading of the Declaration from the back steps. I recommend this. Thomas Jefferson's prose is good to proclaim and stirring to hear.

One year the guests included a charming young Englishwoman, herself an attorney, and as a neighbor submitted the charges against the king she leaned over and murmured, "I feel absurdly guilty."

The only possible answer was a smile and a jingle of ice cubes.

AS AN ENGLISHMAN ONCE REMARKED, YOU wouldn't invite a friend to come over for a thimbleful of beer. I often thought of this when comparing the scope of history—whole vatfuls of it, so to speak—with the size of our books—say, a generous pitcherful.

Choosing heroes and themes for *Those Inventive Americans* was a happy torment of riches, from the waterside hopefuls working on steamboats to the earthbound hopefuls assembling contraptions to fly in. Our living subjects in 1971 included four Nobel laureates in physics and a memorable representative of immigrant inventors, Vladimir Kosma Zworykin from imperial Russia, sometimes called the father of television. He was a pioneer in the technology that has since his time altered political campaigns and moved the Wild West from backyard shootout games into the family den.

"ABOUT THE ONLY THING THAT'S CLOSE OUT here is history," wrote Charles McCarry in *The Great Southwest.* He and a magazine colleague, George F. Mobley, blended their artistry in a fine example of Special Publications' popular one-author-one-photographer format.

George found freshness in world-famous terrain, in wind-etched faces, and in such diversions as the Intergalactic Chicken Flying Contest of Luckenbach, Texas. Mac caught the music of breezes and the Papago language and scores of local voices; he marked the sweep of time from geology to artists' colonies, a stone ax to radio telescopes, the vanished Anasazi to the elusive border jumper.

"When do we come in?" This, a high school history teacher told me the other day, is a question he often hears from Latino students. It may be a natural question in Maryland today, but it probably was not when

McCarry was visiting a region where settlers from Mexico planted Spanish traditions long before *los Estados Unidos* proclaimed themselves in 1776. (Mac evoked that event unforgettably from a lonely camp in the San Juan Mountains.)

"For me, *The Great Southwest* is a book of memories." That was the comment of Don Crump, a stalwart of Special Publications from the start and now himself a heartening memory.

Don, who hailed from Oklahoma, took pride in his Cheyenne ancestry. His mother was born in a tepee, and her mother told "a frightening account of soldiers' bullets whining past" in 1875, in one of the last skirmishes in Indian Territory. "Only in America," says his family: That girl grew up to marry a soldier, an immigrant from Hungary.

NOT EVERY SURVIVOR'S STORY ENDED SO well. Not everyone survived. A chronicle of that era is the 153rd Special Publication, Herman Viola's recent *Trail to Wounded Knee: The Last Stand of the Plains Indians 1860-1890.* It is a harrowing story, the more powerful for the pictographs by Indian artists and the photographs by white contemporaries.

Viola's book gives the reality beyond the old movies, the innocent backyard games. It presents the climax to a struggle for land, obvious as early as 1763, when the British tried to prevent white settlement west of the Appalachians, or 1776, when Jefferson accused George III of stirring up "the merciless Indian savages." I am glad I read it. I feel—not absurdly—guilty.

Probably many of us would disown this story if we could. It would be soothing to think, "My ancestors hadn't even come here then!" or "I wasn't even born before the Bicentennial!" But we inherit all of our history. To accept only the agreeable parts, I think, would be like taking a marriage vow for richer but not for poorer, in health but not in sickness, for better but not for worse. Not a formula for happily ever after.

FOR 1986, THE CENTENNIAL OF THE STATUE of Liberty, our staff prepared a large-format book called *Liberty: The Statue and the American Dream,* published by the Statue of Liberty–Ellis Island Foundation. Leslie Allen wrote a crisp account of the monument and a longer account of immigration, with poignant family details. A separate portfolio stressed the unique fate of African Americans set apart by slavery and stigma. A special brochure announcing the book prompted a challenge from a reader. He was himself African American, he wrote; did we think we had done justice to this theme?

I answered in words along the following lines: The longer I work in this program, the more I hesitate to make such a claim. Our subjects are large, intricate, as subtle as any life; they humble us. I can assure you that we do our best to convey the proper context, the accurate fact, the tang and nuance of detail. It is for our readers to say if we succeed.

I ended my communication to him by saying that I hoped he would examine *Liberty* and see if he wanted to keep it. He wrote a gracious reply, saying he would do just that. I hope he liked it.

As we would say for any book, we hope you like this one.

In the harbor of Charleston, South Carolina, British warships bombarded Fort Sullivan on June 28, 1776. The fort's spongy palmetto logs absorbed the impact, and the British withdrew. Both editions of The Revolutionary War *mixed modern and historical illustrations to tell the saga.*

REVOLUTIONARY WAR (1967 & 2004)

by Bart McDowell & John M. Thompson

Designing a Stars and Stripes To be an Emblem Forever

No one knows for sure who designed the United States flag or whether it flew during any Revolutionary War battle. General Washington was issued no official American flags to fly until the spring of 1783, when peace was being negotiated.

Various heraldic standards began to appear in the early years of the Revolution. One popular motif was the rattlesnake—a native American reptile much feared by European soldiers—on a yellow or red-and-white striped field, often accompanied by the phrase, "Don't Tread on Me." From 1775 to 1777 the unofficial American flag was the Continental Colors, or Grand Union flag. Consisting of 13 alternating red and white stripes with a British Union Jack in the upper lefthand corner, the Grand Union suited colonies still attached to the mother country.

After the Declaration of Independence, the main business of the day was to fight a war. But Congress found time on June 14, 1777, to issue a resolution "that the flag of the United States be thirteen stripes, alternate red and white; that the union be thirteen stars, white in a blue field, representing a new constellation." Flags began appearing with different arrangements—13 stars in a circle, or 12 circling a central star, or (the most popular) stars in horizontal rows. Historians have been unable to verify whether Betsy Ross designed this flag, and no one is certain who first called it the Stars and Stripes. Betsy Ross did make flags for Pennsylvania, but the first we know of her association with the Stars and Stripes is when her grandson claimed in 1870 that she designed it at the request of George Washington. It is likely that Francis Hopkinson, artist and delegate to the Continental Congress, had some say in the design.

The new American flag was first saluted in a foreign port on February 14, 1778, when John Paul Jones sailed the *Ranger* into Quiberon Bay, France. A flag at the battle of Yorktown in 1781 inspired Pvt. Joseph Martin to write, "I felt a secret pride swell in my heart when I saw the 'star-spangled banner' waving majestically."

When Vermont and Kentucky entered the Union in 1795, two new stars and two new stripes were added. By 1818, though, it became clear that as states increased, the flag would be cluttered with stripes. Congress mandated a return to just 13, to represent the original colonies, plus a star for every state. No one put in writing why red, white, and blue were the chosen colors for the flag, but Congress approved them for the Great Seal of the United States, interpreting red to stand for courage, white for purity, and blue for justice.

This flag, opposite, reportedly flew at a Pennsylvania public reading of the Declaration of Independence on July 8, 1776. Below, the Stars and Stripes rose over New York Harbor when the British departed in November 1783.

186 The Revolutionary War

187

Whereas the 1967 edition was a travelogue, the 2004 book (above) relayed anecdotes and artifacts.

In 1967 National Geographic published a book titled simply *The Revolutionary War*. In it the author managed to cover every significant event and personality of the Revolution while weaving in a first-person account of his visits to battlefields and other historical sites.

"The essence of this book is personal involvement," wrote Editor Gilbert M. Grosvenor. Readers were to discover the war and its history by traveling along with the author. In the first excerpt here, the author and his family visit Philadelphia's Independence Hall. Through his children's reactions during the outing, he recounts the creation of the Declaration of Independence.

Nearly 40 years later readers' tastes had changed; a new book in the Special Collection with the same title took a different approach. Instead of a travel narrative on a history theme, it represented the war with a straightforward, condensed history, spending roughly the same amount of text filling out key stories of the Revolution. A first-person presence was no longer desired by author, editor, or even perhaps reader. Authorial intrusion was minimized, or, in this case, gone altogether, in favor of an unfiltered history, perhaps more useful as a pull-off-the-shelf reference. Readers lost the personal touch but gained details about Jefferson and the story of the Declaration.

Declaring Independence

Two writers, 37 years apart, portray the defining moment

Our family celebrated the Glorious Second of July by visiting Philadelphia's Independence Hall [wrote McDowell, traveling with his wife, Martha, and children, Rob, Kel, Tina, and Josh]; we dropped by again on the Fourth. During those visits, we got the feel of time and place.... In 1776, men bitterly, noisily raised their voices here. Delegates quarreled over Jefferson's phrases, deleting some.

The freckle-faced Virginian sat next to Dr. Franklin, "who perceived that I was not insensible to these mutilations," Thomas Jefferson later remembered.

"I have made it a rule," Franklin confided to his young friend, "... to avoid becoming the draftsman of papers to be reviewed by a public body."

At last, on July 4, Congress adopted Jefferson's revised Declaration of Independence.

In 1817 Congress commissioned John Trumbull to paint four large canvases for the Capitol. In this one Thomas Jefferson, flanked by John Adams and Benjamin Franklin, presents the Declaration of Independence to John Hancock.

In winter camp at Valley Forge, Pennsylvania, Gen. George Washington reviews the troops who have not yet fallen to disease, starvation, or cold. This image, used in both editions, tells a story that marked a turning point in the Revolution. Washington's determination during the grim winter of 1777-78 kept the Revolution alive.

"THE REVOLUTION WAS IN THE MINDS OF THE PEOPLE," WROTE JOHN ADAMS IN A LETTER TO THOMAS JEFFERSON YEARS LATER, IN 1815.

"But that old Trumbull painting doesn't show them signing," said Kel.

Delegates waited for an engrossed copy.

On July 8, outside the Hall, the Declaration was read to a crowd of Philadelphians. On August 2, most of the members of Congress signed it—but not all: At least one signed as late as November. And all of the 56 signatures but President John Hancock's and Secretary Charles Thomson's were kept secret until 1777.

"Were they really afraid?" asked Tina, who had always assumed the Founding Fathers were fearless. The last words of the Declaration itself answered her question: "...we mutually pledge to each other our Lives, our Fortunes and our sacred Honor." Together they had committed an act of treason. They knew the risks—death by hanging for themselves, poverty and dishonor for their families—and still they signed. Secrecy was the minimum prudence.

They made nervous jokes of gallows humor. Heavy Benjamin Harrison chuckled; when his turn came at the British noose, he said, his weight would bring him swift mercy.

But the risk was real. Of the 56 signers, 15 had their homes destroyed in the war. Some signers were seized by the British and thrown in jail. Others narrowly missed capture; and still others experienced the heartbreak of seeing their libraries burned, their colts killed, their children taunted as sons of traitors.

"Their *colts* killed?" my daughter asked in shock. It was true. When British soldiers raided Jefferson's farm, they seized all horses big enough to travel—and cut the throats of the foals they left behind. Tina regarded this act as a major atrocity.

Many an American recoiled from the Declaration. Washington's friend Bryan Fairfax sided with his king. John Dickinson, who refused to sign the Declaration, was still willing to fight beside his neighbors.

But the street crowd showed no such brainy restraint. Everywhere, until the last frontier settlement got the news in September, communities were busy with their celebrations.

Typical was Worcester, Massachusetts, where thirsty patriots "repaired to the tavern, lately known by the sign ... King's Arms," reported Isaiah Thomas's newspaper. The royal sign was removed and toasts were offered for "Prosperity and perpetuity to the United States of America" and about two dozen other noble things—including one toast to "Perpetual itching without the benefit of scratching to the enemies of America."

When she heard that one, Tina rolled in mirth—then halted abruptly and counted the toasts.

"They had 13 drinks before that one," she said. "Do you think they were—*drunk?*"

But I read on: "The greatest decency and good order was observed...."

AT THAT MEETING ON JUNE 7, VIRGINIAN Richard Henry Lee introduced three resolutions [wrote John M. Thompson in the 2004 edition].

He proposed the establishment of an American confederation. He called for an official attempt to gain European allies. And he called for a public proclamation "that these United States are, and of right ought to be, free and independent states, that they are absolved from all allegiance to the British crown, and that all political connection between them and the state of Great Britain is, and ought to be, totally dissolved."

That robust announcement would end up, almost word for word, in one of the most important documents in the history of the United States and the world: the Declaration of Independence. The five committee members appointed to create the document agreed that Jefferson was the best writer and appointed him to draft the text. Curiously enough, statesmen of the time considered the issue of alliances more significant than the break with Britain. John Adams, appointed to both the proclamation and the alliance committees, took on drafting the proposed treaty and palmed off the job of writing a document declaring independence.

The 32-year-old planter-statesman assigned to write the draft came up with a remarkably forceful yet eloquent statement of the embryonic nation's hopes and ideals. Incorporating earlier resolutions, as well as political philosophy dating back to 17th-century English philosopher John Locke, the 1,817-word statement asserted that "all men are created equal," and that among the rights all were born with were "life, liberty, and the pursuit of happiness."

JEFFERSON'S NOW CANONIC PHRASES, IT is interesting to note, differ from sources he had at hand. His fellow Virginian, George Mason, penned that colony's Declaration of Rights, which stated that "all men are by nature equally free and independent." And when John Locke listed intrinsic human rights, they included "life, liberty, and property." Jefferson's changes have provided fodder for generations of discussion and debate in classrooms and legislatures.

If a government violates the very rights it is supposed to protect, wrote Jefferson, then it is the duty of the governed to rebel. He backs up the claim of "abuses and usurpations" with 26 grievances against the King, building to an almost journalistic hyperbole: "He has plundered our Seas, ravaged our Coasts, burnt our towns, and destroyed the Lives of our People. He is, at this Time, transporting large Armies of foreign Mercenaries to complete the works of Death, Desolation, and Tyranny." As a result of these outrages, the colonies declared themselves severed from Britain, with the signers pledging "our lives, our fortunes, and our sacred honor."

Members of Congress got a chance to hack at Jefferson's draft a bit. The author wasn't pleased by the cuts, but he was satisfied that his colleagues left it pretty much intact.

One phrase condemning George III for condoning the slave trade was cut: The denunciation seemed hypocritical, but the text did retain the charge that the king was inciting slaves to rebel against their owners.

The decision to declare independence did not come easily. Some patriots—including, for example, John Dickinson of Pennsylvania—opposed the plan vehemently. Representatives from New Jersey, Maryland, and South Carolina argued against independence. Those in favor of it in Pennsylvania had to work outside existing governmental structures, organizing a pro-independence Pennsylvania Convention to counter the strong opposition in the Pennsylvania Assembly, led by Dickinson.

On July 2, 1776, Lee's resolution passed by a vote of 12 colonies, with New York abstaining. John Adams predicted that the day would be forever celebrated. John Dickinson—no Tory, but a conservative who questioned the wisdom of an abrupt break from Britain—chose to miss the vote on July 4, when the Declaration itself, the formal document announcing the resolution, was adopted.

Let there be light: In a reconstruction of Thomas Edison's Menlo Park laboratory in Dearborn, Michigan, a curator lights a replica Edison bulb. An American genius who invented the incandescent lamp and the phonograph, Edison said, "We will make electric light so cheap that only the rich will be able to burn candles."

Those Inventive Americans

(1971)

AGRICULTURE: NEW MACHINES FOR NEW LANDS
Sparks fly as a molten torrent tumbles into molds at Sparrow's Point, Maryland, in a mill belonging to the Bethlehem Steel Company, a major supplier for the automobile industry. In the first half of the 19th century, the growing network of railroads and new factories created a huge market for steel, but not until the 1850's could American mills meet the demand. After the Civil War, however, America came to rival England as the world's leading steel supplier.
Unfinished Oldsmobiles (left) roll along an assembly line in Lansing, Michigan. An outgrowth of experiments with interchangeable parts and mass-production techniques, this line turns out 95 cars an hour. Ransom Olds first applied the system to building automobiles in 1899, nearly ten years before Henry Ford installed an assembly line. By 1904 Oldsmobile production had reached 5,000 cars a year.
Custom-made car nears the end of an Oldsmobile assembly line. Computers guide and time the components—grilles, instrument panels, engines, and optionals—so they reach the right place at the right time. Fenders for a specific car arrive from sub-assembly lines at just the proper moment. The next automobile in line may look entirely different.
62
63

From cars and steel to cyclotrons, American ingenuity fills the pages of Those Inventive Americans.

A celebration of American inventors was a natural choice for a National Geographic Society book. The volume offered portraits of ingenious Americans and their inventions throughout American history. Starting with Benjamin Franklin and his parlor experiments with static electricity, the book moves on to Robert Fulton's steamboat, Eli Whitney's cotton gin, Samuel F. B. Morse's telegraph, Alexander Graham Bell's telephone, Thomas Edison's phonograph and incandescent lamp, and the Wright brothers' flying machine.

Lesser known inventors are covered as well, and what makes the book so interesting are the details about inventions we take for granted now and the stories of the people who gave them to us. One such story is that of Russian-born engineer Vladimir Kosma Zworykin, who more than anyone is responsible for creating television. His wryly recounted experiences encompassing both World Wars reveal a man of remarkable talent and ingenuity. Though he invented many things, he is best known for changing the world with his 1923 iconoscope (camera tube) and 1929 kinescope (cathode-ray picture tube), which together formed the basis of the first all-electronic television system. The long winding road from home-glassblown photocells to modern television should inspire anyone who has worked on a creative endeavor.

The Father of Television

From Joseph J. Binns's portrait of Vladimir Kosma Zworykin

"A few weeks after my enrollment in the Imperial Institute of Technology in St. Petersburg, the police arrived to put a stop to student rioting and disorders. We students barricaded ourselves in a campus building and were besieged for three days. Thus, at the very start of my college career, I had a confrontation with the police which, at that time in Russia, was quite common for a student."

The raconteur is Vladimir Kosma Zworykin, father of television. Fellow members of the National Academy of Engineering in Washington, D.C., are gathered to honor this engineer, scientist, and former student rebel with their coveted Founders Medal on April 24, 1968....

HE WAS BORN JUNE 30, 1889, IN MUROM, Russia, 200 miles east of Moscow, the youngest of seven children. At age nine he started spending his summers as an apprentice aboard the boats his father operated on the Oka River. He eagerly helped repair electrical equipment, and it soon became

Orville Wright flies his biplane for King Alfonso of Spain at Pau, France, in 1909, six years after the Wright brothers' historic first flights. The king promised the queen he would not fly, although he wanted to.

FIRST AND GREATEST OF AMERICAN INVENTIONS WAS, OF COURSE, THE REPUBLIC ITSELF, YET NOTHING IN PARTICULAR INDICATES THAT THE AMERICAN COLONISTS CONSIDERED THEMSELVES ESPECIALLY INVENTIVE.

apparent that he was more interested in electricity than anything nautical.

Upon graduating from high school, he left for the University of St. Petersburg. After attending his first lectures, he resolved to become a physicist—a decision which lasted until his family heard about it. Their view was that in Russia's rising new industries, engineering offered a richer future than physics. Accordingly, Vladimir's father made him transfer to the Imperial Institute of Technology.

He loved the life of a student, even in the setting of restlessness and repression that characterized the decline of Czarist government. His courses included laboratory work in his great love, physics; faculty and students heatedly discussed the new atomic nucleus theory of Ernest Rutherford, the mysterious X-rays discovered in 1895 by Wilhelm Konrad Roentgen, Marie and Pierre Curie's current research in radioactivity.

Boris Rosing, a professor in charge of laboratory projects, became friendly with the young engineer and let him work on some of his private projects: Rosing was trying to transmit pictures by wire in his own physics laboratory. "Needless to say, I was soon there as his understudy," Dr. Zworykin recalls. "It was a glorious three years, and what a perfect school it turned out to be!"

Many scientists were attempting to extend man's sight, as the telegraph and telephone had extended his speech. An outstanding achievement was the mechanical scanner of the German inventor Paul Nipkow, an invention that received the first television patent, in 1884...

Rosing had been quick to see the advantages of an electronic system over Nipkow's mechanical one. He and his young assistant experimented with a primitive cathode-ray tube, developed in Germany by Karl Ferdinand Braun.

"We made almost everything ourselves," Dr. Zworykin recalls, "becoming glassblowers to fashion photocells and amplifying tubes." And in 1910 Rosing exhibited a television system, using a mechanical scanner in the transmitter and the electronic Braun tube in the receiver. Although the system proved impractical, it fired Zworykin's imagination. (Boris Rosing did not live to finish his work. He was arrested during the Russian Revolution and died in exile.)

The lure of theoretical physics drew Zworykin to Paris after he graduated with honors and a scholarship in electrical engineering in 1912. There he studied X-rays under Paul Langevin.... After a year and a half, he was transferred to Officers Radio School, won his commission, and began teaching electronics.

When the Russian Revolution began in 1917 and Zworykin saw that it would disrupt his scientific career, he decided to leave the country, but at first could not get permission. Then the United States refused him a visa. For months he wandered Russia to avoid arrest in the chaos of civil war between the Reds and the Whites.

When an Allied expedition landed in Archangel in September 1918 to aid Russia's northern defenses against the Germans, Zworykin made his way there. Pleading his case with an American official, the earnest young Russian told of the work he would do in

Frames from an 1890s film show a man sneezing. Such early motion picture marvels were viewed through a battery-powered kinetoscope, invented by Thomas Edison's protégé, W. K. L. Dickson.

developing television. He might have made sense to a physicist, but his recital seemed fantastic to the diplomat. Nonetheless, impressed by Zworykin's zeal and personality, he arranged for a visa.

REACHING LONDON SAFELY, ZWORYKIN boarded a ship for America. Traveling first class as befitted an officer and gentleman, he discovered that the other passengers dressed formally for dinner. Not having a dinner jacket, he was chagrined when everyone stared at him each evening as he entered the dining salon. He could not know then this embarrassing situation might one day save his life!

Arriving in the United States in 1919, he soon joined the Westinghouse laboratory staff in Pittsburgh. After trying in vain to persuade his superiors to let him develop an all-electronic television system, he left the company. Eighteen months later he returned, and was given greater freedom to work on his many ideas, especially for television.

The chief components of a modern TV system are the camera at the sending point and the picture reproducer at the receiving point. The camera generates electrical signals that correspond to the brightness (and recently, color) in the transmitted scene. These signals are then processed and amplified so they can be sent over long distances to the receiver, where they are recovered and applied to the picture reproducer. This unit converts the signals into a visible image of the original scene.

A GENERATION OF BOYS LEARNED ELECTRONICS ON MORE-OR-LESS HOMEMADE WIRELESS SETS. MANY WOULD GROW UP TO BE MEN OF SCIENCE AND INVENTION.

In 1923 Zworykin applied for a basic patent on his electronic TV system and exhibited it to a group of Westinghouse executives. "By present standards the demonstration was scarcely impressive," he wrote in 1962. "The transmitted pattern was a cross projected on the target of the camera tube; a similar cross appeared, with low contrasts and rather poor definition, on the screen of the cathode-ray tube."

This performance indicated that his devices were sound—and needed, as he said, *"tremendous improvement"* to be useful. After the demonstration it was suggested that he devote time to "more useful projects." He complied, but he continued to work on electronic television.

On November 18, 1929, at a convention of radio engineers, Zworykin demonstrated a television receiver containing his "kinescope," a cathode-ray tube with the principal features of all modern picture tubes.

And months before that historic session, another event had vitally affected the future of television. Dr. Zworykin met David R. Sarnoff, vice-president and general manager of the Radio Corporation of America. "Sarnoff quickly grasped the potentialities of my proposals," Zworykin later wrote.... A reorganization led to Dr. Zworykin's transfer to RCA in Camden, New Jersey. As the director of their Electronic Research Laboratory, he was able to concentrate on making critical improvements to his system.

Zworykin and his staff began with the TV camera, producing in 1931 an improved version of his "iconoscope," a camera tube. A sensitive screen in its heart builds up an electric charge in proportion to the brightness of the scene at each point, while the scanning beam passes over the rest of the screen. In effect, the screen stores light for each point of the image and intensifies it more than 100,000 times.

Therefore, as the scanning beam hits each spot, it releases a much stronger picture signal than the old mechanical scanners provided.

The iconoscope completed the fundamental elements of a practical, all-electronic television system, and became the mainstay of TV broadcasting until after World War II. Zworykin's "storage principle" is the basis of modern TV.

Starting in 1934, ten years after he became a naturalized U. S. citizen, Dr. Zworykin began to travel extensively for RCA. The beginning of World War II, in 1939, found him in Lebanon, where he managed to get on a plane bound for England. About to sail for the United States aboard the S.S. *Athenia,* he suddenly recalled that his tuxedo was in a trunk he had abandoned in Beirut. The memory of his earlier shipboard embarrassment overwhelmed him, and he decided to wait for a later vessel so he could buy formal wear.

The *Athenia* never reached port. A German U-boat torpedoed and sank her off the Irish coast; among the missing were 28 Americans.

Back in the United States, Dr. Zworykin continued to work. In 1944 the German High Command named him as the inventor of a secret infrared device for the U. S. which could pierce fog and clouds, giving navigators "virtual maps by which to fly." Questioned by reporters, Dr. Zworykin laughed off the story. Curiously enough, he was in

Historical imagery: TV pioneer V. K. Zworykin poses beside a broadcast of the 1969 Apollo 11 splashdown. Atop the television console rests a 1934 version of his "iconoscope" camera tube.

fact working on infrared image tubes that would convert invisible infrared rays into visible light to allow humans to see in the dark without revealing their position. The device made possible the "sniperscope" and the "snooperscope," used by thousands of Allied soldiers in World War II.

After the war, he continued to find new applications for electronics. He imaginatively led such projects as using TV pickup tubes and computers for weather forecasting; computer-controlled traffic signals to prevent traffic jams; and experimental radio transmitters along freeways for automatic driving of specially-equipped automobiles, to eliminate highway accidents.... A humanist, keenly aware that inventions do not automatically serve the public interest, he has suggested that television, the industry he helped to create, may one day strengthen the voice of the people....

"Our first close view of the moon and the planets will, undoubtedly, be through the eyes of television," he wrote in 1954. Pictures sent from satellites in the mid-1960s proved his foresight.

THE GREAT SOUTHWEST (1980)

by Charles McCarry

With the sky for a ceiling and not a wall in sight, a weary cowhand beds down after a long day in the saddle on a West Texas ranch. The cowboy and the open range have long been integral to the mystique of the great Southwest.

Southwestern landscapes spread to include Indians, prospectors, cowboys, farmers, artists, and entrepreneurs.

Special Collection editors sent the veteran writer-photographer team of Charles McCarry and George F. Mobley out to the American Southwest for a book that would cover the region's plains and prairies, cities, mountains, canyon country, desert, plateau country, and Rio Grande Valley. Their efforts resulted in a sweeping canvas that presents both history and modern culture through carefully observed travel journalism.

McCarry served as a speechwriter in the Eisenhower Administration; after a stint in the Army, he worked undercover for the CIA in Europe, Asia, and Africa. Turning to journalism, he wrote for several national magazines, but became famous as a writer of spy novels, including *The Tears of Autumn* (1974) and *The Better Angels* (1979). In our excerpt he shows his skills in a number of ways. Starting on the Fourth of July in Colorado's San Juan Mountains, he leaps in his imagination to the first Independence Day, more than 200 years earlier, and pictures a conversation with a local Indian about events in faraway Philadelphia. The scene gives us a sense of the country's size and how removed the Southwest was from those early struggles. He then adroitly compares nearby mine structures to gold prospectors, neatly handing us an image of the area's Old West history. Cowboy Chet Smith brings that history up to the present day.

Man's Natural Speed

Recalling Independence Day in Colorado's San Juan Mountains

I opened my eyes on the Fourth of July and saw the flag of the dawn—a patch of red sunlight reflected on a field of snow—climbing toward the morning star, which shone for a last moment between the black of night and the blue of day.

If the colors were right, so was the music: the rustle of aspen leaves in a gentle breeze, the rush of a mountain stream in the place where I had made my camp, 12,000 feet above the sea in the San Juan Mountains of Colorado.

I was alone, but of course I was not alone. This was a natural camp, a soft place where a little grass grew on the stony face of the mountain—a place where there was new water, sun-melted the day before, a place where a ledge and a grove of trees provided shelter from winds that still blew bitter cold when the sun was down. Others had camped here: the Ute and those who came before the Ute; the trapper and the hunter, the miner. Their fire circles and their ghostly footprints were all around me.

In my imagination, I saw an American with a feather in his headband, broiling a trout here on July 4, 1776. What would he have replied if, somehow, I could have stepped across 204 years from my morning on the mountain to his and told him what was occurring 1,800 miles to the east in a muggy city called Philadelphia? There, a group of rebellious subjects of a king who resided still another 3,500 miles to the east were solemnly voting to adopt a Declaration of Independence—thereby transforming themselves into Americans and their simple agrarian colonies into a union whose citizens would, in only eight generations, leap from the plowshare to the spaceship. No doubt my original American, on hearing that, would have given me his breakfast, for The People were ever generous and good to madmen.

There had been madness in these mountains. As sunlight tugged at shadow, I caught a glimpse across the valley of the buildings of an abandoned mine. Weatherbeaten, leaning drunkenly, they clung to the hillside as a prospector clings to his dream of gold. Here, abundant gold and silver were realities in the last three decades of the 19th century.

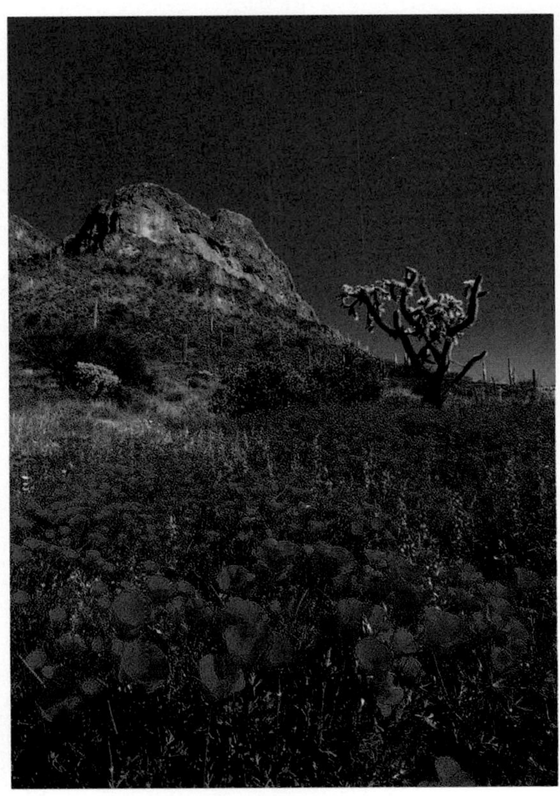

Golden poppies splash a slope of the Ajo Mountains in Arizona's Organ Pipe Cactus National Monument. Uphill from them, a gnarled jumping cholla rises beneath an eroded volcanic butte.

Winding its way to the Gulf of Mexico, the Rio Grande provides water for plentiful crops of citrus, vegetables, and cotton. The lower Rio Grande Valley boasts a year-round growing season.

Although the boom ended long ago, mining continues in the San Juans, and living men still remember the afterglow of the glory days. In Durango, which became a smelting center for the mining region, I heard Arthur Isgar speak of the human cost. "My father died in 1936 at the Gold King Mine," said Art. "He'd been a miner all his life, and he worked all that day and died in his sleep, with two of his sons near him in the same bunkhouse." All four of Art's full brothers were miners a good part of their lives. He chose ranching as a career, and he is the only one of the five still living.

The Spaniards prospected in these mountains, and local legend holds that the Ute and other upland tribes knew of the existence of gold but kept the secret for fear of losing their hunting ground to feverish whites. Mountain men, who came in search of beaver pelts to be made into tall hats for European and American dandies, were hardly more talkative than the Indians, and for the same reasons.

The Spanish law forbade foreigners to carry on trade within the empire of Spain. Trappers risked the fate of one expedition whose furs, valued at $30,380.74½, "the fruits of two years' labor and perils," were confiscated in 1817 by the Governor of New Mexico. But if the authorities in Santa Fe were strict, mountain men weary of isolation found a season in hospitable Taos a highly congenial experience. This adobe town at the southern end of the mountains was, as the popular historian Harvey Fergusson wrote, ... "more than any other place ... the heart of the mountains."

DURING THE LONG PERIOD OF SPANISH dominion, a visit to Taos could be a thrilling business—especially if Utes, Apaches, and Comanches all happened to be in the plaza at the same time, as was sometimes the case, and if they happened to be at war with one another. There was a brisk trade in everything, including human beings. The fiercer Indians sold to the Spaniards, and sometimes to other tribes, the captives they had taken the year before. The practice continued under Mexican and then United States rule: A young, healthy Indian could be bought for $300 even after New Mexico became U. S. territory.

That memory brought a rueful smile to the lips of Fray Angelico Chavez, a Franciscan historian and poet who is descended from one of the first families of New Mexico. "People here boast of the pure Spanish blood that runs in their veins," he told me with a twinkle of scholarly mischief. "But perhaps they get some of their pride from the blood of the Kiowa and Pawnee that were bought from the Comanche and taken as wives—and from those wild Anglo-Saxons who married our women later on."

But on that Fourth of July morning in the San Juan Mountains, I was living, however briefly, the life that men long lived among the peaks—a life alone with nature. Some live it still. In the La Sal Mountains of Utah, I had spent time in a mountain cabin with an ageless cowboy named Chet Smith. Texas-born and Colorado-raised, Chet had been in the country around the La Sals since 1927, and had been working for the family of rancher Hardy Redd for more than 40 years. "I can't live in a town," said Chet, warming up a pot of stew for Hardy and me. "I've got to be out where I can't hear no noise." Chet paused. "Hardy, what's that blankety-blank *hum*?" That "hum" was a machine working underground in a mine ten miles distant. "Too close," said Chet, and served the stew.

The mountain men lived on into Chet Smith's time. He remembers a trapper named Burt Rowel who lived high in the La Sals. The snows can come in October, and they can be deep; there's no getting out once they've fallen. "Burt would kill a

At age 93, desert-weathered artist Georgia O'Keeffe displays "Black Place III," depicting a mountain where she camped one stormy night. The Wisconsin-born artist bought a New Mexico ranch house in 1940.

porcupine when he saw one and hang it up in a tree," Chet recalled. "If he got caught in a storm he was all set—he'd find him one of them froze-up porcupines, cook it, and sleep by the fire under the tree where he'd hung it."

Gone, though, are the days when Chet was a top hand on the Redd ranches and each spring the cowboys would trail hundreds of Herefords through the Paradox Valley to summer pasture in the high country.

"It was a pleasant thing, a cattle drive," Hardy told me. "You'd start early, push along at a steady walk for three or four hours, then let the cattle drift along, grazing. Around noon you might stop for shade from the heat. Finally another couple hours trailing in cool evening; then a campfire and supper, maybe venison, and you'd eat all you could hold. We truck the cattle now. But the pace of a horse following a cow, to me that's more man's natural speed."...

Something more than 400,000 acres of the San Juan National Forest has been declared a wilderness area. "A wilderness ... is hereby recognized as an area where the earth and its community of life are untrammeled by man," reads the Wilderness Act. In 1965, the first year after the passage of the law, 44,700 visitor-days were recorded in what is now the section of Weminuche Wilderness west of the Continental Divide. By 1979, that number had quadrupled to 187,700. The wilderness, in short, is not exactly untrammeled by man.

Backlit by a setting sun, resplendent storm clouds gather over the central Plains, where American Indians hunted buffalo and prayed to the creator for thousands of years. Their way of life came to a quick end as prospectors and settlers pushed into native lands in the late 19th century.

TRAIL TO WOUNDED KNEE (2003)

by Herman J. Viola

Mitch Boyer (above), half Lakota, half French, served as interpreter for the Crow scouts with the Seventh Cavalry. Boyer told the scouts to leave, but he stayed and died with Custer. Also killed that day was Little Brave (below), an Arikara scout.

Goose, shot in the hand at Little Bighorn, was one of the Arikara Indians who agreed to help the Seventh Cavalry in the 1876 campaign.

128

129

Indian scouts who helped Custer and the Seventh Cavalry are part of the story in Trail to Wounded Knee.

To write up one of the more inglorious times in American history, the Book Division assigned a curator emeritus of the Smithsonian Institution, also a former director of the National Anthropological Archives and a man who has been embraced by the Native American community: Herman J. Viola. Viola has authored numerous books on American Indians before and since. His first book for the National Geographic Society chronicled the demise of the Plains Indians. In a single generation, from 1860 to 1890, a proud and resourceful people were decimated and overcome by the U.S. Army. They were the last of the Indians to give up their traditional lifestyle.

The following excerpt is from Viola's chapter on the defeat of the Nez Perce. In the summer of 1877, a faction of about 800 Nez Perce men, women, and children, who refused to settle on a reservation, were hounded by the Army through 1,700 miles of Idaho, Wyoming, and Montana. Several hundred people died in pitched battles or from hunger, cold, and fatigue. Four months of skirmishing and desperate flight ended only 40 miles short of Canada and escape. Viola brings his storytelling ability to bear on this sad tale: Instead of ending with Chief Joseph's famous speech, he gives the final word to an aide to General Howard, a man who had chased down the Nez Perce and yet clearly came in the end to respect them.

Tired of Fighting

The sad, strained days leading up to the massacre

The tragic odyssey of the Nez Perce ended on September 30 in the Bear Paw Mountains, less than 40 miles from the Canadian border. This time, soldiers under Col. Nelson A. Miles surprised the fugitives. Again it was a near thing. Miles ordered a cavalry charge, but the soldiers had to cross 4 miles of open terrain, which gave the Nez Perce time to react.

White Bird set up a battle line of a hundred riflemen. They stopped the cavalry charge dead in its tracks, killing 24 troopers and wounding another 42. U.S. troopers managed to drive off most of the Nez Perce horses, so the Indians were trapped. Even worse, key warriors died in the initial attack, among them old Toohoolhoolzote and Ollokot, Joseph's brother, one of the best military minds in

Inspired by painter George Catlin, Philadelphia artist Charles Deas headed west, settling in St. Louis, where he painted scenes of American Indian life such as this 1845 oil, "A Group of Sioux."

Yankton Sioux in war bonnets toured the sights of Washington, D.C., in 1905, and—perhaps unwittingly—helped promote the Toledo Touring Car. Tribal delegations were often considered exploitable photo ops.

the Nez Perce camp. Surrounded by an overwhelming force armed with cannons, the fugitives had three choices: surrender, fight, or slip away during the night, leaving the elderly and wounded behind.

The Nez Perce were besieged for five days. During that time a storm blew in and heavy snow fell for two days, adding to their discomfort. Two Nez Perce treaty chiefs, accompanying the soldiers, entered the camp and tried to convince the fugitives to surrender, claiming that their people could return to Idaho homelands in the spring. Looking Glass and White Bird wanted to continue the fight; Joseph—worried about the women and children huddled in pits dug for protection from Miles's howitzers—wanted to surrender. As the conference of chiefs broke up, a stray bullet struck Looking Glass in the head, killing him instantly. That night White Bird secretly led as many as 300 of the trapped Nez Perce through the military cordon and into Canada.

AFTER FOUR MONTHS AND 1,700 MILES, the end arrived for the Nez Perce. They fought and defeated several numerically superior armies; they behaved with dignity and restraint along the way; they committed few atrocities and paid for the supplies and ammunition they obtained from farmers and merchants. Embarrassed military commanders began to believe they were chasing a "Red Napoleon." But Napoleon himself could not have done much better, given the handicaps the fugitives faced. Not only were the whites against them, but so were many of the tribes to whom they appealed for assistance. Indeed, warriors from several tribes joined the Army in the chase, attracted by the desire for fine Nez Perce horses as much as by the opportunity to earn war honors once again, even if on behalf of the white man.

On the afternoon of October 5, 1877, Joseph ended the struggle. "I am tired of fighting," he said. "Our chiefs are killed. Looking Glass is dead. Toohoolhoolzote is dead. The old men are all dead. It is the young men who say yes or no. He who led the young men [Joseph's brother, Ollokot] is dead. It is cold and we have no blankets. The little children are freezing to death.... Hear me my chiefs! I am tired. My heart is sick and sad. From where the sun now stands, I will fight no more forever." All the Nez Perce leaders deserve credit for the brilliant campaign, but when the end came, only Joseph was left, and he receives all the acclaim for the campaign.

Joseph surrendered on the promise that he and his followers could return to Idaho. But the government ignored that promise and sent them instead to Oklahoma Territory. There they remained until 1883, when a few widows and orphans were allowed to return to Lapwai and the remaining Nez Perce Indians were sent with Joseph to the Colville reservation in northern Washington. None of Joseph's children went north with him. All had died in Oklahoma.

For the Nez Perce, these troubles had been a civil war, pitting family against family, band against band. The majority were already adjusting to the new order, so most did not suffer the psychological trauma that devastated their more militant neighbors on the Northern Plains. Like the Sioux, many Nez

Blind and near 90, Chief Red Cloud of the Oglala Sioux maintained a dignified aspect.

Perce—Joseph among them—sought an explanation and escape from their difficulties through dreamer religions. Their prayers, though, did not take the violent twist of the followers of the Ghost Dance, the dreamer religion that soon swept through the Sioux tribes in the late 1880s and raised suspicions among government officials, culminating in the massacre at Wounded Knee.

As for Joseph, for the rest of his life he pleaded to return to Idaho. The white people who lived in his former homeland objected, so he remained in Washington until his death in 1904. On the news of Joseph's death, an aide who had fought under General Howard wrote an appropriate epitaph: "I think that in his long career, Joseph cannot accuse the Government of the United States of one single act of justice."

CHAPTER THREE

World History & Cultures

Introduction by George E. Stuart

Writers and photographers traveled around the world, creating titles for the Special Collection. From Iran to Iceland, Tahiti to Tikal, the stories and images abounded, bringing the world into sharper focus for millions of readers.

For nearly 40 years, from 1960 to 1998, George Stuart was staff archaeologist for the National Geographic Society. During that time he edited and wrote for the magazine, chaired the Committee for Research and Exploration, and worked as a cartographer for the Map Division. As an archaeologist, he has done fieldwork at North American and Mesoamerican sites. He lives in western North Carolina, where he serves as president of the Boundary End Archaeology Research Center, a study center and library dedicated to Maya and Mesoamerican archaeology, epigraphy, and iconography.

I first saw Tikal through the age-dimmed windows of an old DC-3—a cluster of five great stone pyramid-temples rising as sunlit islands in a vast dark green sea of unbroken rain forest. It was 1968, and my family and I had booked seats on the early morning flight from Guatemala City to the famed Maya ruins in the remote lowland region north of the capital.

Seven of us traveled together: my wife, Gene, and four children—three boys and a girl ranging in age from 3 to 13—along with photographer Gordon W. Gahan. It was a scary flight—they all are for me—but at the time it was the only easy way to get to Tikal. As our plane finally dipped toward the dirt airstrip, I could see the thatched roofs nearby—the archaeologists' camp and, probably, the Jungle Lodge, where we would spend the next week.

Only an hour or so after landing, we found ourselves walking in single file, following a shaded trail beneath the high canopy of rain forest, led by the legendary guide, Clarence Massiah. All was quiet for a while, until the monkeys in the treetops above began screaming their protests at our invasion of their territory.

Before our visit, I had carefully read all the available guidebooks and reports on Tikal and had corresponded with the University of Pennsylvania archaeologists who were excavating there. None of this had adequately prepared me for the daunting reality of the place.

We followed winding trails along ravines and among the mounds and pyramids. A few were restored, at least in part; others were untouched, towering overgrown heaps of rubble, sometimes with parts of walls or stairways showing through. Most of these structures were arranged to form large plazas or smaller courtyards, all now largely overgrown with dense bush.

In the cleared Great Plaza, we stood and contemplated the imposing stone stelae and altars carved with figures and hieroglyphic texts. Nearby rose the incredibly steep Temple I, far too slippery to climb safely—or so it seemed to my cautious eye. All of us simply stood in wonderment as we began to realize the scope and achievement of the Maya who had built here one of the greatest cities of world antiquity between 2,500 and 1,000 years before.

OUR FAMILY'S TRAVELS THROUGH AMERICA'S past had begun earlier that year, toward the end of my first decade of working as the staff archaeologist for the National Geographic Society.

Robert L. Breeden, director of the Special Publications division, knowing of my background in American archaeology, asked if I would be interested in writing a summary of the topic for the popular book series. He added, almost casually, that the work would necessarily be a firsthand account, so I would be free to visit any archaeological site I needed to see in

WITH A WEAK SMILE, I RESORTED TO WHAT HAS BECOME MY FAVORITE RESPONSE TO ANY QUESTION ABOUT CULTURE: "IT IS JUST THE WAY WE DO IT."

person, with my whole family, of course, and at Society expense! I was stunned.

The results of that family trek, spanning the archaeological riches of the much of the United States, Mexico, and part of Central America, appeared in 1969 as *Discovering Man's Past in the Americas,* the 15th volume of the Special Collection, with Gene and me as co-authors, illustrated by a roster of master photographers including Lyntha Scott Eiler, Otis Imboden, and Bates Littlehales.

OUR VISIT TO TIKAL REMAINS BUT ONE OF many, many special memories I have kept from my 30-year involvement with the Special Collection book-publishing program. As an anthropologist I especially remember the more than a dozen volumes dedicated to looking at the incredibly rich world of human culture, defined as the sum total of learned behavior, including everything from ways of subsistence to religious beliefs.

The titles of those works speak for themselves: *The Incredible Incas* by Loren McIntyre, *The Mighty Aztecs* and *America's Ancient Cities* by Gene S. Stuart, *Clues to America's Past* by Douglas W. Schwartz and other experts—and many others. Together the four volumes sampled in the chapter that follows reflect the sheer scope of the variety of human culture as it was in different times and in different places, and how some succeeded while others failed: recurring themes in the Special Collection titles about world cultures.

Writing effectively about culture presents a supreme challenge to anyone who attempts it. The reason: Each of us carries the baggage of bias and idiosyncrasy of his or her own culture, and this tempers or affects our ability to accurately describe, much less explain, the behavior and beliefs of others whose ways of life differ from ours.

Realization of this fundamental problem of cultural observation came to me suddenly through a trivial episode that took place on a spring afternoon in 1974, in the village of Cobá, in the northeastern part of the Yucatán Peninsula. At the time my family and I lived in a sturdy house of pole and thatch in the rural settlement where I had come to help map the vast expanse of ancient Maya ruins in the surrounding forest. The six Stuarts had only recently just settled in to a dramatically new way of life as the only newcomers in a community of some 350 Maya. On the day in question, *we*—the strangers—became the primary focus of village curiosity.

A DAY OR SO BEFORE EASTER, WE DECIDED it was time to dye eggs for the occasion, and we had brought packets of powdered dye from the United States in anticipation of the need. From one of our neighbors who ran a small general store, we had purchased a few surplus eggs—ever a rarity in the settlement. These we had carefully taken home, boiled over the open fire of our hearth, and allowed to cool for a few hours in the shade.

We then gathered in the front yard to properly prepare Easter eggs. Soon our neighbors gathered to watch this curious ceremony. Finally, one came forward and asked politely why we were coloring our eggs.

I tried to explain, but soon saw that my attempt was going nowhere, for I myself really had no idea why I was coloring eggs. Did I know then that the egg was a symbol of resurrection associated with the season, or that it had a history of complex associations with the hare that eventually became the Easter Bunny in western European tradition? Of course not! (But I made certain to read about this later.)

Finally, with a weak smile, I resorted to what has become my favorite response to any question about culture. It was once uttered by an old Seneca in answer to a query from an anthropologist about the meaning behind a ritual he had recently observed: "It is just the way we do it."

THE CHAPTER THAT FOLLOWS PRESENTS excerpts from four books in the Special Collection that deal with the extraordinary variety of ways in which human beings "do" their customs and ways.

In *Nomads of the World* (1971), Mohammad Bahmanbegui, then director of Iran's Office of Tribal Education, gives us a vivid and loving narrative of his own people, the Qashqā'ī shepherds of the Zāgros Mountains, the rugged border area bordering the Persian Gulf and Iraq.

At the moment in time when the book was published, nearly four decades ago, the wandering life of the Qashqā'ī centered on herding and rug weaving in a culture that had masterfully adapted to its environment. Soon, as we now know, this very area would serve as the setting for the momentous changes that have taken place since Bahmanbegui wrote.

In *The Vikings* (1972), Howard La Fay re-creates the epic of the remarkable Scandinavians who raided, traded, and settled the vast area of the North Atlantic and Mediterranean worlds from Malta to mainland America. Howard wrote of the modern descendants of the Vikings as well.

In *Voyages to Paradise* (1981), Will Gray retraces the travels of Capt. James Cook, one of the most remarkable and able explorers to come out of Europe in the 18th century. In three epic voyages between 1768 and 1779, when he met his death on a Hawaiian beach, Cook observed and described the many varied and now long-lost ways of life in Polynesia and the northwest coast of North America. Gray's summation of Cook's achievement shows how this observer of human ways literally changed the world.

The Mysterious Maya, which Gene and I first published in 1977, was based on our many years of travel, beginning with Tikal a decade earlier and ending in Cobá, where we lived our daily lives with these remarkable people. In the excerpt that ends this chapter, you will witness a *Chachaac* ceremony held by a Maya shaman to help bring rain to a drought-stricken village, along with other incidents of life that took place not long after the episode involving our Easter egg rite.

As you might imagine, living in Cobá for the better part of two years, like all of our travels among the Maya, had an enormous and lasting effect on our family. Perhaps the most important lesson of all that we, the other observers featured in this chapter, and, hopefully, their readers learned comes down to one simple yet profound conclusion: Other people live differently and believe different things, and it's all right, for in the long term only mutual respect among cultures can guarantee the continuation of peace and life on this planet.

Lifeline in a monochromatic void, a train of Lapp nomads and their reindeer-hauled sleds cross the vast emptiness of a snowbound plateau in Norway.

Nomads of the World (1971)

Silver-white sword hilt of wedding regalia indicates the bridegroom's presence among kinsmen as Deva, 16, arrives in a bullock cart (below) at his bride's camp outside Kapasan. The solemn groom (right), engaged since childhood and kept from seeing his betrothed, will not look at the face of his bride, Kakku, until the second day of ceremonies. Then they get acquainted during games, such as competing to find a ring in a pan of cloudy water (left); in one game he removes her veil. Two more days of ritual, feasts, and teasing jokes await them at his camp. Usually the bride then rejoins her family to grow to womanhood. But Kakku, 16, stayed with Deva to live in his family's cart-home.

Evocations of ceremonies, occupations, and pastimes show how the world's nomadic cultures survive.

A book on the world's nomads made sense for the National Geographic Society to publish for a couple of reasons. First, it cataloged a vanishing way of life. Second, it appealed to people's natural wanderlust. As in the best travel writing, furthermore, the book time and again went beyond the presentation of foreign cultures; it made readers respond on a gut level, examining their own lives.

In the book's foreword Leonard Carmichael, chair of the Society's Committee for Research and Exploration, writes, "an ancient appeal motivates not only the nomads who figure in this book, but also the modern city-dweller as he turns his car for a Saturday outing on the open road." Thus we instinctively understand the roving Bedouin of Arabia, Pygmies of Central Africa's Ituri Forest, and Guajiro Indians of Colombia.

In this selection Mohammad Bahmanbegui, director of Iran's Office of Tribal Education, writes about the shepherds of the Zāgros Mountains in western Iran from lifelong experience. He lived in a tent until he was 13, migrating to an urban area only once a year.

"Every bend in the track, every hill, pass, ravine, every watering place I knew," writes Bahmanbegui. His lively account of visiting the Qashqā'ī tribesmen to give exams to the children is made poignant by his prediction that their nomadic ways could not survive much longer.

Hardy Shepherds and Their Future

Thoughts as Mohammad Bahmanbegui returns to his people

Swirls of dust followed my Jeep as it bounced along the rocky track. I was now more than 300 miles northwest of Shīrāz, crossing a succession of rises in one of the plains spreading between the sharp stone ridges of the Zāgros Mountains of Iran. For miles I had seen nothing on these hot, dry expanses except the peaks rimming the tableland, an occasional village of one- or two-room mud houses, tan like the earth, and a few black rectangles of Qashqā'ī tribesmen's tents, menaced only by wandering columns of whirling dust devils. (Most authorities now prefer Qashqā'ī [khosh-khy-ee] to the older "Kashgai" or "Gashgai.")

Then I saw ahead under the cloudless bright sky a patch of green, the one I was looking for. My brother Nader in his big tent at that grove of trees would be watching for my dust clouds, like smoke signals. I smiled with pleasure to picture our numerous cousins running from their tents to Nader's when they heard his shout.

Sharing a communal platter, Bedouins of Saudi Arabia eat rice and camel meat in silence, using their right hand only. These wanderers often travel 1,200 miles a year in search of good grazing pastures.

Kuchi *nomads of Afghanistan set up camp, a tradition interrupted in 1971 by drought in the Hindu Kush. Forced to remain in winter camp, their sheep faced starvation.*

AS THE EDGE OF THE SUN APPEARED OVER AQ DĀGH, OUR WHITE MOUNTAIN, CAMELS ROSE WITH HIGH-PITCHED STACCATO GRUNTS, AND THE PROCESSION OF ANIMALS AND PEOPLE BEGAN TO MOVE.

Even before I came to a full stop by the long row of guy ropes—each trimmed with a large red, blue, or green tassel—steadying the poles along the open front of Nader's tent, I was reaching out of the jeep to clasp hands with my relatives. Their wide grins matched in jauntiness the turned-up flaps of their tan felt tribal hats.

"Khōshgalling! Welcome!" Nader said in the first language I learned as a child, the Turkish dialect of the Qashqā'ī. And then he added in Persian, our national language, *"Qadam bar cheshm!* Your foot up in my eye!" This means, "I like your coming so much, I'd feel happy even if you kicked me in the eye!"

Nader's wife Shahnaz came hurrying around the corner of the long tent. She pulled at a filmy white mantle, a *sarandāz,* held by a purple scarf around the crown of her head—though Moslem, our women go unveiled. The hem of her full and shimmering red skirt danced to her quick steps. *"Salām!* Hello! You've finally come!" she said. "We'll kill a lamb to roast and we have partridges on the skewers ready to cook for kebab. Nader shot them this morning."

Of course all my relatives knew I had come on business. As head of Tribal Education for Iran, I give examinations to the children of the tent schools, white portable umbrellas with no furniture or equipment except a blackboard propped up on two sticks. "Where is Fazel, the teacher?" I asked.

"He's bringing the tent," Nader answered. "Come sit down and have a glass of tea." We sat cross-legged on the brightly patterned Qashqā'ī rugs covering the tent floor, and leaned against a 40-foot-long mound of goods and supplies covered with beautiful handwoven carpet-cloths. My cousin Ali started a small fire in a shallow hole just outside the tent, and brought out pot, glasses, and sugar lumps broken from a long loaf.

ARRIVING AT KOHNARCHEH, TEN MILES west of Semirom, always gives me the feeling of coming home. Many of my earliest memories center on this summer campsite of my family.

I recall, for example, my joy and relief when as a four-year-old, tied for safety to a horse and saddle nearly every day for two months during our spring migration, I saw in the distance our little hill and its few scattered poplars. Tricklets of spring water run through short grass near the tent and down the slope toward the rocky bed of a brook.

How many times have I stooped to wash my hands and look out toward our three towering colored mountains, all part of the Zāgros range? Āq Dāgh of whitish rock stands to the east; Goy Dāgh, green with shrubs and grass in spring, rises in the west; in the north looms Qara Dāgh, stony black.

Scores of green spots like Kohnarcheh—usually owned by Qashqā'ī families of considerable prosperity and standing—brighten these monotone highland plains. In the past, ownership of vast acreage here gave great economic and some measure of political power to the *Kadkhodās*, or clan chieftains; the *Kalāntars*, or those hereditary chiefs above the Kadkhodās; and especially to the *Khāns*, or hereditary leaders of the five tribes of the Qashqā'ī.

And in order to preserve this power, these tribal leaders used to arm themselves and their peoples.

But during the last two decades, beginning in the early 1950s, the disarmament of Iranian tribes, the distribution of land, and the nationalization of pastures have changed all this. Now loaded guns no longer stand in every Qashqā'ī tent, to be used against the government or neighboring tribes. Now much of the Khāns' vast lands and numerous villages with their farms have been parceled out by the government to individual families, village peasants or nomadic tribesmen.

Onetime tribal nobles or their families drive jeeps and trucks from their houses in Shīrāz or Kāzerūn or Firūzābād to the Zāgros to pass the summer in the cooler climate. While their wheat and barley crops mature on their southern farms with citrus and date orchards, they tend apple trees and vegetables on their northern land, watered by springs or deep wells, and send their hundreds of sheep and goats to nearby grasslands. They have no official role, but act as spokesmen for and still have some influence among their people—a fact officials make use of in administering tribal affairs.

In festival finery, a Bororo cattle herdsman of Niger expects good luck with women.

WITHIN SOME MILES OF NADER'S GREEN hill, about 50 families of the Bahman-Beg-lu clan of the Amaleh tribe live in scattered groups of tents. Like most of the other 25,000 Qashqā'ī families, they depend on free grazing for their animals. Their herds average about 70 animals, with perhaps 40 sheep and 30 goats, both of which supply meat as well as milk for making cheese, yogurt, and butter. The sheep also yield wool and the goats the long, black hair woven into tentcloth.

I can look at the size of a Qashqā'ī tent, at the number and quality of rugs in it, at the height and length of the mound of baggage piled neatly at the back, at the richness of the cloth in the women's attire—and how far their skirts stand out with petticoats—and, from just those observations, give a close estimate of family income.

Inevitably, with every move of the government to modernize and develop Iran, good grazing lands have shrunk. Roads constructed in the pasture areas have cut into the grass. The sprawling, smoking cement factory at Shīrāz blocks a top-grade migration route; gardens and grain fields of village farmers stretch out across more and more traditional pastures of the tent-dwelling Qashqā'ī.

All this, added to the effects of frequent years of drought, has made nomadic shepherding less and less able to feed millions of sheep and goats and hundreds of thousands of pack animals. I believe, in fact, that within 25 years the migratory way of life will end for most of my people.

THE VIKINGS (1972)

by Howard La Fay

As though harking to his Norse past, young Bjørn Skår, arms full of turnips, pauses at a call from his father. A younger son unlikely to acquire the family farm, he might have joined the Vikings had he lived a thousand years ago.

Captured during the sack of her father's city, Popa, daughter of the Count of Bayeux,
before Hrolf the Ganger in his camp. Hrolf married his beautiful prisoner.

Vivid artwork by Louis S. Glanzman complements the text to bring the story of The Vikings *to life.*

Of enduring fascination, the Vikings—those Scandinavian raiders, merchants, and settlers of the ninth to the eleventh century—left a legacy of seafaring bravado and terror from Byzantium to Newfoundland. For a long time, annals and sagas filled in the blank spaces left by unwritten (or unfound) records; later, archaeologists began piecing the Vikings' story together. A *National Geographic* magazine article on the Vikings led to a book by journeyman writer Howard La Fay.

La Fay remarks of his travels, "My own exploration of the Vikings' world revealed its vastness and its infinite variety. I saw the remains of their dwellings and boat sheds beside piney Newfoundland forests. I sailed in their wake along the windswept shores of the Caspian Sea. I followed them from the long Arctic nights of Iceland to the soft breezes of the Bosporus. And I duly found their faint traces—runic inscriptions, crumbled longhouses, magnificently resurrected ships of war." He traveled in search of current lifestyles, known history, and the echoes of myths and legends in that part of the world.

In this excerpt, La Fay visits a noted historian who happens to be the president of Iceland, and recounts the twilight of the Vikings, when Christianity replaced Thor and the other Norse gods. Though a more or less bloodless coup, the transformation required the work of miracles—or so say the records.

Twilight of the Heroes

Tales of the quest for the ancient sagas

I was in an eight-story building, one of the newest in Reykjavik, capital of Iceland, when suddenly the structure shuddered violently. A distant explosion, I thought, or perhaps a low jet. But the spasm continued through a long, ugly 20 seconds. I watched people dashing for the exits. Not until the final, convulsive shudder did I realize that I was experiencing my first earthquake. It proved to be the most violent shock recorded in earthquake-prone Reykjavik in several decades.

The tremor forcibly reminded me that Iceland is still in its geological youth. The island is still, in effect, suffering growing pains.

Geysers (the word derives from Old Norse) spew from the surface of the inner highlands. Glaciers, relics of the still-waning Ice Age, creep past smoldering volcanoes. And in 1963 the ocean south of Iceland suddenly spurted ash-laden clouds and the island of Surtsey rose full-blown above the surface, a geologic Aphrodite of black lava.

From the ninth to eleventh century, Hedeby served as a trading center on Jutland's Baltic coast. Norse merchants hosted visitors who bartered silver for slaves, silks for furs, and wine for swords.

In the depths of the Icelandic winter, dawn doesn't break until almost noon. It was still pitch dark at 10 a.m. on a December day when I was received in his office by Dr. Kristján Eldjárn, famous historian and President of Iceland.

I asked Dr. Eldjárn's opinion of the historicity of Iceland's most revered product, the sagas.

"There is general agreement," he said, "that the sagas mix fiction with historical elements. The difficulty lies in determining which is which.

"Icelandic culture stems to a very large degree from the Viking Age. Our language is the most important and most obvious example. Our natural resources haven't improved; we still farm and fish for a living. Nor has the structure of our community changed in any essential way.

"When in the year 1000 the Althing adopted Christianity as the official religion, it was the pagan Thorgeir of Ljosavatn who announced that all should be baptized. And all were. There was no bloodshed, no persecution. Icelanders are still just as devoted to democratic procedures."

THE TWILIGHT OF THE NORSE GODS foreshadowed the twilight of the Vikings. Christianity's ultimate triumph, when it came, shattered ethical patterns and codes of conduct throughout Scandinavia. The process of conversion was slow, fitful, and often suffered serious reverses; but once the kings and jarls accepted baptism—as they did in increasing numbers at the beginning of the 11th century—the old gods lost Valhalla.

In 831, barely 40 years after the Vikings burst upon the western world, the Christian Church mounted a spiritual counterattack. The emperor of the Franks, Louis the Pious, in an action promptly confirmed by the papacy, named Hamburg "as the metropolitan see for all the barbarous nations of the Danes, the Swedes, and likewise the Slavs and the other peoples living round about."

The bishops of Hamburg thereafter dispatched waves of missionaries into the North. Though the harvest of souls was slight, many an evangelist won a martyr's crown. Adam of Bremen recorded the fate of one Wolfred, an Englishman, who "entered Sweden and with great courage preached the Word of God.... He proceeded to anathematize a popular idol named Thor which stood in the Thing of the pagans, and at the same time he seized a battle ax and broke the image to pieces. And forthwith he was pierced with a thousand wounds for such daring.

But there were exceptions.

Poppo, "a holy and wise man" according to Adam—and, from the evidence, a gifted showman—scored a spectacular success in Denmark. "Since it is the way of barbarians to seek after a sign, he straight way and without hesitation held a red-hot iron in his hand and seemed to be unharmed. Although it would appear that every delusion of error should by this act easily have been removed from the minds of the pagans, the saint of God is said once again to have manifested another miracle—if you will, a greater one—in order to clear away that people's paganism. For he clad himself in a waxed tunic and, standing in the midst of the people, directed that it be set on fire in the name of the Lord.

"Then, with his eyes and hands lifted up to heaven, he so patiently bore the spreading flames that, after his garment was entirely consumed and reduced to ashes, his cheerful and pleasant countenance gave proof of his having not even felt or suffered from the smoke of the fire. Because of this unusual miracle many thousands then believed through him and to this very day Poppo's name is extolled by the peoples and in the churches of the Danes."

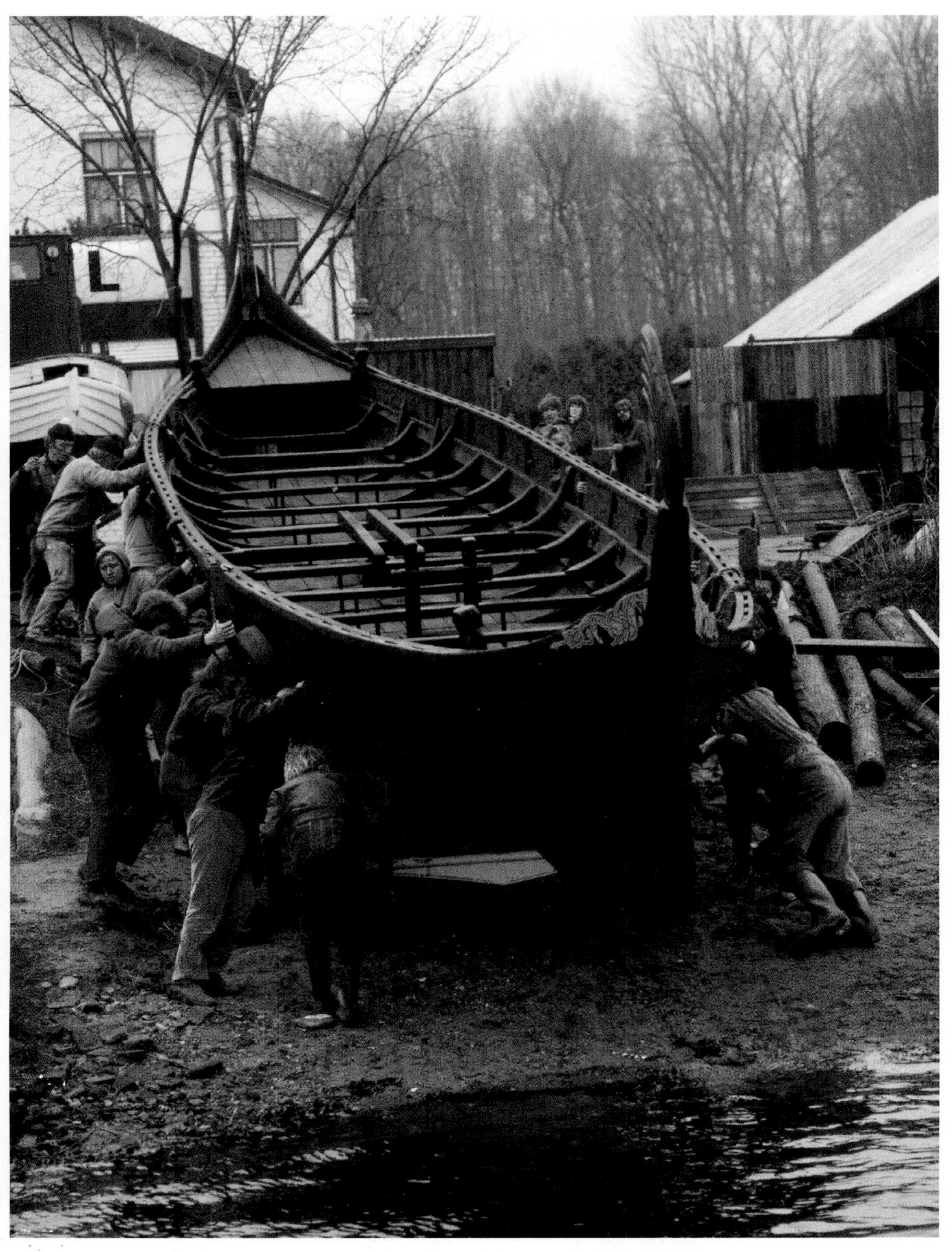

Danish scouts launch the Sebbe Als, *a replica of a small Viking warship discovered at Skuldelev in Roskilde Fjord in 1962. With authentic lashed (rather than nailed) strakes, the sail-and-oar-powered ship proved seaworthy.*

A Hawaiian priest ceremonially offers Captain Cook a baked pig. The Hawaiians saw Cook as an incarnation of Lono, god of peace and bounty. The staff with flowing cloth, symbol of Lono, resembled the English masts and sails, and Lono was to return by sea.

Voyages to Paradise (1981)

by William R. Gray

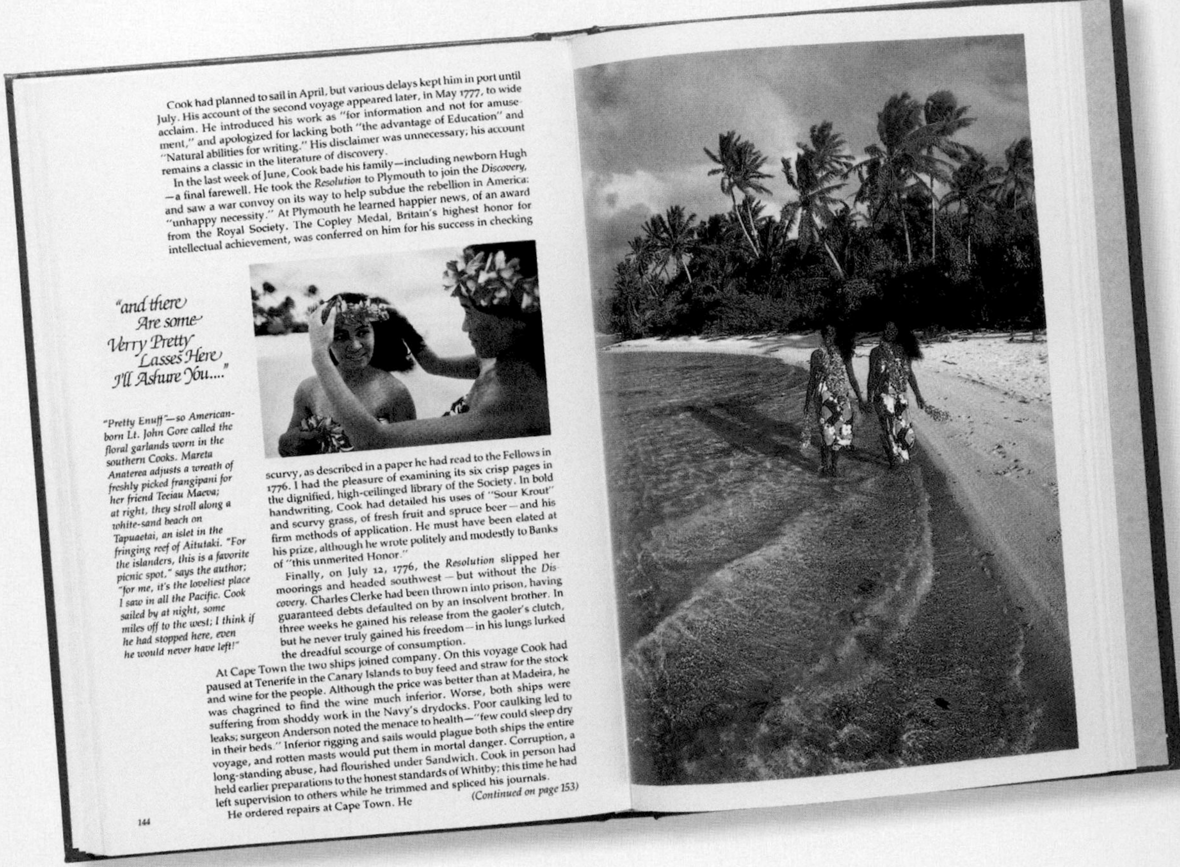

Cook had planned to sail in April, but various delays kept him in port until July. His account of the second voyage appeared later, in May 1777, to wide acclaim. He introduced his work as "for information and not for amuse- ment," and apologized for lacking both "the advantage of Education" and "Natural abilities for writing." His disclaimer was unnecessary; his account remains a classic in the literature of discovery.

In the last week of June, Cook bade his family—including newborn Hugh —a final farewell. He took the *Resolution* to Plymouth to join the *Discovery,* and saw a war convoy on its way to help subdue the rebellion in America: "unhappy necessity." At Plymouth he learned happier news, of an award from the Royal Society. The Copley Medal, Britain's highest honor for intellectual achievement, was conferred on him for his success in checking

"and there Are some Verry Pretty Lasses Here I'll Ashure You...."

"Pretty Enuff"—so American-born Lt. John Gore called the floral garlands worn in the southern Cooks. Mareta Anaterea adjusts a wreath of freshly picked frangipani for her friend Teeiau Maeva; at right, they stroll along a white-sand beach on Tapuaetai, an islet in the fringing reef of Aitutaki. "For the islanders, this is a favorite picnic spot," says the author; "for me, it's the loveliest place I saw in all the Pacific. Cook sailed by at night, some miles off to the west; I think if he had stopped here, even he would never have left!"

scurvy, as described in a paper he had read to the Fellows in 1776. I had the pleasure of examining its six crisp pages in the dignified, high-ceilinged library of the Society. In bold handwriting, Cook had detailed his uses of "Sour Krout" and scurvy grass, of fresh fruit and spruce beer—and his firm methods of application. He must have been elated at his prize, although he wrote politely and modestly to Banks of "this unmerited Honor."

Finally, on July 12, 1776, the *Resolution* slipped her moorings and headed southwest—but without the *Dis- covery.* Charles Clerke had been thrown into prison, having guaranteed debts defaulted on by an insolvent brother. In three weeks he gained his release from the gaoler's clutch, but he never truly gained his freedom—in his lungs lurked the dreadful scourge of consumption.

At Cape Town the two ships joined company. On this voyage Cook had paused at Tenerife in the Canary Islands to buy feed and straw for the stock and wine for the people. Although the price was better than at Madeira, he was chagrined to find the wine much inferior. Worse, both ships were suffering from shoddy work in the Navy's drydocks. Poor caulking led to leaks; surgeon Anderson noted the menace to health—"few could sleep dry in their beds." Inferior rigging and sails would plague both ships the entire voyage, and rotten masts would put them in mortal danger. Corruption, a long-standing abuse, had flourished under Sandwich. Cook in person had held earlier preparations to the honest standards of Whitby; this time he had left supervision to others while he trimmed and spliced his journals. He ordered repairs at Cape Town. He

(Continued on page 153)

144

William Gray's text and Gordon Gahan's pictures bridged the distance to Captain Cook's 18th-century world.

One particularly adventurous title in the Special Collection traced the voyages of one of the world's greatest explorers, Captain James Cook (1728-79). In three journeys across the Pacific, the English navigator discovered and charted New Zealand, Australia, and Antarctica, before finally being killed by Hawaiian natives.

To retrace his life and accomplishments, the National Geographic Society sent photographer Gordon W. Gahan and writer William R. Gray out in search of pictures and stories. They were gone for nearly a year. By dugout canoe, island schooner, horseback, and seaplane, they visited all the places in the South Pacific that had been visited by Cook during his voyages.

"It was a life-changing experience for me," Gray recalled, "because I really got to know James Cook as a person. I wasn't just looking at him through a lens 200 years later. I'd read all his journals and then traveled to the exact places, some of which are extremely remote.

"That's what the National Geographic Society did—they allowed us to have that latitude and the financing to go to places where very few other people could go. I really became a student of Pacific exploration."

This excerpt is from Gray's prologue, in which he lays out the scope of Cook's accomplishments and of his own plans for following in the wake of a man who opened up the world.

As Far As Any Man Can Go

Recalling Captain Cook's South Sea voyages

Rampaging gales bullied the blue Pacific, pushing violent breakers onto jagged coral heads. Trapped by wind and current in a maze of reefs off New Caledonia, the crew of the little sailing ship *Resolution* faced a perilous night. At any moment she could be driven onto the rocks and shattered. "I realy think our situation was to be envyed by very few except the Thief who has got the Halter about his Neck," one man recalled.

Throughout that dark night, the heart-stopping cry of "Breakers ahead!" rent the tropic air. The captain, a veteran of exploring the Pacific Ocean, snapped orders that kept his ship tacking away from danger.

In the morning he wrote in his journal: "Daylight shewed ... that we had spent the night in the most eminent danger havg had shoals and breakers continually under our lee at a very little distance from us."

Brilliant seamanship and a brilliantly disciplined crew had rescued the ship from disaster. Any ordinary commander would have set sail immediately for the open sea, thankful to escape that tangle of reefs.

But this was no ordinary commander. James Cook, a superb sailor, also possessed a wide-ranging scientific curiosity. He had approached this dangerous shoreline because he had noted unusual objects spiking the land—columns of rock, or bizarre trees. "I was now almost tired of a Coast I could no longer explore but at the risk of loosing the ship and ruining the whole Voyage, but I was determined not to leave it till I was satisfied what sort of trees those were."

So he edged along through treacherous shallows, to anchor near an islet with a cluster of the trees. With his expedition's botanists, Cook went ashore and marveled at one of the strangest plants in the South Pacific—*Araucaria columnaris,* once *cookii.* It soars as tall as two hundred feet, but its branches rarely exceed six.

For the moment Cook was satisfied—he had investigated those puzzling trees, he and his companions had sampled the island's plant and animal

Off the coast of Tahiti, a three-masted square-rigger sails at sunset, recalling the sturdy ships that carried James Cook and his crew across the Pacific.

IN HIS COMPETENT, PRACTICAL WAY, CAPTAIN COOK CAME TO SYMBOLIZE THE HUMANE EXPLORER. HE HAD TAKEN MANKIND TO THE LIMITS OF THE GLOBE, AND HE HAD STIRRED IMAGINATIONS EVERYWHERE.

life, and he had made his usual accurate observations of latitude and longitude. After gathering a few last botanical specimens, Cook turned the *Resolution* toward the south.

A SOFT-SPOKEN MAN OF SCIENCE, A STRONG-willed man of the sea, James Cook, in three globe-girdling voyages from 1768 to 1779, explored more of the Pacific Ocean than any man before him had done. In so doing, he discovered a myriad of untracked islands, he immeasurably expanded many fields of knowledge, and he stirred the imaginations of people around the world.

Born in humble circumstances in 1728, Cook ascended to the forefront of public and intellectual life in England. Early in his career, he evinced characteristics that aided his rise: dogged perseverance, navigational expertise, uncanny leadership skills, marked resourcefulness and ability to make decisions, and a general competence in many areas of learning.

"James Cook was one of the great men of the 18th century," historian Michael E. Hoare told me in Wellington, New Zealand. Dr. Hoare's academic honors include a term of study as a "James Cook Fellow."

"Cook came to the fore at an extremely important moment in history," he continued. "Technological, scientific, and medical discoveries were burgeoning—many beneficial to long voyages of exploration.

"The 18th century was the Age of Reason, in which a desire for knowledge of the natural world was rekindled. It was also a time of romantic vision, when the thought of discovering new lands and peoples was appealing.

"In addition, the British Empire was poised for great expansion. The Seven Years War between England and France had ended in 1763. The victory propelled Britain into a period of extraordinary activity. Captain Cook's successes, I think, were caused by the conjunction of an intelligent, practical, and capable man with the situation and the times that called for one.

"We cannot, of course, overlook the factor of luck. And Cook was fortunate to have excellent crews and some of the world's most respected scientists on his expeditions. But he was truly a remarkable man and one whose significance will never fade in the study of history."

WITH VETERAN NATIONAL GEOGRAPHIC photographer Gordon Gahan, I pursued the wake of this remarkable man for nearly a year.

Our travels took us about the vast Pacific Ocean—from the northern tip of Alaska to the southern tip of Tasmania, and to most of the island groups in between. We traveled to England, to the moors of North Yorkshire where Cook spent his childhood, to the North Sea ports where he learned the crafts of sail; to the Maritime Provinces of Canada where he matured as a commander and as a scientific observer. We journeyed to Tahiti and New Zealand—two of Cook's favorite refuges; to Australia; to the many South Pacific paradises that he discovered; to the ice in Bering Strait; and finally to Hawaii, where he met his death.

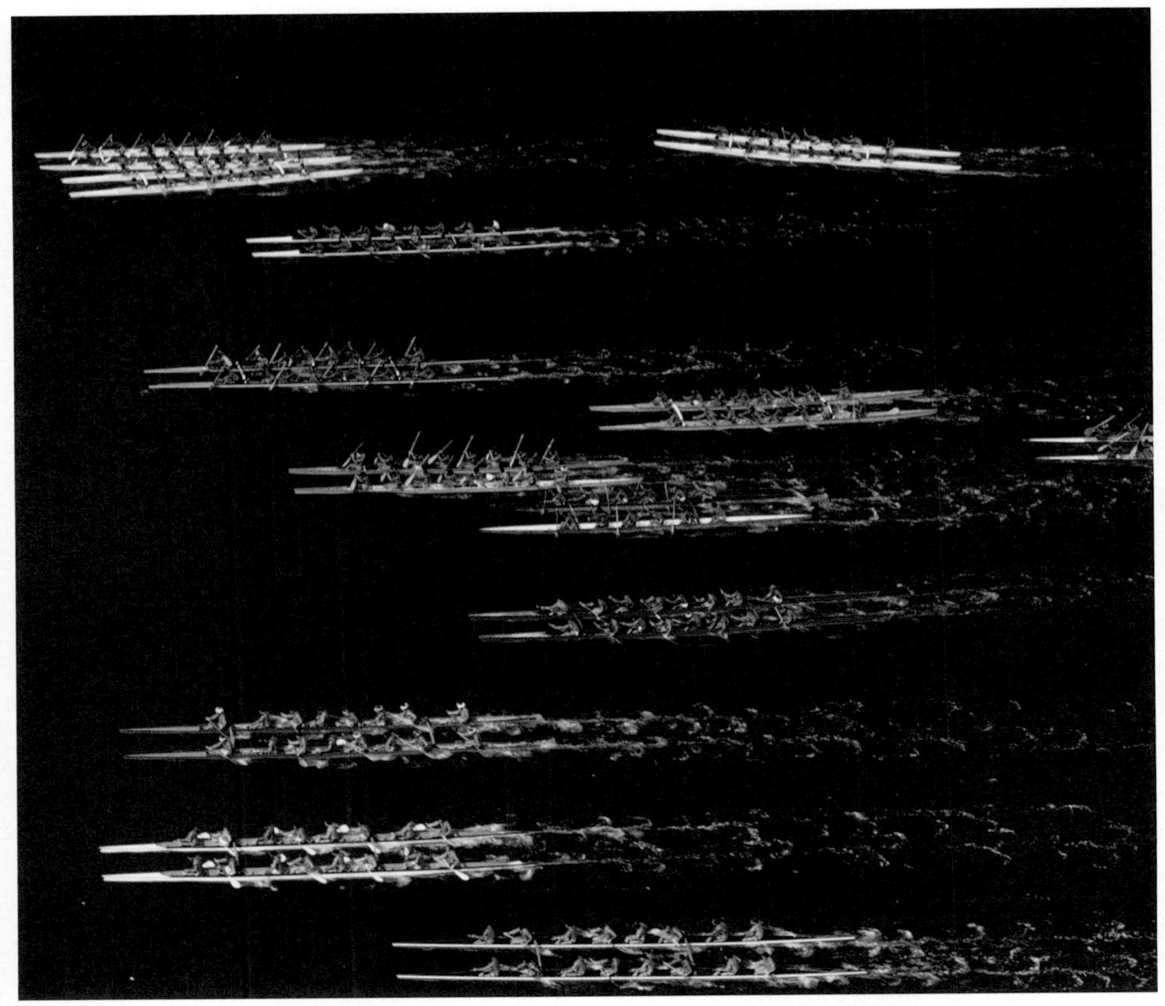

Double canoes race off Tahiti's southern coast. Lighter and faster than the wooden double canoes of Cook's time, the boats recall a traditional past that Polynesians still celebrate proudly.

With every mile, with every landfall, I marveled anew at the accomplishments of James Cook. Although Ferdinand Magellan had crossed the Pacific nearly 250 years before Cook, and the Portuguese, Spanish, Dutch, French, and English had explored parts of it, the Pacific Ocean in 1768 remained an enormous mystery. Few reliable charts existed.

"To me, the thought of Cook and his men setting off into the total unknown is quite terrifying," Rear Admiral D. W. Haslam, Hydrographer of the Royal Navy, told me in his office in Taunton, England. "Month after month—for years at a time—Cook navigated uncharted waters, often in abhorrent conditions of wind and weather. It's incredible! He surely had a seventh sense for the sea.

"He safely guided those small wooden ships—not much bigger than Thames River barges—through frozen seas packed with icebergs and through tropic seas filled with coral. He faced all the conditions dauntlessly."

Even today he is a legend throughout the Pacific. One venerable islander from Tonga, whose

Coconut oil gives a sensuous sheen to a Tahitian dancer's skin (top); such women beguiled the crew sailing with Capt. James Cook, but Cook himself refused their overtures. Botanist William Stearn of the British Museum (bottom left) displays specimens collected by Cook and others on his voyages. Cook Island dancers (center right) perform with the kind of grace and style that impressed the English explorers. A grass-fringed resident of Tanna in the New Hebrides (bottom right) watches an initiation rite, little changed since Cook's time.

Polynesian forebears were among the best navigators in the world, said flatly, "Besides Jesus Christ, Captain Cook was the greatest man who ever lived."

COOK'S NAME GRACES A PICTURESQUE town in Australia, the highest mountain in New Zealand, a jewel-like strand of islands in the central Pacific, a mountain-rimmed inlet in Alaska, scores of other geographic features. But that came as a tribute from those who followed him. He named his discoveries after his patrons in England, his crewmen, even his ships. Cook was modest, hardworking, taciturn.

A large, rawboned man, he had a certain stolidity of character. He strove to be just with his men—although at times he revealed a violent temper. In an era when impressment was the surest way to form a ship's company, men willingly sailed with Cook. Although some called him "the despot," most respected and even loved him.

The same held true for the islanders he met. Captain Cook treated them as fairly as he did his men, and generally they returned his kindness with veneration. Problems, of course, arose, but usually from misunderstandings in the collision of two disparate cultures. Cook kept detailed journals of his voyages, with careful observations on places and peoples and keen interpretations of various events. Only by implication, as a rule, did he disclose his personality.

Occasionally, however, the sheer excitement of what he had accomplished inspired him, and his pride became evident. On his second voyage, after sailing far south of the Antarctic Circle, Cook revealed this of himself: "Ambition leads me not only farther than any other man has been before me, but as far as I think it possible for man to go…"

THAT ADMISSION INDEED ILLUMINATES James Cook's character. To survive the perils of the Pacific Ocean—storm waves that dwarf a ship, coral reefs that crush a hull, sun that blisters the skin, cold that transforms rigging into flesh-shredding cables of ice—James Cook had to be ambitious, and to know himself well.

Most of our intimate knowledge of Cook comes from those who wrote about him: members of his expeditions, friends and associates in England, and biographers, especially John Cawte Beaglehole of New Zealand. Professor Beaglehole, who died in 1971, devoted his long career to the study of James Cook. He edited and published the journals, and he wrote the definitive study of the great explorer's life.

In "those few elected spirits, such as Cook," mused Dr. Beaglehole, "is the complete equipment of genius, and fortune coincides with their appearance, and the face of the world is changed."

As we traced him across the Pacific, Gordon and I quickly discovered the awesome degree to which Captain James Cook had changed the face of the world.

Twilight of the ancients: The formidable Pyramid of the Magician rises in Uxmal, a Maya city that flourished on Mexico's Yucatán Peninsula from about A.D. *700 to 1000.*

THE MYSTERIOUS MAYA (1977)

by George E. Stuart and Gene S. Stuart

"Out of the shadow arose a vision from a fairy tale," wrote Alberto Ruz Lhuillier (below) when he discovered the splendid tomb beneath the Temple of the Inscriptions. Directing excavations at Palenque in 1949, Ruz found a secret staircase under the temple floor. After four seasons' work clearing the rubble-clogged passage, he reached the burial chamber of the ruler he called "8 Ahau." A five-ton limestone sarcophagus lid (opposite) nearly filled the dark crypt. In exquisite bas-relief, it shows the fleshless jaws of an Underworld monster reaching toward a half-reclining man—probably the dying ruler.
82

Photos by David Alan Harvey and Otis Imboden portray the mystery and beauty of the Maya.

National Geographic archaeologist George Stuart and his wife Gene, a staff artist, brought more than two decades of experience and expertise to the writing of *The Mysterious Maya* in the mid-1970s, based on both research and fieldwork with various Native American peoples.

The Maya had one of the most advanced civilizations in the Western hemisphere before European contact. They dominated Mesoamerica, producing pyramid temples, elaborate gold and copper work, and hieroglyphics. At the time of the Stuarts' book, the Maya numbered about two million, their lives still centered on agriculture. They spoke more than a score of languages.

This excerpt is from a chapter by Gene Stuart. Living with her family in a Maya village in Mexico's Yucatán Peninsula, she was able to see firsthand how the people had adapted to modern life while keeping their culture intact.

When they pray for rain, a Roman Catholic priest presides, but they also pay tribute to a native pagan deity. Stuart notes the offerings, as well as who brings them, and how the supplicants themselves are not above indulging in these much appreciated little luxuries. She keeps the tone respectful yet strikes a humorous note when the *Chachaac* ceremony, intended to lift everyone's spirits, leaves them nauseated. With her sharp eye for telling detail, Stuart brings readers into the circle.

Summer in Cobá

Memories of family life with the Mexican Maya

For two summers my family and I lived in the village of Cobá, Quintana Roo, near the eastern coast of the Yucatán Peninsula of Mexico. There, I became fully aware of the dependence of farmers on the behavior of nature, sometimes ideal and benevolent, sometimes cruel and capricious. Despite ceremonies loyally performed for them, the gods are generous or they are not.

In 1974, the rains came before mid-June. Crashing afternoon and evening storms dumped rapid-flowing rivulets on the newly planted fields. Harvest that year was bountiful. More than enough corn to last the year. Enough left over to sell.

But during the second summer, not even a light shower had fallen by late June. Clouds built up, turned dark; and, helpless, we saw them drift to the north or eastward out to sea. The men of the village said they would not plant their cornfields if rain did not come in ten days. We waited. Hot wind swept black dust through the pole walls of our house. By noon every day our heads throbbed from the heat and we sought a cool haven under our roof of thick

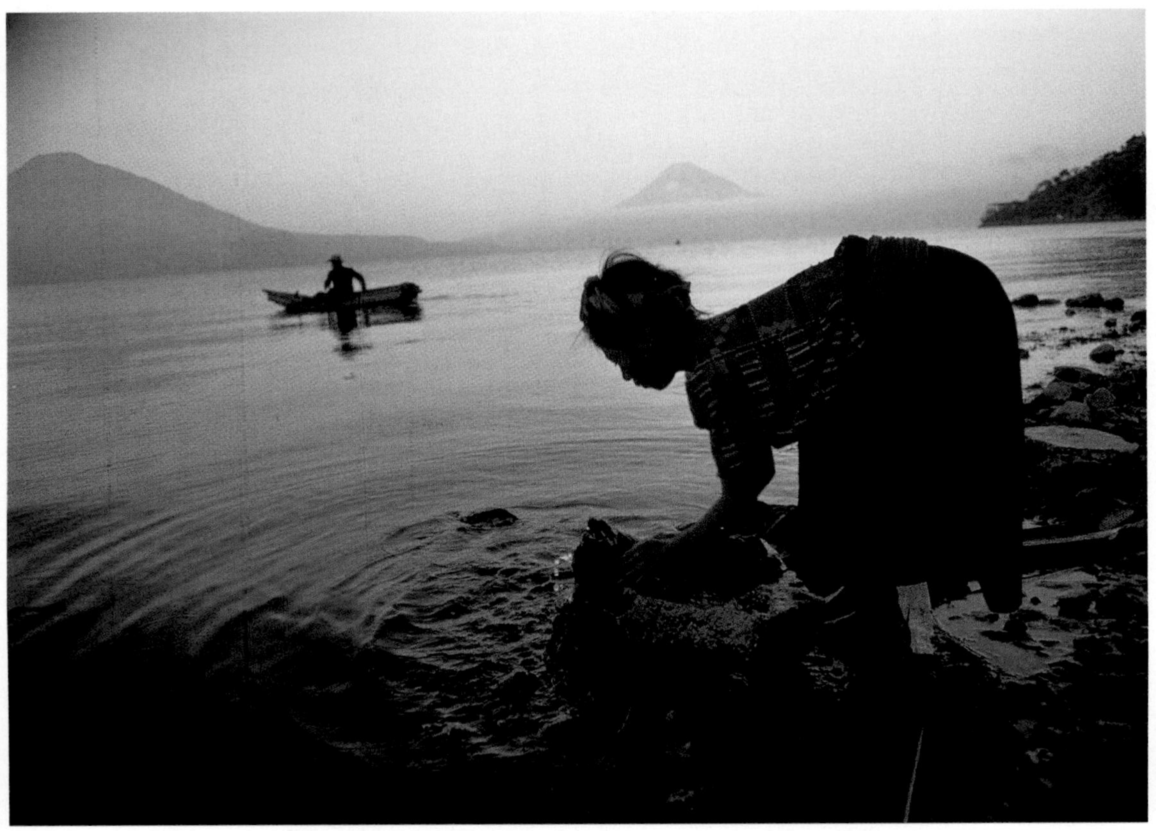

Sunrise at Lake Atitlán finds a Maya woman cleaning clothes and a fisherman paddling his boat; rimmed by volcanoes and steep hillsides, the highland lake has long been a center of Maya culture.

Distinctive fabric colors and clothing designs (top) mark this Maya family as residents of the farming community of Sololá, near Lake Atitlán. Heedless of threatening skies (bottom), a boy rolls his hoop on a bluff above the lake.

palm thatch. Sometimes a sleek mare and her little foal with a startled scrub-brush of a mane trotted along the road; their hoofs made a hollow sound against the dust and porous limestone underneath. Jacinto May showed us his watermelon patch—little shriveled melons the size of limes.

The men began to speak of the rain god, Chaac, and plan a *Chachaac* ceremony to ask his favors. They chose a day. The village women ground corn and squash seeds for food offerings. I boiled extra drinking water, certain that after the ceremony it would rain hard and often, and my outside cooking fire would be useless.

ON THE APPOINTED DAY, A MAYA PRIEST from a nearby village arrived at dusk. Word swept through Cobá that he would let women attend the Chachaac ceremony. I was amazed, for ceremonies for rain and planting are exclusively the sacred charge of men. This was a ritual that I might never again be privileged to attend. We asked the men to suggest appropriate offerings.

"Candles, beer, cigarettes or soft drinks. A hen if you have one."

We didn't, but a village store was still open. Laden with cigarettes and Coca-Cola, George and I, with our daughter Ann and sons Greg and David, followed them along a path into the high bush. It wound through ruined Maya temples and palaces and into an ancient courtyard. Dark breadnut trees, heavy with Spanish moss, circled a clearing, and there in the center stood an altar made of poles and freshly cut branches. Arches, also made of branches, stood at each of the four cardinal directions. In front of each arch was a pole, with a beeswax candle thrust into the splayed top end.

The priest was a gentle man, middle-aged, and like all the northern Maya, immaculately clean in

Hunters and their dogs head out into the forest near Labná, in the Yucatán, hoping to bag deer, wild pig, and birds. Some Maya hunters still make offerings to the gods.

his blue work pants and orange shirt. He motioned us to place some of the cigarettes on the altar. The other offerings lay to one side. We spoke in whispers and scattered ourselves in a semicircle outside the area of the altar and arches, choosing fallen stones from the ancient temples to sit on. The priest took small gourd bowls from a plastic shopping bag. He hung some in the arches and arranged the others on the altar on a ritual bed of *chimché* leaves. One, he placed underneath, then filled them all with water.

Darkness closed our sacred clearing into a small circle of candlelight as the air calmed to solemn stillness. No one moved, no one spoke. I sat with my youngest son, David, beside the wizened roots of a breadnut tree. Near us lay a trough made from a hollowed log and covered with a sheet of plastic. The priest moved to the trough, quickly took something from it and slipped it into a gourd. At the altar he stirred the contents with a small bundle of tightly bound leaves.

In reaching into the trough he had pulled aside the plastic cover, and in the candlelight I saw a design burned deep into the wood—a cross. It was then I noticed a small brass crucifix on the altar. For a loincloth the Christus wore a skirt like the old Maya men still wear, but made of white cloth and embroidered with red flowers like a *huipil* [dress].

The priest knelt on a dusty feed sack in front of the altar and began to pray. His voice was low and steady—so low that I could not hear a distinct word, but I knew that he spoke Maya and there was no need for him to speak loud, for this was a priest

EACH GENERATION OF THE MAYA PEOPLE HAS SEEN NEW IDEAS, CHANGE, MOVEMENT. IN ANCIENT BELIEF, THE PAST IS THE PRESENT AND FUTURE, EVER REPEATING.

speaking to the rain god, Chaac, and what was happening at the moment was between them.

An assistant knelt behind him, and I thought how much like a Catholic mass it looked—a priest kneeling at an altar with his acolyte. And then suddenly it seemed to be a Catholic altar. The branches intersecting over the middle formed a dome. I realized it was like a Byzantine church made of branches. The four arches of the four directions were the four wings of the church. I smelled incense. Someone had thrown it onto a shovel filled with glowing embers. And then we were on our feet and the priest's voice rose strong above ours as he began in Spanish, "Hail Mary, full of grace."

I stood behind Mexican archeologist Antonio Benavides and saw his face in profile as he prayed with the priest. Pale skin, dark wavy hair, close-cropped beard and dark heavy-lidded eyes. The Spanish conqueror, Francisco de Montejo, must have looked much like that when he landed on these shores and the ancestors of this very priest fought in desperation to keep the Spaniards from their land.

Our prayers continued. Finally the priest dipped his bound leaves in a gourd and scattered the now-blessed water in the four directions across the altar. We found our fallen temple stones again and rested. The men poured some of the blessed water into a bucket of more water, mixed it with ground corn, and passed gourds of the drink to all of us.

"What is it?" asked David.

"*Zacá*, a holy drink—a sacred drink for Chaac," I answered.

"Oh." He began to drink in short, serious gulps.

The ceremony continued. As the priest prayed in Maya, young boys sat beneath the altar imitating frogs.

"*Woh, woh, rana, rana,*" their voices rose in a plaintive cry for rain.

We chanted the Christian prayers in Spanish. "Our Father's, Hail Mary's," over and over again. Then we rested and drank another gourd of zacá. Near midnight the moon rose white and full above the eastern arch. Liquid in the trough began to make intermittent bubbling noises. It was a fermenting mixture of water, honey, and bark from a *balché* tree. Between rounds of prayers the men sometimes drank beer or shared a cigarette from the altar.

Often the exhausted priest fell asleep.

When it was time to begin again an assistant touched his arm gently and whispered, "*Nohoch Tata*—great father."

EACH ROUND OF PRAYERS LASTED 45 minutes, and there were nine in all. At dawn the rounds were complete. But already the priest had taken out his polished sacred divination stones and spread them across the feed sack. He examined them carefully, then slowly shook his head.

"There will be no rain for Cobá."

As the sun rose, the leaves on the altar wilted, the candles burned to molten stumps, and the men prepared the feast. They placed thick cakes of corn dough, layered with ground squash seeds and marked with a cross, into a large pit lined with hot stones. They covered them with palm leaves, then

Clad against the cold, yet barefoot, women wait to watch a fiesta in Tenejapa in the Yucatán's Chiapas highlands; distinctly differentiated roles for women and men have changed little over the centuries.

filled the pit with dirt. While the bread baked, chickens bubbled in a caldron of broth, blood, and spices.

The priest's assistants and the frog boys politely served us each four gourds of balché, a gourd of Coca-Cola, then balché mixed with Coke. Waves of nausea began to sweep through me. The food was placed on the altar and dedicated to Chaac; then the first course was served: ground yellow corn mixed with bright yellow chicken feet on a banana-leaf plate. We could not stay. Of our family, only Greg remained in the clearing.

The balché had not fermented enough to be alcoholic and hallucinogenic as it is supposed to be, but it is in all its stages both purgative and emetic. For the rest of the day I draped my cleansed soul and purged body in a camp chair while George ministered to all of us. Ann lay sprawled on the cool tile floor at the Mexican archaeology camp next door, unable to move. I had found David deathly pale and exhausted beside the trail, hanging limp, with his eyes closed, knees buckled, arms dangling listlessly, and his chin wedged into the fork of a little tree. Ann and I have probably attended our last Chachaac ceremony. But Greg and young David may well be part of such a night again.

In the following days we watched the sky anxiously, hoping the prediction was mistaken.

A few showers fell in late July; then rain stopped until autumn.

That year, no corn grew in the milpas of Cobá.

CHAPTER FOUR

Travel & Exploration

Introduction by Sam Abell

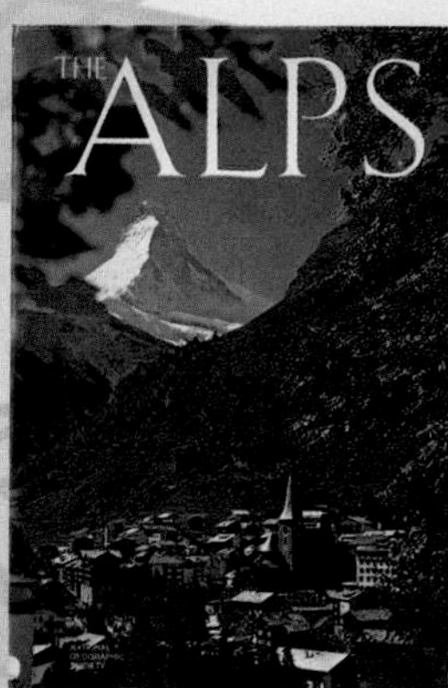

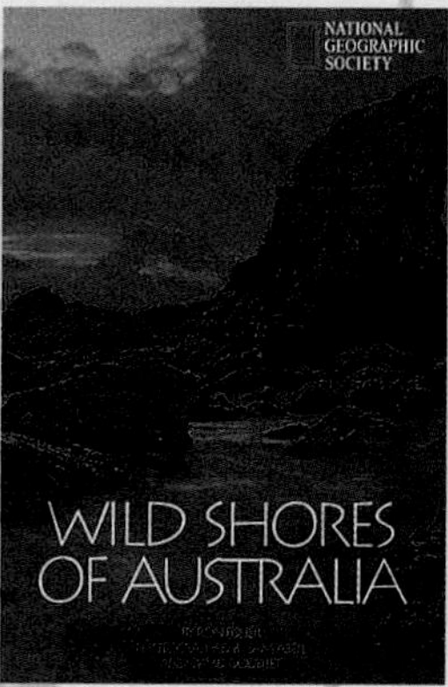

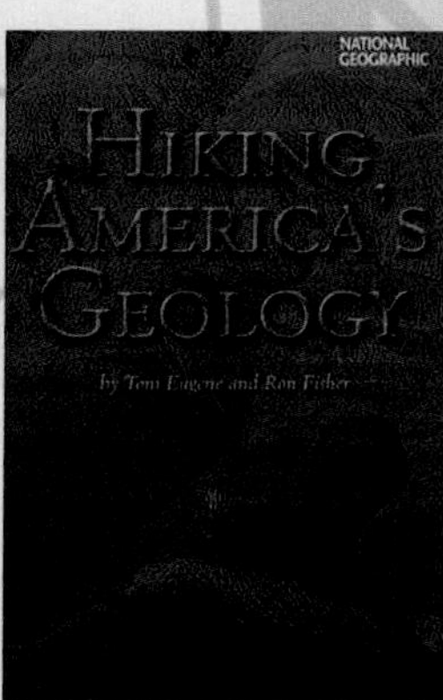

Near and far, familiar and exotic—National Geographic's Special Collection reflected a rich world of travel and adventure on every continent. Often the authors and photographers found thrills or faced dangers, taking readers along on every escapade.

In Sam Abell's 30-year career as a photographer, he has traveled around the world for National Geographic *magazine and the Society's Book Division. In 2002 he collaborated with Leah Bendavid-Val on a retrospective book,* Sam Abell: The Photographic Life. *His work was the subject of a one-man exhibition at the International Center of Photography in New York. He is the author of* Seeing Gardens *(2001) and* The Life of a Photograph (2008). *He lives in Crozet, Virginia, with his wife, Denise.*

From a photographer's perspective, working on a book in the Special Collection was just like working on a *National Geographic* magazine assignment, only better. What could be better than working for the magazine with its legendary length of time in the field? *More time in the field.* Competitive pressure to perform for the magazine? *Less pressure on Special Publications.* The magazine lasts a long time in people's homes and offices? *Books last longer.* You are in good company with other photographers in the magazine? *You have a book to yourself.*

So in my 30 years as a photographer at the National Geographic Society, I divided my work almost equally between the magazine and the Book Division. I was the photographer for four full Special Publications and contributed chapters for six other titles as well as providing the photographs for four larger-format books. Of all that time spent, the work done on Special Publications was, truly, the most special.

I met my wife, Denise Myers, while working on *The Pacific Crest Trail* (1975). She was hiking the trail in the summer of 1974. I was working with writer Will Gray (who would eventually become director of the Book Division). Will and I weren't hiking all of the trail; we were "high-pointing" it—concentrating on those sections that had the most potential to provide material for Will's storytelling and my photography. It was a common and practical strategy.

Still, over two summers we hiked 1,500 of the 2,600 miles of the mountainous trail that stretches from Mexico to Canada and traverses the Sierras, the Cascades, and the North Cascades. Hiking 1,500 miles with a dual load of camping and camera gear is no small feat, but I was not particularly proud of myself. My admiration was reserved for the so-called through-hikers. These were the individuals who set forth to hike the entire trail, from south to north, in one continuous six-month summer. Will and I were drawn to these hikers for their camaraderie and for their stories.

This led us into a trail friendship with Denise and her hiking companions. We first met by chance at a hot spring in the dry hills of southern California, where they had stopped to rest, resupply, and heal blistered feet. Weeks later we met again by accident in the Sierras, then met by arrangement several more times on the trail.

Will and I knew the trail was a test. At first, it was a straightforward physical test, and many would-be through-hikers drop out in the first 500 miles. After that it's a test of fortitude and, in Denise's case, a test of faithfulness. She'd made a promise to her partners, and she was keeping it. So despite having their packs and gear stolen and having their last companion drop out at the end of California, Denise and Hal hiked on. As our two parties slowly made our way up the trail that summer, my admiration for Denise grew into affection and from there into love. Sometime in the

I LEARNED HOW TO TRAVEL BY
WORKING ALONGSIDE MY NATIONAL GEOGRAPHIC
COLLEAGUES FOR THREE DECADES.

early snows of autumn Denise crossed over the Canadian line and into my life.

We were married in 1976 and for the next 20 years we traveled together on National Geographic assignments. Many of those memorable assignments were for Special Publications—books in the Society's Special Collection.

ASKED TO NAME HER FAVORITE ASSIGNMENT, Denise would probably say the Galápagos *(Majestic Island Worlds,* 1987). Asked to name my favorite place on Earth, I'd name a knoll in the Yukon from which it seemed the whole elegantly sloping Arctic Plain lay at our feet *(Canada's Wilderness Lands,* 1982). Ask either of us how we truly got to know our home state of Virginia, and we'd say by hiking through it on the Appalachian Trail (*Mountain Adventure,* 1988).

All these assignments have one meaningful thing in common: The writer on them was Ron Fisher. Ron was a staff writer and editor for Special Publications for 25 years. He may well have more bylines in Special Publications than any other writer. A number of those bylines we shared.

Our first assignment together set the standard by which we worked. The assignment was to do a book on canoeing in America. At the time I'd just finished the Pacific Crest Trail book and was still smarting from the fact that I hadn't walked all 2,600 miles of the trail. To my mind, that was the most authentic editorial approach.

I determined that there was a right way to undertake the fieldwork of the new book. It was to do all the rivers and lakes we selected. "All" meant beginning at the headwaters and canoeing to the mouth of each river. (In reality, this turned out to be impractical or impossible; we were able to do it just twice.)

In the case of lakes, it meant paddling all the historic canoe routes beginning, in our case, with the legendary—and lengthy—Route of the Voyageurs in northernmost Minnesota. This is the water path blazed by pioneering French Canadian fur traders bringing canoe loads of beaver pelts to market through the vast interconnected system of lakes and rivers in what is now interior Ontario. Retracing their route from International Falls, Minnesota, to Lake Superior would take three weeks of wilderness travel.

MEANWHILE, RON WAS PLANNING HIS version of the book, beginning with its fine title, *Still Waters, White Waters* (1977). He was quietly concentrating on the "still waters" part of the book's title—his apprehension of white water didn't appear until our fraught shakedown outing on the roaring Nantahala River in North Carolina came to a premature end.

We set that aside and in the fall of 1975 left National Geographic in a VW bus. It would be 14 months before we returned for good. In Minneapolis we picked up two 18-foot wood and canvas canoes and headed north to the Boundary Waters Canoe Area.The structure of our trips became the structure of the book. It was a grandly circular, clockwise structure beginning and ending in autumn and in the north, the natural home of the North American canoe.

After the Boundary Waters, we canoed the Allagash in Maine, the Okefenokee Swamp in Georgia, and the Suwannee River in Florida. In summer we went down Indiana's Fox River, the Buffalo in Arkansas, and Utah's placid and turbulent Green River. Then to the historic route of Lewis and Clark on the Upper Missouri in Montana, finishing with a month in Wyoming on Yellowstone Lake and Jackson Lake at the foot of the Tetons.

But the big trip was a three-week paddle down the Noatak River in the northwest corner of Alaska. It was the canoe trip of a lifetime. Years later, when I mentioned to Ron that the Noatak trip was my favorite, he said "Aren't you misremembering that trip? The guide lied. He'd never been down the river and told us there were no rapids. You capsized and lost most of your camera gear. We ran out of coffee, then food. You fought with the guide, then fired him at the first Eskimo village. We were cold, tired, and hungry. Our last night was spent on the open ocean." All true—and, like all bad trips, a good story, but only part of the story. The rest was beautiful and funny.

At the headwaters in the Brooks Range, we read at night under the waning influence of the midnight sun. Near the end of that journey, we saw the northern lights. In between we floated through the vast silence of America's last unbroken wilderness. An owl flew around my head. On a gravel beach I picked up an unusual rock: the tooth of a woolly mammoth. We saw mountain goats, caribou, and grizzly bears eating blueberries. When we were hungry, we fished and ate blueberries like the bears.

Ron lost his favorite New York Yankees T-shirt. I lost most of my cameras and long lenses. But I learned to use the camera I had and made new pictures, ones I still look at today.

And yes, we did end up alone at night on the Arctic Ocean, trying to reach the Kotzebue. It was harrowing—but memorably beautiful as well. A stunning sunset, then deep darkness, and with it the enlivening, edgy sense of the unknown. But what I felt there, and remember now, was our sureness. By noon we were strong canoeists, and when we had to lash our canoes together that night in the open ocean to transfer partners, we did it smoothly.

Later on the beach we "danced a jig of joy," in Ron's words. We had done the Noatak, from the headwaters out to the ocean. That night Ron found his missing Yankees T-shirt. He'd been wearing it.

TRAVEL IS THE SUBJECT OF THIS CHAPTER, and my colleagues at National Geographic were thoughtful travelers. I learned how to travel by working alongside them for three decades.

From Ron I even learned how to arrive on assignment. Twenty years had passed since *Still Waters*. *Australia* was to be our last book together. I had hastily flown in overnight and groggily gone to bed. Sometime later in the day I awakened and looked out at a parking lot, only dimly aware of where I was.

Ron had taken leave, boarded a cargo freighter that accepted passengers, and set forth across the Pacific. For three weeks our faraway island steadily grew closer until one sparkling afternoon Ron's ship sailed under the mighty Sydney Harbor Bridge, passed the Opera House and dropped anchor on the *Wild Shores of Australia*—the title of our book. He'd arrived by ship, as sailors had for three centuries. Now he was ready to write.

THE ALPS (1973)

Snow blankets the Bavarian village of Kochel, sunlight sparkles on the distant summit of the Heimgarten, and a frosty mist tingles the air above a family strolling a well-packed hillside lane.

High in the Valle d'Aosta at the hamlet of Graines, farmer Vincent Willermin (below) and his black-clad wife, Elena Borbey, watch their nephew Walter Revil, staff in hand, at his summer task of helping with the cattle. Two watering troughs and a dungheap flank the path. Animals occupy the ground floor, with family quarters above; the farthest door leads to a storeroom containing feed grains for the stock, cornmeal, potatoes, hard rye bread, and homemade sausage. Such stone farmhouses keep a long-established regional pattern. Architecture provides one of the few consistencies in an area where borders have shifted often, where villages only miles apart speak different languages.

136

137

A team of writers and photographers delivered up a host of delightful scenes and friendly natives in The Alps.

A book celebrating the magnificence of the Alps, one of the world's great mountain ranges, came out in 1973. To accomplish this mission in a reasonably short time, staff writers and photographers dispersed themselves among picturesque villages and snow-bound fastnesses, and together they put this alpine holiday of a book together. Each country sharing the Alps got its own chapter—Switzerland, France, Liechtenstein, Germany (Bavaria), Italy, Yugoslavia (Slovenia), and Austria.

North Carolina native Mary Ann Harrell wrote the book's introduction, stressing the idea that though small by Himalayan or Andean standards, the Alps are nonetheless tremendous in their wealth of romance, their traditional grandeur, and their place in human history. Various chapters of the book touch on geology here and there, but the real focus of its pages are the friendly people and the breathtaking beauty of the region.

Harrell's light, conversational style sets the tone for the entire volume. Let others climb the Matterhorn, she says, content to gaze on and enjoy its beauty. Even when quoting what other writers have to say about the Alps, there's no straining after effect. The same goes for the paragraph about the mountain chain's dimensions. She simply gives you what you need to know, packing your rucksack with a sweater and tasty snacks, and off you go along the high and winding Alpine trail.

Heidi's World

From Mary Ann Harrell's opening chapter on the great mountains

"Come on, you *have* to climb at least one," a friend insisted at Zermatt. I was delighted with the village and the view—"the very sanctuary of the 'Spirit of the Alps,'" says a 1903 guidebook on Switzerland. And I was entirely content with hikers' paths that don't force you to hang on with your hands. My friend had just completed a practice climb on one of the easier peaks before he took on the 14,690-foot-high Matterhorn. He had not quite convinced me when the conversation drifted to the problem of replacing his sunglasses.

"They fell off."

"Why didn't you pick them up?"

"They fell 900 feet."

That was convincing.

You don't necessarily have to climb the Alps to enjoy them. "Playground of Europe," climber and

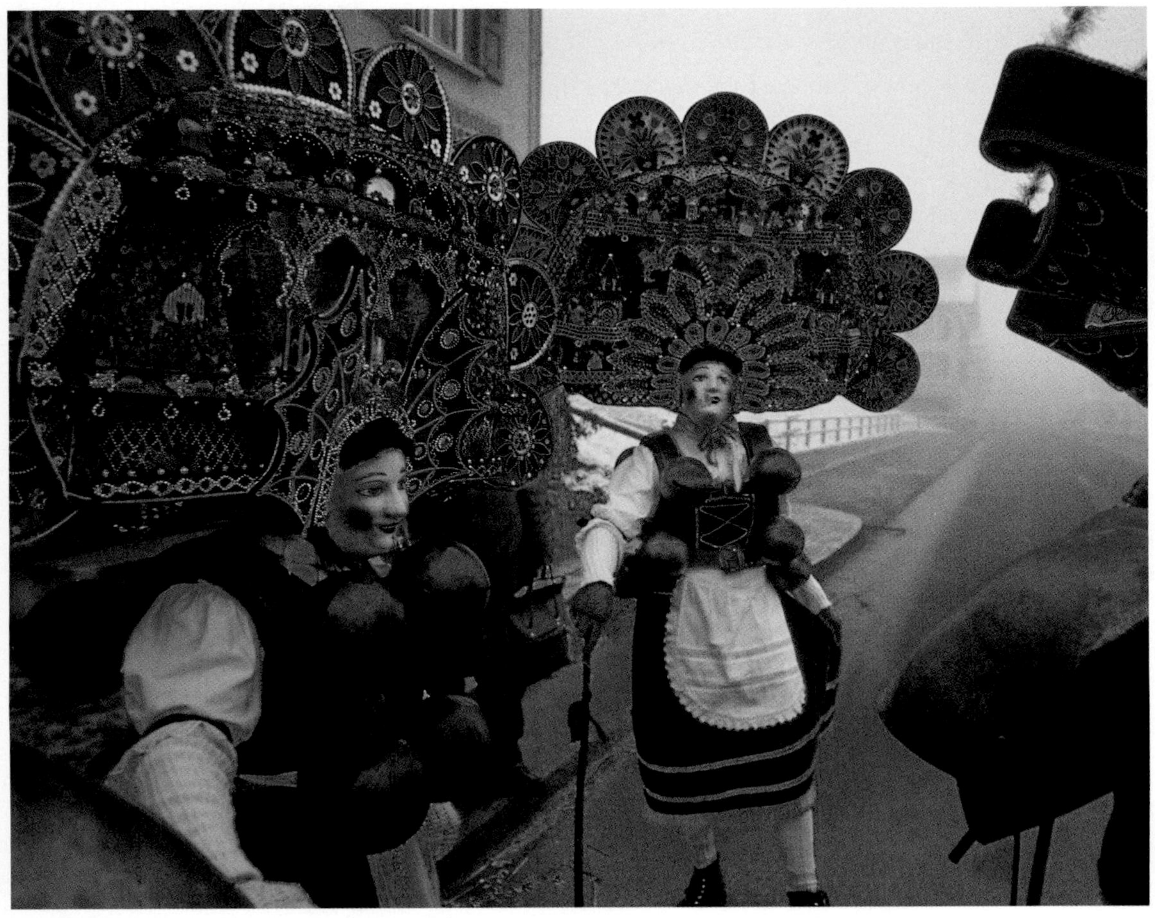

Dressed to impress, merrymakers at the Silvester-Klausen festival in the Swiss town of Herisau disguise themselves in masks and elaborate headdresses. Similar traditional Alpine fetes can be found throughout the region.

FOR MILLENNIA STRONG MEN HAVE MET THE GEOGRAPHIC CHALLENGE OF THESE "SAVAGELY BROKEN ROCKS," AS LIVY DESCRIBED THEM IN HIS HISTORY OF HANNIBAL'S JOURNEY.

scholar Leslie Stephen called the Alps a century ago. Now the phrase would be "Playground of the World."

From the Maritime Alps with their views of the Mediterranean to the Vienna Woods, from Bavaria to Lake Bled, the mountains sustain an empire of entertainment. Bikini-wearing skiers in Italy, hitchhiking students, architecture buffs, music lovers assembling at Salzburg, climbers from Mexico or Japan, Middle Westerners game enough to stretch their throats on a yodel—all of them can find diversions in the diversity of the Alps.

LONG BEFORE I EVER SAW THE CLEAR dazzle of Alpine snowfields, I met the high pastures and white peaks as part of Heidi's world. Like so many other children, I knew that "the Alps" meant the life of the herdsmen. In fact, I saw my first snow mountains as a backdrop for the formal gardens by Lake Como; goat-herding seemed wildly remote from the neatly trimmed hedges, the stone figures in classic drapery, and the living figures in casual drip-dry with garlands of cameras.

As an introduction to the human variety of the Alps, it was perfect.

"In the Rockies," says a colleague, "you're aware of a land that goes on for hundreds of miles; in the Alps you're aware of a life that has gone on for hundreds of years—how a particular village or city has developed its own ways over the centuries."

Dimensions alone cannot account for the richness of the Alps. This whole range would fit easily into Virginia and West Virginia combined. Measured along the arc from Nice to Vienna, the length of the chain is some 650 miles. Its width is surprisingly narrow, averaging only 100 miles. Overall, the Alpine area occupies 80,000 square miles: modest, as mountain systems go. In contrast, the Rockies extend roughly 3,000 miles in length, with a maximum width of 350 miles or so. The young Himalayas run some 1,500 by 150 miles.

Nevertheless, the Alps may well be the most famous of major mountain ranges and are certainly the most thoroughly examined. Here, in the 19th century, the scientific study of mountains began. Thus the Alps became a standard—but this, warns geologist Rudolf Trümpy of Zurich, can be misleading, considering the complexity and great variety of mountain-building events.

Why mountains ever rose at all has perplexed and distressed men in the past. Although the Scriptures speak of the Lord's holy mountain, early Jewish and Christian scholars often blamed the origin of mountains on sin. Some cited the disobedience of Adam and Eve; others, Cain's murder of Abel; others, the general corruption that provoked the flood in Noah's time. Nothing less calamitous could have replaced good farmland with useless heaps of rock and ice.

But beauty? Anyone who visits the Alps must keep memories of scenes that brought absolute exultation. I recall such classic vistas as the Matterhorn beyond the glaciers from Gornergrat; but most vivid of all is a single white summit, sunlit above a valley in gathering dusk, unforgettable even though its name has faded with the name of the

In the village of Appenzell in northeastern Switzerland, near Heidi country, an elderly man gazes out from a sliding window of his 200-year-old home (top), his face almost as weathered as his house's wood trim. An Alpine festival at Aeschiried (bottom) offers a break from the toil and tedium of harvesting and herding. The midsummer festival lets visitors enjoy Swiss traditions but serves primarily as an excuse for locals to gather in celebration. Herdsmen's 12-foot-long alpenhorns resound; neighbors join together in yodeling and group singing.

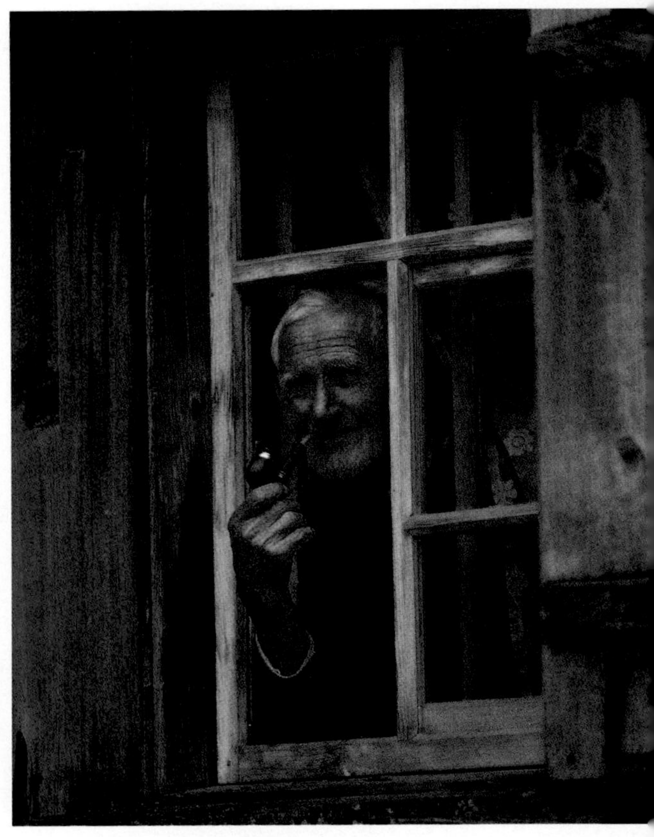

Swiss restaurant that served delectable fresh-caught trout for dinner that night.

Yet for generations men found the Alps—and other mountains—ugly. Latin poets called the Alps "frozen" or "savage" if they wrote of them at all. Compiling adjectives for mountains in the 1670's, an Englishman included a few like "lovely, star-brushing," but more in this vein: "insolent, surly, barren, pathless, melancholy, forsaken, crump-shouldered."

Probably the fatigue and risk of travel inspired some of this. A young Welshman wrote in 1621: "I am now got over the Alps ... I had crossed and clambered up the Pyreneans to Spain before; they are not so high and hideous as the Alps." In 1646 diarist John Evelyn, riding muleback in Switzerland's Simplon Pass, found it "very steepe, craggy, & dangerous ... onely inhabited with Beares, Wolves, & Wild Goates."

Travel was still tiring, however, when 18th-century visitors seeing the Alps for the first time declared themselves "rapt" in the face of the sublime, and when 19th-century strangers marveled at the vast glories of the Alps and leafed through the pages of Byron or Shelley for words to express so great a thrill:

"All that expands the spirit, yet appalls / Gather around these summits."

Or: "...all seems eternal now."

Relics of an ancient forest protrude from sand dunes on Fraser (or Great Sandy) Island in the Coral Sea, off the east coast of Australia. Sandblows helped build Fraser, the world's largest sand island, 76 miles long and up to 15 miles wide. More than 230 species of birds live here.

Wild Shores of Australia

(1996) **by Ron Fisher**

Heavily hunted for many years, sea lions find
refuge on Kangaroo Island. Rocky beaches along
southern Australia once teemed with fur seals and sea
lions. With few natural enemies, they were easy prey;
tens of millions were killed in less than 30 years.
The future of the island's glossy black cockatoo (above)
remains in doubt: Probably only 180 survive,
victims of shrinking habitat and competition from bees
and possums for nesting places in hollows of trees.
118
119

Splendid images of maritime life vie for attention with a spellbinding text in Wild Shores of Australia.

A circumnavigation of the entire continent of Australia was Ron Fisher's assignment in the 1996 book *Wild Shores of Australia*. The shoreline winds around the country that is also a continent for some 22,800 miles, stretching a full 30 degrees of latitude from northern to southern coastline. Fisher called his Australian junket "a ride on a splendid carousel."

From dazzling white beaches packed with swimmers and surfers to wild rocky shores, from the steamy tropics of Kakadu in the north to the buzzing cities in the south—Ron Fisher took his readers along on a richly varied adventure in the best of the National Geographic Society's travelogue tradition.

Fisher makes the point that while visitors tend to associate Australia with its outback, the vast majority of its population lives near the ocean; the history and culture of this island country are tied to the sea. Fisher's easygoing style matched well with the artistry of photographers Sam Abell and David Doubilet.

In the following extract, Fisher relates his meanders around the neighboring cities of Fremantle and Perth in remote Western Australia. He visits a crocodile park and a maritime museum and takes a drive up the rugged northwest coast. With a nose for a good story, he deftly recounts the memorably gruesome tale of one of the country's oldest known shipwrecks.

The Golden West

Encounters with wrecks, crocs, and long, sandy beaches

Fremantle is one of those confusing Australian coastal cities with no square blocks, streets that unexpectedly become one-way, and abrupt dead ends. It's an aspect of the coastal cities I learned to recognize: They were built to conform to their waterfronts. So I floundered around for an hour or two, trying to find the Western Australia Maritime Museum, for I knew it told the story of the wreck of the *Batavia,* Australia's second oldest known shipwreck.

The *Batavia* was a merchantman of the Dutch East India Company that wrecked on the arid Abrolhos Islands some 275 miles north of here on June 4, 1629. The commander, the senior officers, and some of the passengers set off in two small boats to look for water, leaving 268 people behind. There followed three months of rape, murder, and debauchery as one faction of survivors made war on the other. The commander, instead of finding water, took a month to sail to Batavia—now

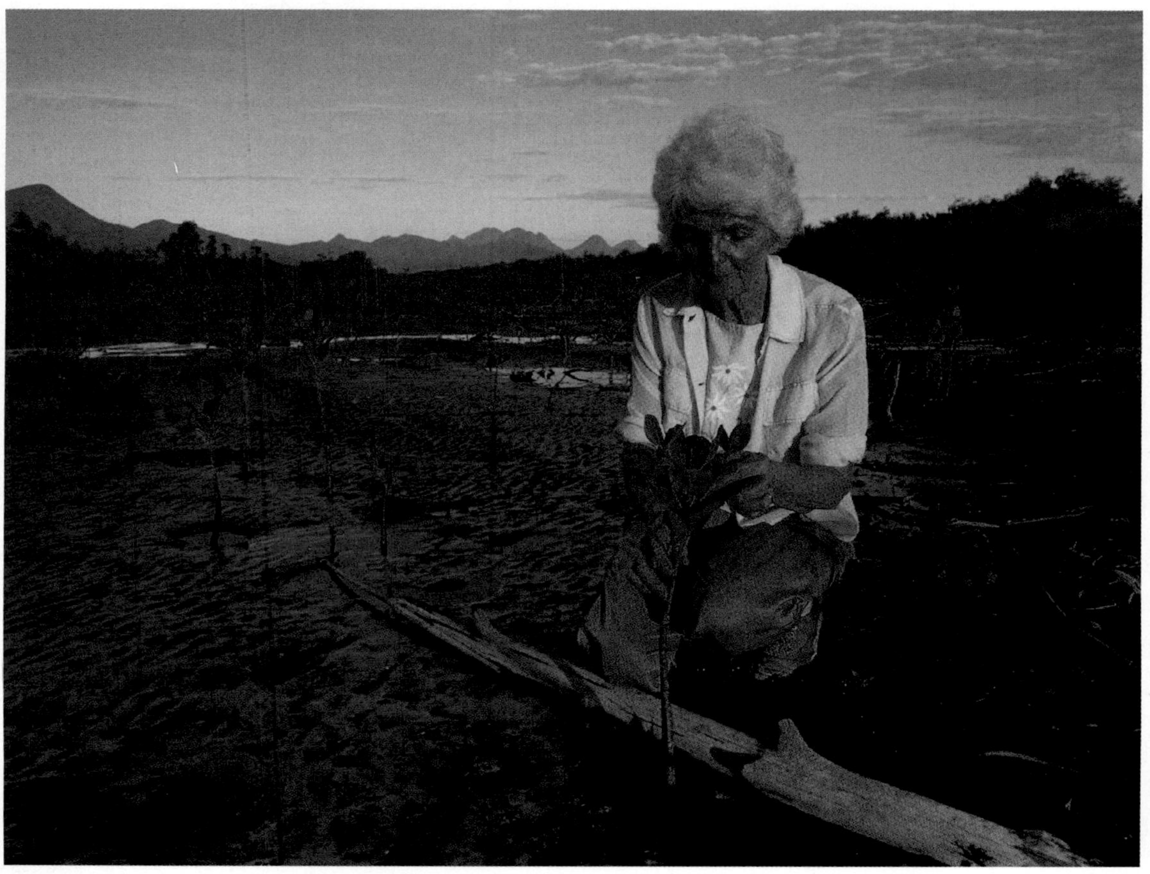

Ray of hope: Environmental crusader Margaret Thorsborne plants new mangrove seedlings in a bulldozed forest on Queensland's Hitchinbrook Channel. The mangroves will provide vital shore stabilization and habitat.

Jakarta—and 63 days to return to the wreck, where he barely avoided being ambushed and killed himself by the mutineers. He found 125 men, women, and children murdered and the rest terrorized.

The bones of the *Batavia* moldered in obscurity for centuries until 1963, when a fisherman led divers to the wreck. Excavations during the 1970s recovered much material, which is now housed in museums in Fremantle and Geraldton.

In Fremantle, surviving hull timbers have been reassembled and artifacts such as coins and pottery are now displayed in glass cases. Most striking are the 137 sandstone blocks raised from the *Batavia.* They puzzled archaeologists until someone fitted them together into an impressive portico intended for the castle in Batavia. Reassembled now, the portal looks like something from the set of a Cecil B. DeMille movie.

I VISITED THE FREMANTLE CROCODILE Park and noticed a sign advertising the Hard Croc Café. Croc farms and parks have sprung up in several areas of Australia, largely in response to the animals' near extermination by hunters. Both species—the so-called saltwater and the freshwater—were nearly gone from their range in northern Australia by the time bans on hunting were imposed between 1962 and 1974. There are now thought to be some 60,000 freshwater crocodiles in Australia and upwards of 60,000 salties in the Northern Territory alone.

Now farms around the country raise crocodiles commercially, both for their meat and more especially for their skins. The park in Fremantle had finches flitting around and just above the creatures' pools. "If they fly too low, the crocs'll have a go at them, said owner Don Wieringa. There were saltwater crocs penned there—including Bismarck and Rasputin. In Rasputin's pen was a sign that read: "Rasputin's my name, Gus to my friends. I'm the one with the big smile. I'm an amiable sort of chap. My mate thinks so too. I came from Wyndham in the northwest, but I'm happy here. See my new teeth growing?" As I watched, one of Gus's eyes slowly closed, then just as slowly opened again—a sinister wink.

I made it a point, whenever I talked with people who worked with crocodiles, to ask: "Do you dream about crocodiles?"—because they seemed to me the sort of beasts that might populate nightmares.

Anna, at the Fremantle croc park, said, without a flicker of hesitation, "All the time. They sort of get into your head, and you can't get rid of them."...

Mike Osborn, then manager of the Wyndham Crocodile Farm, couldn't shake hands with me when I first met him because his right hand was swollen and covered with big red stitches, the result of a bite a few days before. "I dreamed about crocs the night before I was bitten," he said, "but it's my first bite in a year." His wife, Anne, interrupted: "The first bite in a year that's *needed stitches.*" A six-footer had gotten him while it was being moved to another pen.

FREMANTLE'S NEAR NEIGHBOR TO THE north—Perth—has the west coast of Australia pretty much to itself. The nearest other state capital—Adelaide—is 1,315 air miles away. With Fremantle, Perth was host city to the America's Cup competition in 1987, just four years after the Australians took the cup from the U.S. for the first time in 132 years. The city gained momentary fame some years earlier when it turned all its lights on during the night of February 20, 1962, as a friendly gesture to astronaut John Glenn, who was orbiting the earth in his Mercury space capsule.

The black swans that caught the eye of an early Dutch explorer—he named the river the Swan—still

Ever on the alert, a wallaby pauses for a drink in the muddy Ord River, one of several crocodile-infested streams draining the rugged, remote north coast.

attract visitors to Lake Monger in Perth. The city prides itself on being the friendliest and most relaxed capital in Australia, with perfect weather and sublime beaches. And it's the right size for a city, big enough to satisfy urban needs but small enough to explore comfortably. Because of its proximity to the Orient, Perth is the Australian city where I saw the most Asian faces while strolling around town.

NORTH OF THE CONFUSED TANGLE OF Fremantle and Perth, Australia's Route 1—a highway that runs virtually all the way around the country, clinging as closely as possible to the coast—once again brings order to chaos and makes circumnavigating the country easy. It carried me northward, toward the rugged and exotic northwest coast....

In the desert country there, limestone spires rise dramatically from the bare sands.

Another 155 miles up the highway is the city of Geraldton, a favored holiday destination of Perth families.... Giant fig trees shade the entrance to the building that houses its maritime museum. Inside, I said to the woman at the desk, "What's the best thing in your museum?"

"It's all interesting," she said. "But you must watch our video. I'll rewind it."

"What's it about?" I asked.

"Oh," she laughed, "I can't give away the plot."

The video was about the *Batavia.*

Walrus bulls mass on an Alaskan beach in Togiak National Wildlife Refuge. The walruses fatten on mussels and clams in the summer and then migrate north. Low-flying planes can stampede the herds, causing injury or death, and the refuge has secured legal protection against careless pilots.

Natural America (1998)

by T. H. Watkins

HIGH PLAINS STORM
broods over an isolated house on BLM
lands near Medicine Bow, Wyoming. Those
who tried to stake their claim in plains
country were among the many thousands
who saw the "leftover lands" west of the
Missouri River as a dream of opportunity
—a dream that often was dashed by an
inhospitable climate.

The grand spectacle of nature, dwarfing the works of man, is Natural America's *theme and clarion call.*

By late in the last decade of the 20th century, the environmental movement had grown so urgent that it was not enough to present a book on the natural world and simply gush. True, readers had become numb to scolding about the planet's poor health, but editors of National Geographic's Special Collection felt that in subtle ways they had to remind people that wild places and animals remain only because we allow them to. A book on the natural world of America was set into motion, intended to celebrate the fact that the United States was a leader in land conservation.

Selected to write the book was T. H. Watkins, the Wallace Stegner Distinguished Professor of Western American Studies at Montana State University. Watkins took the opportunity of writing the essays that make up the book to explain why conservation is a good idea. Besides being beautiful, he reminds us, the natural world is our inheritance as well as our future. In his essay titled "The Safety Valve," he tells us that we need wilderness for our health, if not our very survival.

"As strenuous challenge or contemplative retreat, the parks and other units of the national lands offer welcome respite from the world, a safety valve for body and spirit," he writes. "And where's the price tag when a small girl from Harlem stands surrounded by a bright swarm of monarch butterflies at Great Kills Park on Staten Island? Such a moment is worth nothing—and everything."

America's Safety Valve

On the value of the national parks and forests

Gentle pursuits have much to recommend them. In the national forests alone, where there are more than 133,000 miles of hiking trails, including nearly 6,000 miles of the National Scenic Trails System, at least 30 million hikes take place every year. The Bureau of Land Management (BLM) does not keep figures on the number of miles of trails its lands hold, but 28 million people engaged in what the agency calls "trail activities" in 1996. The National Wildlife Refuge System had 5.4 million trail visits that year....

All of this activity suggests that millions of Americans are seeking renewal by getting as close to the land as their feet will take them. And many of those same millions are letting their feet do the walking in what may be the single most important thing the national lands can offer the poor, addled human spirit in the way of recreation: wilderness, designated wilderness, federal wilderness, American wilderness. No other nation on Earth has anything to compare with the National Wilderness Preservation System of the United States. Like jazz and the Bill of Rights—like the national lands themselves—officially classified wilderness is a uniquely American idea, found only on these lands.

Recently, considerable discussion has arisen over the question of just how "wild" designated wilderness truly is, given that human beings have

With the roar of geothermal falls for company, a fisherwoman casts a line in the Firehole River at Yellowstone National Park. Such pursuits have measureless value.

Explorers glide through a saw-grass swamp in Everglades National Park in craft similar to those made by the Seminole. Most of the area's Indians are long gone, as are millions of wading birds.

THE CITIZENSHIP OF LAND, LIKE THE CITIZENSHIP OF THE SOCIAL CONTRACT THAT BINDS US WITH THE CONSTITUTION, CARRIES WITH IT RESPONSIBILITIES AS WELL AS RIGHTS.

been in and on the land ever since the first peoples emigrated here from Siberia, perhaps 20,000 years ago.

As they moved down the continent, splitting up into language groups, and splitting up again into nations called tribes, they set fires to create better hunting grounds. They grafted one plant species onto another to engineer something they could cultivate and eat. They carved hunting and trading trails through wilderness or over plains. They built irrigation works and huge burial mounds, and erected whole cities made of earth. They did any number of things that to one degree or another altered the land in measurable ways.

That being the case, this argument goes, designating certain pieces of landscape worthy of protection because they contain a relic of "primeval" America is illogical at best. What we are protecting is not a place but an idea.

As it happens, the Wilderness Act of 1964 doesn't say anything about "primeval" or even "pristine." What it does say is this: "A wilderness, in contrast with those areas where man and his own works dominate the landscape, is hereby recognized as an area where the earth and its community of life are untrammeled by man, where man himself is a visitor who does not remain...." That seems good enough for most of those who think that such areas still are as close to the truly wild as most people are ever likely to get. As Wallace Stegner wrote, "We simply need that wild country available to us, even if we never do more than drive to its edge and look in. For it can be a means of reassuring ourselves of our sanity as creatures...."

I can attest that sanity is the point. Though I reside now in a small western town surrounded by mountains, I spent 37 years of my life in large cities, walled off from all but the most cursory connection to the natural world. True, San Francisco and Oakland in California did have San Francisco Bay, but even when I lived there in the 1960s and 1970s, the Bay was threatened by development. Only a grassroots citizens' movement kept its shores from being filled in and built upon. New York City has Central Park, but that is an entirely manufactured place. Washington, D.C., where I lived for nearly 16 years, has big old white oaks and maples lining the streets and ornamenting the city's squares and circles, but all were planted by humans long ago and have a regimental character; only the 1,754 acres of Rock Creek Park hold at least a suggestion of wildness.

But even in my big-city days, my work as a writer enabled me to hop airplanes to someplace wild fairly often. The sudden feeling of freedom and anticipatory excitement that came over me when I stepped out of the airport in Salt Lake City, got into a rental car, and headed for the canyon country of southern Utah was as real as it is indescribable.

Every single time I did so—not every now and then, but every single time—whether heading for the Escalante River or pointing myself toward the backcountry Rockies or the California desert or the Everglades or any other place that holds a wilderness treasure, I felt as if I were coming home.

America's striking desert landscapes include fields of prickly pear cactuses in Big Bend National Park, Texas (above), and an ancient spiral petroglyph in Arizona's Saguaro National Park (below).

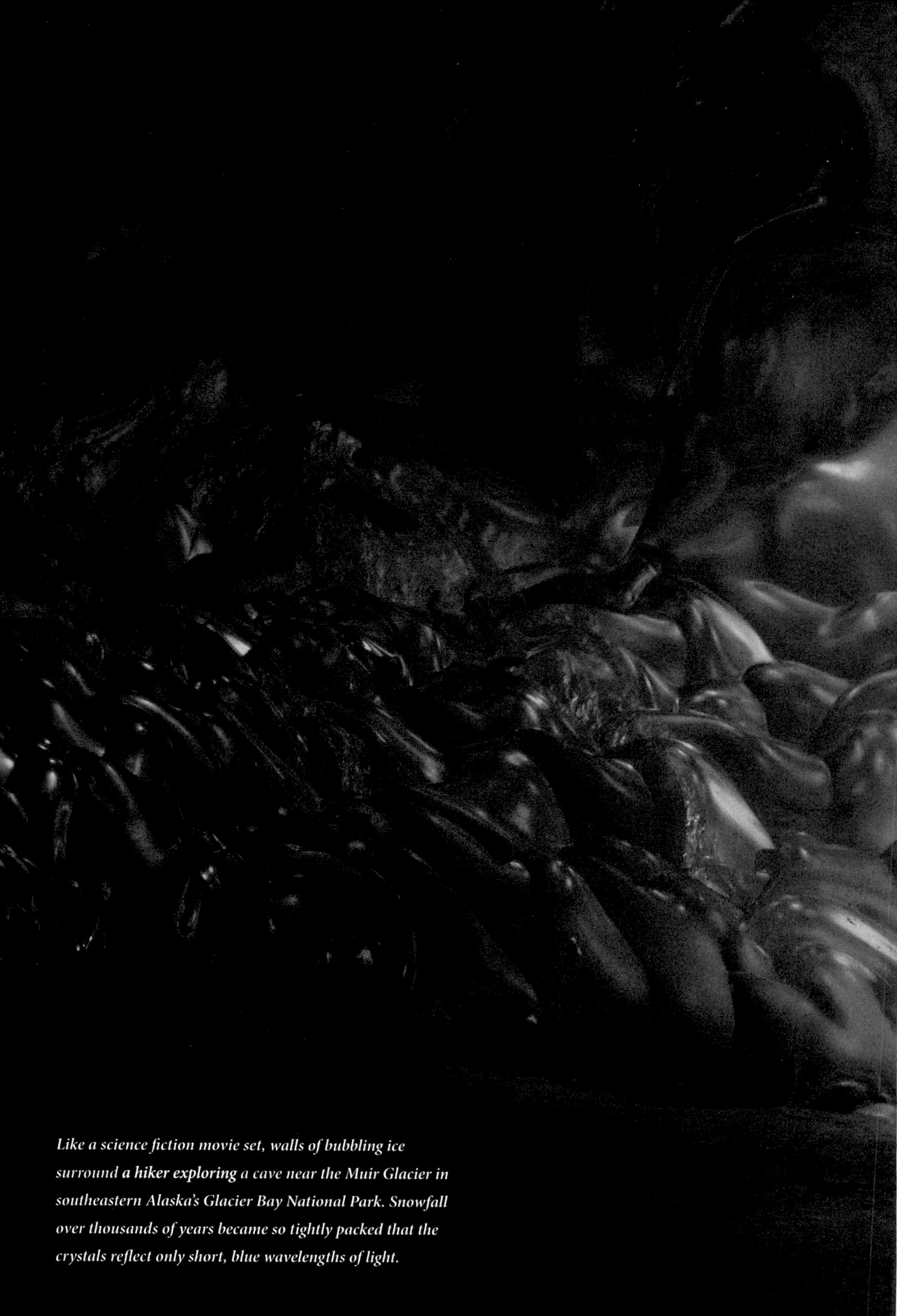

Like a science fiction movie set, walls of bubbling ice surround **a hiker exploring** *a cave near the Muir Glacier in southeastern Alaska's Glacier Bay National Park. Snowfall over thousands of years became so tightly packed that the crystals reflect only short, blue wavelengths of light.*

HIKING AMERICA'S GEOLOGY

(2003) **by Toni Eugene and Ron Fisher**

KINGS CANYON: A packtrain picks its way down slippery slopes in Sequoia and Kings Canyon National Parks. Hikers traverse sharp peaks and snowfields at the mountain crests, alpine meadows and groves of giant sequoias at lower elevations.
Hiking America's Geology
California's High Sierra

Hiking America's Geology *guides readers through some of the nation's most breathtaking scenery.*

The idea for this 2003 volume was to take readers to places where they could see the exciting processes of geology at work—processes that we usually think of as slow and imperceptible. Chapters chronicled journeys to Alaska's Glacier Bay National Park, where calving glaciers scour out steep-walled fiords; to California's Yosemite National Park, with its sheer cliffs and plummeting waterfalls; to Colorado and Utah's dinosaur country; and to Acadia National Park on the rock-jumbled coast of Maine.

Perhaps the most dramatic example of the ongoing handiwork of American geology was portrayed in the first chapter, titled "Hawaii's Mountains of Fire." Author Toni Eugene—a National Geographic staff member for more than 20 years—hiked through Hawaii Volcanoes National Park on the Big Island of Hawaii. Wrote Eugene, "The volcanoes that form the heart of Hawaii create as they destroy, constantly changing and reshaping the island."

Hiking a fiery realm of craters, lava fields, and rain forests, Eugene and her friend, Camille, at one point behold an amazing early evening spectacle—a brilliant eruption a few miles from their trail. Eugene's polished writing (ornamented thanks to her ear for fascinating, subject-specific words, like "clinkery") bubbles over at times into childlike enthusiasm. She seems to be saying to readers, in effect, come on out and see all this for yourself—the message of all good travel writing.

At the Volcano's Edge

From Toni Eugene's encounter with Hawaii's dynamic flow

We began to familiarize ourselves with the Hawaii Volcanoes National Park, starting at Crater Rim Drive, which rings the cliff-walled summit caldera of Kīlauea, one of Hawaii's youngest and most active volcanoes.

Geologists define a caldera as a steep-walled depression at a volcano's summit. It forms when the magma reservoir below the mountain shrinks. Unsupported, the floor of the volcano collapses, leaving a depression. A crater, smaller than a caldera, can form by collapse or explosion.

Kīlauea Caldera is some three miles wide and 400 feet deep; within it, Halemaʻumaʻu Crater is 3,000 feet in diameter. We made several hiking forays from Crater Rim Drive, all of them short and easy. Devastation Trail, about a mile round trip, passes over an old lava flow. White skeletons of *ʻōhiʻa lehua,* a native tree of the myrtle family that can grow to spectacular heights, littered black and broken fields; bright ferns and ʻōhiʻa lehua seedlings covered with pink blooms, tiny starts of those tall trees, sprang from stark black rock.

Like a furnace from the underworld, fiery lava pours from a rift on Kīlauea in Hawaii Volcanoes National Park. Overnight hikers sometimes see the molten glow in the distance.

TWO HUNDRED YEARS AGO
THIS LANDSCAPE DID NOT EXIST,
AND TWO CENTURIES HENCE IT WILL BE NO MORE.

After patient searching, I found examples of Pele's tears—tiny droplets of black volcanic glass formed as molten rock is blasted upward then cools as it falls to Earth—and fine golden strands called Pele's hair—volcanic glass formed when thin filaments of molten lava are carried by the wind.

HALEMAʻUMAʻU, THE LEGENDARY HOME OF Pele, the Hawaiian goddess of fire, is only a five-minute walk from Crater Rim Drive, across a field of steaming vents, called solfataras, where reeking sulfur gases seep to the surface of the volcano. When Mark Twain visited here in 1866, he noticed the stink of sulfur—"strong," he allowed, "but not unpleasant to a sinner." Sulfur crystals cling to the rock around the solfataras, and the acidic gases color the surrounding rock. Steam escaping from one hole was so hot I had to yank my hand away.

A wilted lei tribute to Pele ringed a small boulder near the crater; a White-tailed Tropicbird soared on

Bear tracks cross a sandbar at Alsek Lake in Alaska's Glacier Bay National Park. Along the far shore, icebergs as big as houses were shed from Alsek and Grand Plateau Glaciers.

In Utah's Arches National Park, the South Window offers a porthole on hikers and distant Turret Arch. The park's 2,000 sandstone arches provide timeless vantages onto nature's spectacular stonework.

wings spanning three feet above the dark gray and black expanse. Pele's home has changed in size and depth since 1924, when it was 1,500 feet in diameter. During the last major Halemaʻumaʻu eruption, in 1967, lava filled the crater to within a hundred feet of the rim, then receded. A solidified circle of rock, reminiscent of a bathtub ring, indicates how high the lava reached.

In the afternoon, Camille and I hiked the four-mile Kīlauea Iki Loop Trail. Kīlauea Iki, or little Kīlauea, is an ancient crater that, like Halemaʻumaʻu, collapsed to form a depression when molten rock drained from below the volcano.

As we approached Kīlauea Iki, hikers below straggled like ants across seemingly barren blackness, and wisps of steam wafted lazily upward. Steep switchbacks led 380 feet down through a junglelike forest of tree ferns and ʻōhiʻa lehua to the crater floor. A bubbling lava lake in 1959, the floor looks now like a scene from *Star Wars* or *Planet of the Apes:* a steaming one-mile expanse of inky crust.

Camille and I struggled over jumbled sections of aʻa, one of two types of Hawaii's basaltic lava. Aʻa, more viscous than the other Hawaiian lava, pahoehoe, breaks into loose, jagged pieces as it flows downhill. The clinkery rubble is sharp, and chunks roll underfoot; hiking over it demands constant attention. Pahoehoe, which contains more gas than aʻa, has a smooth and ropy surface. It brings to mind quick-frozen brownie batter, and walking on it is easier on the legs....

THE VOLCANOES THAT FORM THE HEART OF HAWAII CREATE AS THEY DESTROY, CONSTANTLY CHANGING AND RESHAPING THE ISLAND.

About four miles into the hike, we began skirting Makaopuhi Crater, a giant double-lobed pit some 500 years old. The rain was falling so hard it was difficult to see in front of me. Our ranger guru Ruth had advised us to take plenty of water on this excursion, as none was available. We carried six quarts—12 heavy pounds!—each.

With rain falling in torrents all around us, I had little desire to drink, but drink we did, partly just to lighten our load and partly to rest a while. Ahead the trees grew nearer and the terrain appeared to change.

BEYOND MAKAOPUHI, THE PATH WOUND through a dense rain forest of ʻōhiʻa lehua and gigantic tree ferns that slowed but did not stop the deluge from reaching us. Mud replaced rock, and we slid into the late afternoon. Big raindrops plopped on my glasses, and we jumped wide puddles. Leaves brushed us, depositing yet more water on glasses and ponchos. The greenery was thick, and the trail was narrow.

We fought our way past branches and brush, feeling overwhelmed by the foliage—yet this rain forest is young. In 1840, a pahoehoe flow flooded the entire area. After that, it looked much like the bleak terrain Camille and I had just traversed. Those tough little ferns and ʻōhiʻa lehu seedlings we had admired in Kīlauea Iki make fast headway, given ample rain.

As we rounded a bend in late afternoon, we passed a rickety building surrounded by a lava-rock wall. A wooden sign noted that it had once been a *pulu* processing mill. Pulu, the golden fibers that grow on hāpuʻu tree ferns, was gathered, dried, and baled here in the 1800s, then shipped throughout the Pacific and to North America for use as pillow and mattress stuffing.

The light was dimming and the rain beat down as Camille and I trudged past the remains of the pulu mill. The forest thinned, and then the trail entered a broad meadow. By dusk, the rain had slowed down to a drizzle and we stopped to adjust our packs.

"My God," breathed Camille, and I followed her gaze. To the northeast, beyond Nāpau Crater, rose a column of bright orange lava several stories high. Gray clouds, shot with incandescent pink, billowed around it. Sparks of red and orange and chunks of black rock fountained against a slate sky. Struck silent, we watched for several minutes. Finally, as the rain increased to a torrent and twilight approached, we hurried upslope to make camp.

IT WAS STILL POURING IN THE NEAR-DUSK light. Everything was soggy: sleeping bags, clothes, food, us. Discouraged, we rushed to get the tent up and tossed our packs inside just as darkness fell.

At the ledge facing Nāpau, we checked on our volcano. The fiery column was gone, replaced by a ribbon of orange that divided the night. Even from this distance, we could see the river of lava move and change shape as it rolled down an invisible hillside.

We stared, mesmerized, in the cold rain, as the light show continued. We felt no tremors. Finally, exhausted, shivering, and wet, we took shelter in our little tent.

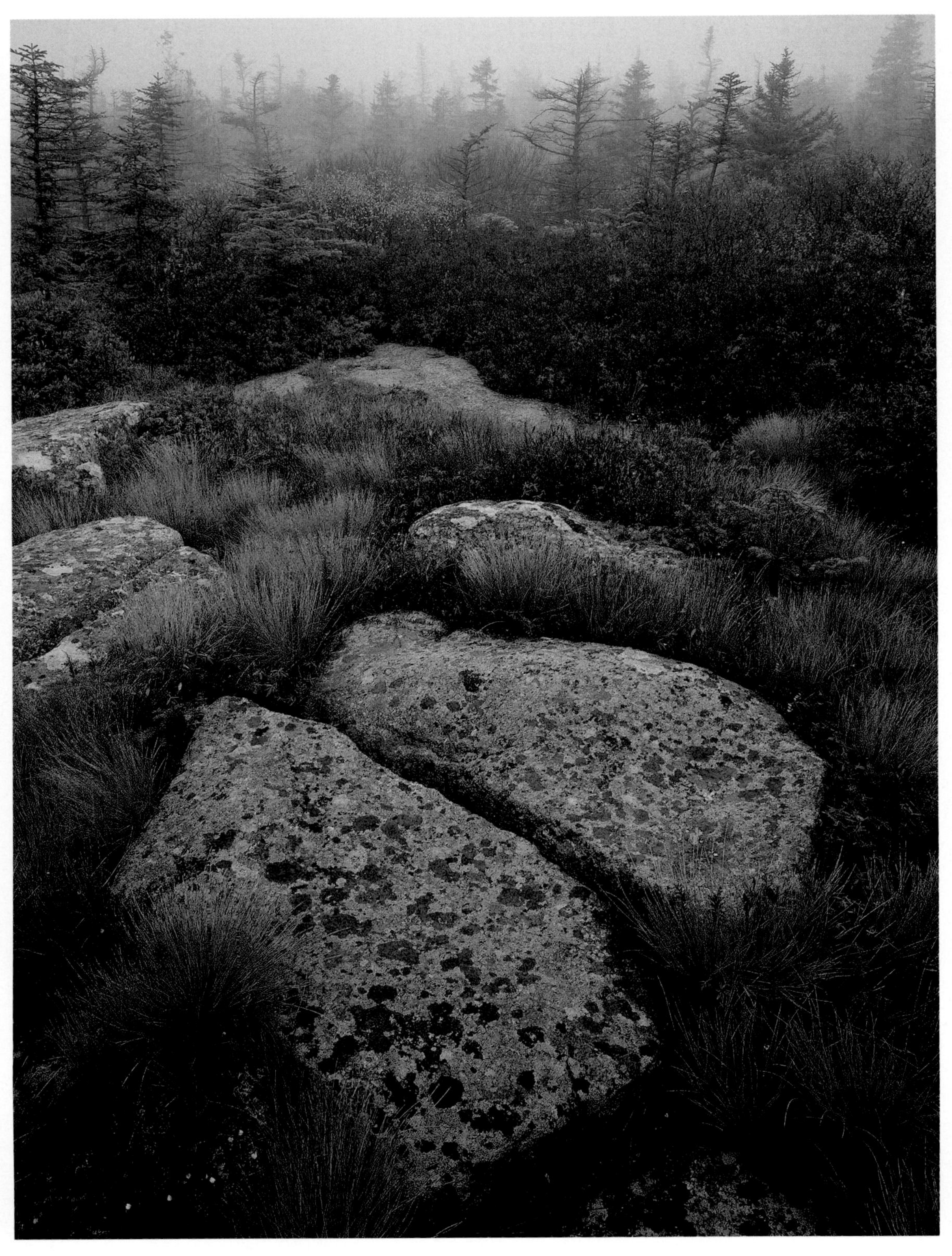

Lichen in paisley patterns coats granite boulders in Maine's Acadia National Park. Named for 681-foot-high Acadia Mountain, the rocky coastal park features 120 miles of hiking trails.

CHAPTER FIVE

Nature & Science

Introduction by Leslie Allen

As part of the National Geographic Society's continuing mission to inspire people to care about the planet Earth, books about the natural world and about cutting-edge science have held an important place in the Special Collection lineup through the years.

Leslie Allen is a nonfiction writer with a special interest in science, natural history, and environmental issues. She has contributed to 17 books published by the National Geographic Society; 10 of those were part of the Special Collection, including her own Wildlands of the West *(2002). She also wrote National Geographic's* Liberty: The Statue and the American Dream *(1995). She lives in Washington, D.C.*

You can't tell a Special Publication by its cover, as they say. Each one has an untold backstory, invisible to most readers—a story of bumps, roadblocks, and other challenges that spring up on the road to publication. The lost rolls of film … the waterlogged notebooks … the missed deadlines … the new discovery that suddenly changes the whole story. And then there's Ivory Tower Syndrome.

A snippet of an old letter from the late editor Merrill Windsor does not mince words in defining it. His correspondent, a world-famous scientist, had just turned in the first draft of a chapter. Windsor wrote to him:

> *As presently drafted, the chapter isn't the inviting, absorbing, first-person account that it needs to be.... Certainly it is packed with valuable information, but the presentation is pretty forbidding for lay readers.... We want* Frontiers of Science *to be quite the opposite: personal, informal, and as nontechnical as possible....*

Merrill Windsor was a great editor and a kind man, but standards were standards. His marching orders reflected an overall mandate when it came to Special Publications devoted to science and natural history: Hard science could, and would, sparkle with liveliness for a general audience. Education and entertainment needn't elbow each other out of the way. Many eminent scientists who contributed to Special Publications already knew this, applying a feather-light touch to the weightiest material. The rest, like the scientist who received Windsor's letter, and later turned his piece into a strong human-interest story, learned on the job.

Of course, not everyone who wrote memorably on scientific or technical subjects for the series came with a string of peer-reviewed journal articles to his or her name. Luis Marden (born Annibale Luigi Paragallo) never went to college, although by the time he was 19, he had published a book on color photography, learned Egyptian hieroglyphics, and taught himself five languages.

National Geographic photographers were still lugging 200 pounds of big cameras, tripods, glass plates, and other gear into the field when Marden arrived at headquarters in 1934 with a little Leica hanging from his neck and introduced 35-millimeter color photography to skeptical staffers. Soon Marden himself became the embodiment of the intrepid, pith-helmeted "Geographic man"—while, thanks largely to him, high-contrast Kodachrome became the standard at the National Geographic Society.

Next he turned his attention to underwater photography, still in its infancy. After World War II, other photographers had succeeded in making color photographs underwater—but only in very clear, very shallow water. Going deeper, first reds, then oranges and yellows faded out; in depths of more than about 30 feet the undersea world turned almost monochromatic.

MORE AND MORE VOLUMES PUBLISHED BY
THE NATIONAL GEOGRAPHIC SOCIETY BEGAN TO SHARE
AN IMPORTANT THEME: THE CONNECTEDNESS OF ALL LIVING BEINGS.

Photographs taken there looked black and white with a bluish tint.

In *World Beneath the Sea* (1967), an early Special Publication, Marden relived the challenges of capturing the riot of undersea life in color. Innovating with correcting filters helped, but Marden decided that what he really needed was auxiliary lighting. He set out with marine explorer Jacques-Yves Cousteau aboard the latter's *Calypso,* armed with 600 flashbulbs.

Marden was no trained scientist, but he reveled in the kind of trial and error that is basic to scientific discovery. Seawater seeped through his flashbulbs' metal bases and they short-circuited; at other times, bulbs imploded when Marden touched them and their jagged edges cut him badly. Like the best scientist-writers, he paused to sketch humor, as when a tag team of the ship's cooks, engineer, surgeon, and Cousteau's wife attempted to repair the bulbs with melted wax. Looking down on a calm sea at night, the bulbs flashing underwater were, he thought, like fireflies and heat lightning rippling along the horizon.

Luis Marden's breakthroughs revolutionized underwater photography. They helped shape coverage in *Undersea Treasures* (1974), *The Ocean Realm* (1978), and other Special Publications. But that wasn't his only photographic legacy. A pilot and science fiction enthusiast, Marden was also passionate about space. During a stint with NASA, he pioneered space coverage for the Society. His innovative images of rocket launches and astronauts, among others, influenced Special Publications such as *Man's Conquest of Space* (1968) and *The Amazing Universe* (1975).

The Amazing Universe was astrophysicist Herbert Friedman's first book, written after a long career at the cutting edge of solar physics, aeronomy, and astronomy; he also pioneered the use of x-rays to analyze materials. He was known especially for creating simple, elegant experiments that answered complex questions, and his straightforward, down-to-earth writing style reflected that.

Friedman also knew how to inspire ordinary readers with his personal tales of trial and error. He emphasized the proximity of success—his own "beginner's luck" launching a rocket one year—to abject failure—watching his rocket burn and crumple on the launchpad the following year. And, as if warning us not to take any of it too seriously, he frequently reminded us of our insignificance in the greater scheme of the universe—a universe whose known dimensions seemed to expand constantly, thanks partly to advances in measurement pioneered by Friedman himself.

Scientists at the pinnacle of their fields connected with the readers of Special Publications by bringing knotty concepts down to their level. As geophysicist J. Tuzo Wilson said, "Most scientific journals are incomprehensible to the layman"—though he believed passionately that ordinary readers appreciated science when it became accessible to them.

In *Frontiers of Science* (1982), he furthered his cause with vivid imagery. Explaining continental drift, Wilson likened continents to "frozen rafts." He explained the Earth's layers in terms of bread crusts and soft butter. Readers got a grip on concepts of tectonic movement when Wilson wrote about opening and closing desk drawers. It wasn't necessarily easy to square the image conveyed by this author with that of the man who was perhaps the 20th century's most honored geophysicist.

Wilson brought a brand of humility to his tectonic tales. When he became a convert to the theory of continental drift in the 1960s, it was so unpopular that defending it verged on professional suicide. Undaunted, Wilson published dozens of articles expanding upon the theory—and planting himself in the middle of controversy. By 1982, he noted with surprise and understatement in *Frontiers of Science,* his theories had become widely accepted in the scientific community.

THEY WERE NOT UNIVERSALLY ACCEPTED among Special Publications readers, however—nor, over the decades, was any statement that presupposed evolution as fact or the age of the Earth as more than a few thousand years. Almost every chapter in volumes focusing on science and natural history stirred protest in some quarter. Researchers and editors of those volumes always braced themselves for a barrage of returns and letters from unhappy readers following a new book's release. Each received a respectful answer.

Although scientists and others who wrote on science periodically waded into controversy, no one framed an argument in starker terms than the renowned ecologist Raymond Dasmann, writing in *As We Live and Breathe: The Challenge of Our Environment* (1971). Dasmann called man "a geological force that moves and shapes the surface of the Earth," and pointed an accusing finger directly at Americans, who "have misused their land and plundered its resources."

A year before *As We Live and Breathe* appeared, the U.S. Environmental Protection Agency came into being. That same year, passage of the Clean Air Act of 1970 dramatically strengthened federal law dealing with air pollution; a year after publication, the Clean Water Act of 1972 did the same for water pollution. But Dasmann urged his readers to go further, and to think what seemed practically unthinkable: "that it is not necessarily good to grow bigger, to produce more, to travel faster, if this means the air will become unfit to breathe and the water too foul for human use." To think big, we need to think smaller, Dasmann asserted, even though "sustainability" would not become a household word for more than another three decades.

The National Geographic Society never published another Special Publication focusing entirely on environmental issues, but more volumes on ostensibly different subjects began to share a theme that Ray Dasmann had introduced: the connectedness of all living beings to each other and to their environment.

A few of those later books—*Vanishing Wildlife of North America* (1974) or *Animal Kingdoms: Wildlife Sanctuaries of the World* (1995), among others—could be shelved neatly under "natural history." But many more, like *Yellowstone Country* (1989) or *Natural America* (1998), were hybrids that fused the political and social to the natural world. As years passed, readers were asking for, and getting, more books focusing on conservation. But as the threats loomed ever larger and grimmer, readers still wanted solutions—or at least hope. They wanted to experience, in words and pictures, the possibility in nature's beauty.

Off the coast of Baja California, a diver swims through a forest of giant kelp. The largest of marine plants, giant kelp can grow two feet a day, reaching two hundred and creating a tangled canopy, the fronds buoyed by spherical gas bladders.

World Beneath the Sea (1967)

He flipped a switch and the submarine's exterior lights blazed a trail through the water. The sea came alive. I saw a circus of color: red gorgonians, yellow sponges, and purple sea urchins on greenish-gray corals. Small fish pranced unafraid in the sudden brightness. An octopus sprawled on a sandy ridge. And all around us swarmed a host of tiny creatures—jellyfish, worms, crustaceans, and the young of crabs, lobsters, and fishes.

Falco gaily revolved the jets to swoop and climb. Then he reversed the flow to slow down and we hovered beside the reef. Cousteau had told me that despite the saucer's grunting and whining when under power, it did not frighten fish away, but attracted them instead. I wondered if they saw the submersible as an engaging clown of a clam, a great yellow clam with staring, curious eyes that refused to stay put on the bottom where it belonged.

We zoomed downward and began to glide over the bottom. I was completely disoriented. I guessed our direction as northwest, but the compass needle indicated east by southeast. Falco pressed on as confidently as a householder in the dusk of his own backyard.

"*Regardez la grosse langouste,*" he said. I didn't see any big lobster. Seconds later it came into the arena of light, waving long antennae. My pilot had seen it beyond in the gloom. Turning to starboard, Falco skimmed above a cluster of gesturing

Drained of water, the ocean beds emerge as a spectacular region unrivaled by anything on land. Towering peaks, plunging canyons, and plains flat as tabletops remain undisturbed by erosion of wind and rain. Ships' echo sounders mapped this underwater world, bouncing electronic signals off the bottom, measuring the time between pings, then automatically charting depth profiles. The Mid-Oceanic Ridge, crisscrossed with fracture zones and grooved by a rift valley, winds for 35,000 miles through all of earth's oceans. On either side, broad basins and plains stretch to the shallow continental shelves.

PAINTING BY HEINRICH C. BERANN BASED ON BATHYMETRIC STUDIES BY BRUCE C. HEEZEN AND MARIE THARP OF THE LAMONT GEOLOGICAL OBSERVATORY

18

The pages of World Beneath the Sea *brimmed with excitement over a final frontier: the ocean floor.*

One could hardly imagine an anthology of National Geographic Society excerpts that did not include the work of Mr. Geographic himself: Luis Marden.

For 64 years, Marden roamed the globe in search of adventure and good stories for *National Geographic* magazine, and he exemplified the intrepid explorer of a bygone era. A multitalented photographer, writer, filmmaker, diver, sailor, navigator, and pilot, Marden learned five languages and Egyptian hieroglyphics as a teenager, then went to work at a Boston radio station instead of going to college. His first adventure for *National Geographic* took him to the Yucatan Peninsula, traveling by tramp steamer and Model T Ford.

In 1957 Marden discovered and photographed the remains of Captain Bligh's *Bounty* off Pitcairn Island; he later retraced Columbus's journey to the New World. On assignment, he often disappeared into unknown corners of the world for months at a time. The restless wanderer turned in his last story in 1998, at age 85; he died five years later.

Marden contributed a chapter on the development of underwater photography to the Special Collection book titled *World Beneath the Sea*. This was appropriate, since he himself had helped pioneer underwater color photography, as well as other photojournalistic technologies. In this excerpt he vividly recalls his work underwater with explorer Jacques-Yves Cousteau.

Cameras Below

Luis Marden recalls the early excitement of underwater photography

The first undersea color photographs ever published appeared in the January 1927 *National Geographic* and marked a milestone in the history of photography. At that time, Charles Martin, an ingenious technician and innovator, headed the National Geographic's Photographic Laboratory. The Society sent him to Dry Tortugas, and he returned with "eight autochromes of genuine sub-marine life; the first ones ever taken," as he reported triumphantly.

Nearly 30 years passed before the publication of another undersea color photograph.

After World War II ended, the Aqua-Lung came on the world market, and increasing numbers of amateur divers began to go down into the sea. At once they tried to take cameras with them, to show the stay-on-lands what the clamor was all about. The first problem was simply that of keeping the camera dry. All kinds of clever makeshifts appeared, from cameras encased in Mason jars to

A diver with gold doubloons shows that undersea exploration can yield lucrative results. A 1960s treasure hunter found a wrecked Spanish treasure fleet but avowed that the "real treasure lies in our having touched hands with history."

IT IS AN UNCANNILY BEAUTIFUL SIGHT TO LOOK AT A CALM SEA ON A DARK NIGHT WHEN UNDERWATER PHOTOGRAPHERS ARE AT WORK. A CIRCLE OF SEA A HUNDRED FEET IN DIAMETER BRIEFLY FLASHES FIREFLY GREEN, LIKE HEAT LIGHTNING ON THE HORIZON.

cameras looking through a glass port in rubber hotwater bottles. Only a few divers had the skill or means to attempt a proper case of metal or plastic through which camera controls of film advance, focus, iris diaphragm, and shutter speeds would be workable.

By that time I had obtained my first commercial underwater housing, a sea-green metal cylinder made in Venice. For some time I had been trying to make color photographs under the sea. Martin and [ichthyologist William H.] Longley had taken their color pictures in crystalline water 10 to 15 feet deep. Lighted by that stupendous flash overhead, the brilliant color of the coral reef came through faithfully. But as depth increases, the thickening blue-green filter of seawater, interposed between the sunlight and the bottom, absorbs the colors of the spectrum. First the reds, then the oranges and yellows, disappear, until beyond 30 feet or so, the diver walks or swims in a monochromatic blue-green world.

IN SHALLOW CLEAR WATER, THE EYE ADJUSTS to the prevailing blue and can still see some reds and yellows, darkened and degraded from their surface brilliance. My first pictures disappointed me, because they looked like black-and-white photographs tinted blue-green. Unlike the human eye, the photographic emulsion does not possess the power of adaptation, and all the warm colors were drowned in blue light.

I used correcting filters to hold back the excessive blue, and got fairly good photographs in the limpid waters of the Mediterranean, provided I did not go too deep. But I soon learned that to make really good three-color pictures underwater I had to use an artificial light source close to the subject. Flashbulbs seemed ideal, and in 1955 when I accompanied Captain Cousteau aboard *Calypso* during his filming of *The Silent World,* I took along 600.

Cousteau later recalled our experience: "Our divers wonder how a man can fire that many bulbs in only four months. They soon discover how. Hardly have we left the Suez Canal before Marden begins diving with stout Émile Robert as bearer.

"Robert goes down carrying Marden's second camera and a large string bag of flashbulbs, which floats above him like the envelope of an 18th-century balloon. It is not long before Marden is crying for more bulbs and we radio for a fresh supply.

"The bulbs, when under pressure, develop leaks in the metal bases. Water seeps inside, short-circuits the lead-in wires, and makes firing uncertain. Marden is chagrined, but the *Calypso* team comes to his rescue. At night we see a strange scene in the mess. The ship's cook heats water; the second cook melts wax in the water; my wife, Simone, cleans the bulb bases; the engineer drills two tiny holes in the base of each bulb; and at the end of the production line stands the ship's young surgeon in his white tunic. With the delicacy of a brain surgeon he injects liquid wax into the holes to insulate the wires.

"Luis's expenditure of bulbs taxes the production rate: It is a race between manufacturer and consumer. We treat 2,500 bulbs before the voyage is over."

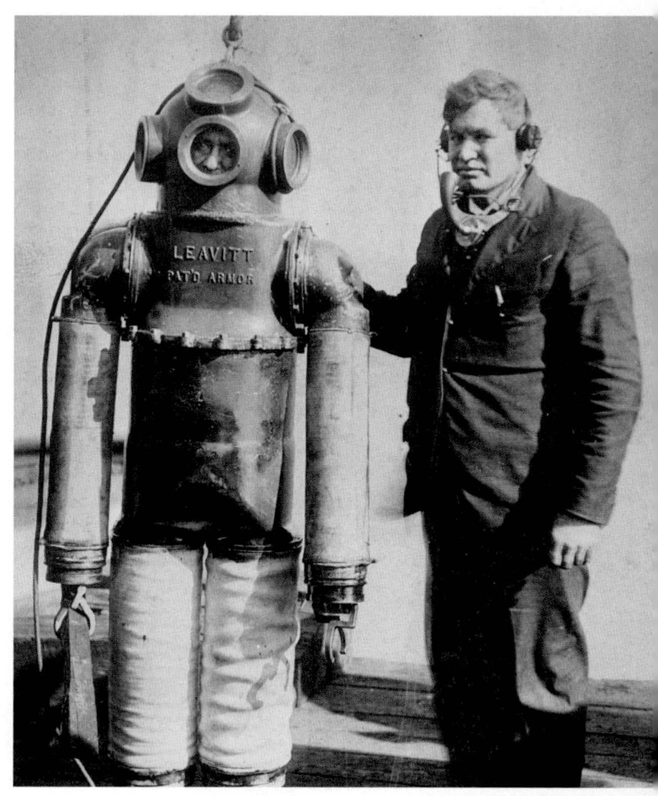

The history of oceanographic exploration is full of hopes, challenges, and people willing to take great risks. In 1922 diver Benjamin Leavitt (top) publicized his intentions to dive in a semi-armored suit and salvage the Lusitania, *a British luxury liner torpedoed by a German submarine seven years earlier. His plan failed for lack of funds. Naturalist William Beebe enjoyed greater success. Here he squeezes from the steel bathysphere (bottom) that took him and designer Otis Barton (at left, wearing shorts) to a record 3,028 feet below the ocean surface in the waters off the Bermuda coast in August 1934.*

Most of them worked. But at depths of a hundred feet or so, something else happened: The bulbs sometimes imploded, shattering violently inward, instead of outward as in an explosion, and driving the fragments of glass into my gloved hand like bullets. The pure oxygen that fills flashbulbs is at a pressure less than one atmosphere, so their thin glass walls undergo strain even at relatively shallow depths. After firing weakened the glass by developing minute cracks in it, some bulbs imploded when touched.

This happened to me the first time as I swam above a sunken ship at 90 feet in the Red Sea. When I took hold of the bulb to remove it from the reflector, I heard a dull report and felt a numbing pain lance through my right thumb. A wisp of greenish "smoke" slowly curled upward; it was my blood, drained of its bright red at this depth.

Weeks later, when another implosion left a neat scar on the middle finger of my right hand, tracing the exact curve of the big bulb, I started to search for some kind of protective glove. But the stoutest leather was ineffective against the tremendous impact of the shattering glass. A chain-mail glove made for butchers provided the answer. Now I handle even the jagged bases of shattered bulbs with impunity.

With burning refuse for a backdrop, children search for treasures amid trash in a Florida dump.

As We Live and Breathe (1971)

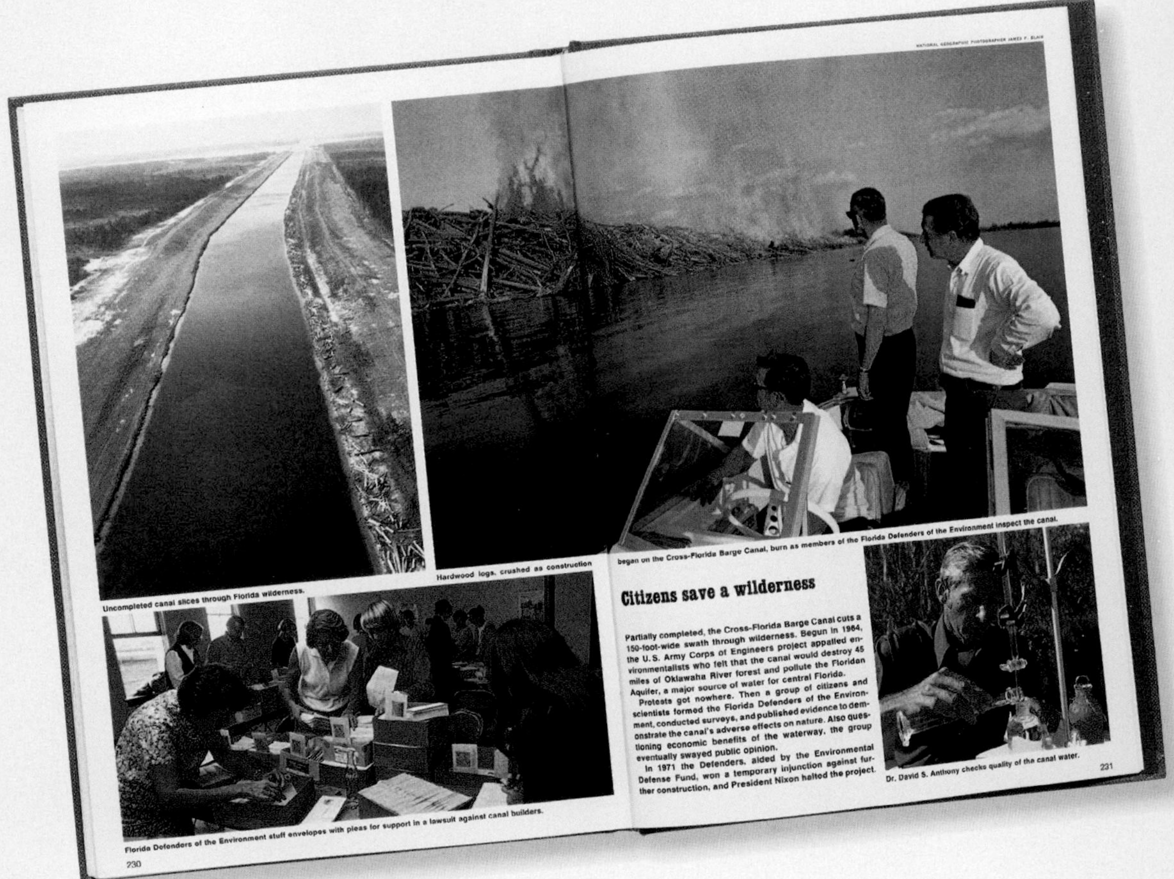

Uncompleted canal slices through Florida wilderness.

Hardwood logs, crushed as construction began on the Cross-Florida Barge Canal, burn as members of the Florida Defenders of the Environment inspect the canal.

Florida Defenders of the Environment stuff envelopes with pleas for support in a lawsuit against canal builders.

230

Citizens save a wilderness

Partially completed, the Cross-Florida Barge Canal cuts a 150-foot-wide swath through wilderness. Begun in 1964, the U.S. Army Corps of Engineers project appalled environmentalists who felt that the canal would destroy 45 miles of Oklawaha River forest and pollute the Floridan Aquifer, a major source of water for central Florida.

Protests got nowhere. Then a group of citizens and scientists formed the Florida Defenders of the Environment, conducted surveys, and published evidence to demonstrate the canal's adverse effects on nature. Also questioning economic benefits of the waterway, the group eventually swayed public opinion.

In 1971 the Defenders, aided by the Environmental Defense Fund, won a temporary injunction against further construction, and President Nixon halted the project.

Dr. David S. Anthony checks quality of the canal water.

231

Compelling images coupled with text by top ecologists and writers sounded an early environmentalist alarm.

With *As We Live and Breathe,* National Geographic's Special Collection turned to humanity's abuse of the land and air. Though its objective was couched optimistically in the subtitle, *The Challenge of Our Environment,* the book cast a critical eye on the nation's rapidly deteriorating rivers, soils, and forests. The authors stated in no uncertain terms that smog was polluting the air, farm and factory waste were fouling our waterways, and that our own affluence was threatening the quality of our lives. Chapters in the book chronicled how the American environment had gone from pristine to dirty and how the nation was attempting to address some of the problems produced by industrialization.

One of the founding fathers of environmentalism, conservation biologist Raymond F. Dasmann wrote the book's introduction, from which the following excerpt is taken. Written nearly 40 years ago, its content is still relevant today.

Since then, many rivers have been at least partially restored, DDT has been banned, and other progress has been made, but the long-term damage caused by an excess of greenhouse gases, predicted well over half a century ago, is only just beginning to be addressed. We are more aware of the problems, yet we more vitally need solutions than ever before.

At the end of his essay, Dasmann poses questions we are still asking: "Can the damage be halted? Can the situation be repaired?"

At War With Their Own Land

Ecologist Raymond F. Dasmann on Americans and the environment

The road ahead shimmered in the heat. Withered stalks of last year's cotton crop and an occasional wind-contorted, leafless tree traced eerie patterns across the landscape in the bright sunlight. The view as we drove down the San Joaquin Valley past desolate fields, abandoned cars, and filling stations did nothing to cheer our spirits.

My wife and I were taking what we thought might be our last trip through California before moving to the East Coast. We had known the valley for most of our lives and had seen it change over the years.

It was a time of reminiscing—and of disappointment. The valley had always had its dust storms and its ground-hugging fogs, but now an unnatural pall of dirty air hung over the land. It blurred the sun and sky and enveloped us in a dreary, oppressive haze.

As I looked back from the Tehachapi Mountains, which separate the valley from southern California, all I could see was an endless cloud of smoke and

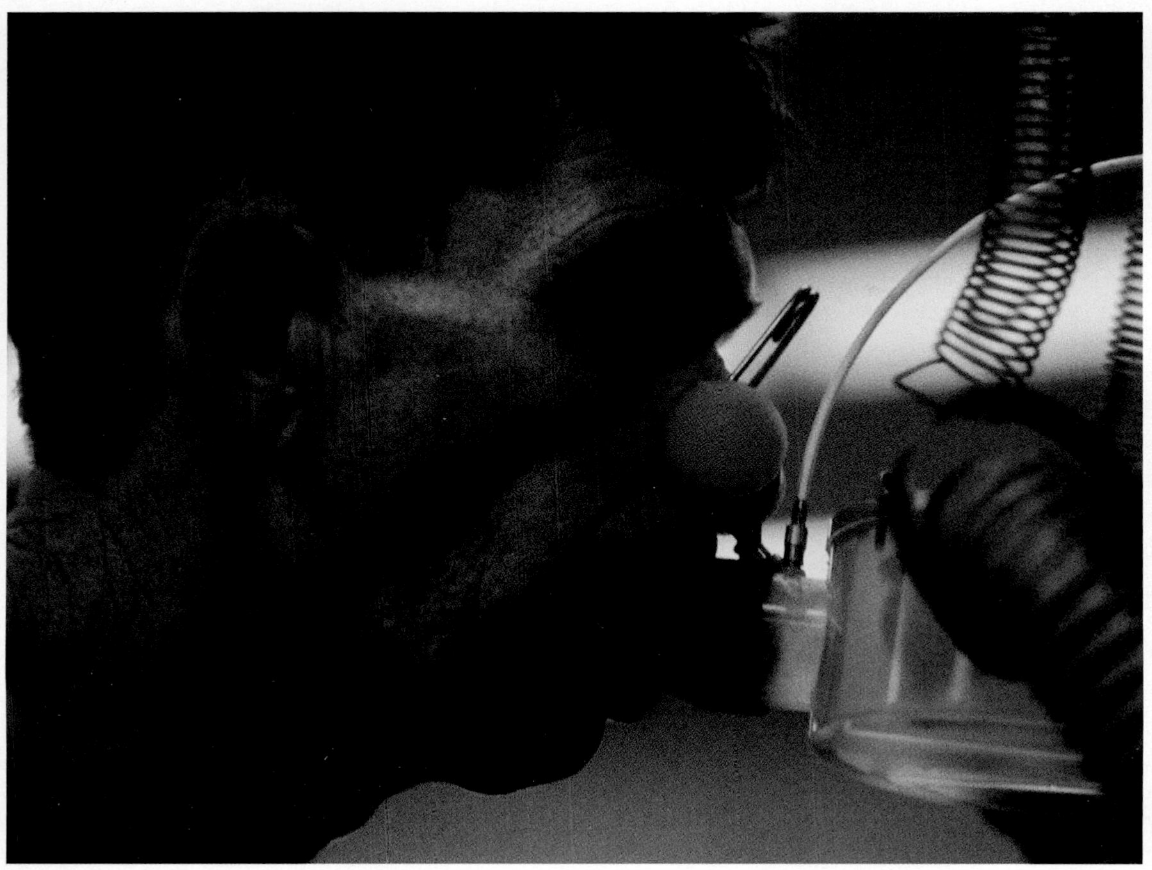

In a black-lung research program, a West Virginia miner breathes through a tube while walking a treadmill. Hundreds of thousands of miners have been disabled by black lung, a disease caused by inhaling coal dust.

A western Kentucky landscape bears the ugly scars of strip-mining, whereby successive layers of a hillside's surface are removed. This area was graded and reseeded, yet erosion continued and acid runoff tainted man-made ponds.

gases. Ahead, below the blanket of brown haze, lay Los Angeles, one of the cities that made the word "smog" famous.

The valley had changed within my lifetime and now seemed an alien place. And so had the cities that I had known as a youngster. The charm and glamour of San Francisco, for example, still cast a spell on me, but the city was more fun and to me a far better place when we crossed the bay on ferryboats instead of on a bridge clogged with cars. It was more exciting to go to the zoo on the old streetcars that rocked past sand dunes than it is to whiz over the concrete freeway. In those days boys and girls could go almost anywhere, in daylight or dark, in safety.

I have seen many changes alter the face of California. In the springtime my family took Sunday drives to see the orchards south of San Francisco. I remember endless vistas of fruit trees in bloom—plums and pears, peaches and apricots. Today houses have sprouted where those trees once grew. Elsewhere, too, cities have spread relentlessly into farmlands.

THE SPANISH, WHO SETTLED CALIFORNIA IN the 18th century, called the San Joaquin "Valley of the Tulares." But the marshes where the tall reeds, or tules, once grew are no more. They have been drained and plowed. The old lakes have disappeared; the rivers that fed them are now dammed, their waters trickling through ditches to irrigate orchards and fields. The wilderness had to go from some of the valley. Herds of elk can't live in wheat fields, and coyotes aren't welcome in the suburbs.

Our farewell trip through the valley took place in 1965—in the decade when the fight against pollution became a popular cause. Pollution had been around a long time, but we accepted it as a price we paid for progress, for smoking factories meant jobs. "I like pollution," a lumberman from northern California once told me. "Those pulp mills have the good green smell of money."

But in the 1960s pollution became a greater problem and more widespread. Chemical pesticides not only killed insects and conquered malaria, but carried by wind, they also permeated the earth, accumulating in the soil, seeping into the rivers, poisoning our wildlife. Bloated fish—white bellies up—washed by the million onto riverbanks and the shores of lakes. In places brown pelicans, prairie falcons, and peregrines laid eggs with shells so thin they never hatched.

IN 1967 THE OIL TANKER *TORREY CANYON* rammed into a reef off the coast of Great Britain, disgorging millions of gallons of crude. Spills and blowouts of offshore oil wells also fouled the Gulf of Mexico, the Santa Barbara Channel, San Francisco Bay, Long Island Sound, and the waters off Cape Cod.

Other hazards threatened the oceans. Scientists at the Scripps Institution of Oceanography at La Jolla, California, said they could find man-introduced radioactivity in a 50-gallon sample taken anywhere in the ocean. Water they tested also contained lead at seven to ten times the natural level. Another study revealed that ocean fish are almost universally contaminated with DDT and other pesticides.

Inland, ponds and the Great Lakes, brooks and rivers served increasingly as dumping areas for industrial wastes and sewage. During the summer of 1970, Government health officials warned thousands of Vermonters to boil their drinking water because of contamination. The oily, chocolate-brown Cuyahoga River, which drains the acids, oils, and wastes from Cleveland's industries into Lake Erie, burst into flame.

DURING THE DECADE OF THE 1960S, AIR pollution, a problem most frequently associated with Los Angeles, also became a fact of life in other American cities. Sulfurous fumes from smelters and power plants fouled the once crystal-clear air of the Southwest. Smog stunted the growth of orange and lemon trees in California and mottled spinach leaves in New Jersey.

"Killer smogs" hit New York City in 1953, 1963, and 1966. During smog alerts, death rates rose and respiratory diseases increased. Was air pollution the cause? No one could say with absolute certainty.

It was in these recent years that the Smithsonian Institution surveyed the amount of sunlight reaching Washington, D.C.

The study showed that the amount of direct sunlight had declined by 16 percent since 1907, presumably because of air pollution. In other areas dust, soot, and aerosols were shading the earth and reflecting some of the sun's energy back into space. From 1900 to mid-century the burning of oil and coal had caused the carbon dioxide level in the atmosphere to rise by 11 percent.

Carbon dioxide lets the sun's rays enter, but it blocks the heat radiating from the earth's surface. Scientists puzzled over whether such a "greenhouse effect" might prevail and raise temperatures enough to melt the polar ice cap, or whether increased dustiness might bring on another ice age. Climatologists called for worldwide programs to monitor the atmosphere to find out what really was happening.

Those who knew the dangers of pollution voiced concern. In her book *Silent Spring*, biologist Rachel Carson warned in 1962 that the careless use of pesticides was upsetting the balance of nature.

All at once the whole Nation seemed to be awakening to an increasing, but neglected, menace. Newspaper headlines became more and more disturbing: "Dirty Air Forecast as a Houston Peril," "Virginia Is Warned of DDT in Shellfish," "Pollution Linked to Ills of the Young." Scores of new books and television documentaries analyzed the problems created by noise, industrial wastes, the population explosion, and power plants.

Thousands upon thousands joined citizens' groups to fight for clean air and water.

Congress created the Council on Environmental Quality to advise the President and coordinate federal environmental activities. Then President Richard M. Nixon established the Environmental Protection Agency, EPA, in a reorganization that brought programs scattered throughout the Government into one agency. EPA was charged with the responsibility to set up, monitor, and enforce federal antipollution standards.

An awareness spread through the country that it is not necessarily good to grow bigger, to produce more, to travel faster, if this means that the air will become unfit to breathe and the water too foul for human use. Pogo, the small, baffled philosopher possum of the comic strips, uttered his now famous words: "We have met the ENEMY and he is US."

We are all polluters. We drive cars when we can walk. We pay developers to drain marshes and pave over our parks. We buy more gadgets. We demand more throwaway bags, bottles, and cans. To change the situation ultimately, we will have to change ourselves. But, if we wait until each person reforms, it may be too late. Some of us feared that the human

An early planned community, Sterling Park, Virginia, situated 28 miles west of Washington, D.C., was begun in 1962. The mushrooming of suburban developments has led to heavy infrastructure demands.

weakness and greed implied in Pogo's words could delay efforts to control pollution. In the meantime, we sought immediate ways to fight pollution. We wanted laws to protect the environment, and the power to enforce them....

THE POLLUTION PROBLEMS OF TODAY ARE acute and accelerating in intensity, and, fortunately, so is public concern. Therein lies the hope for the future, but the problem is one of time.

In the 19th century Americans ignored the havoc wrought on forests, wildlife, and rangelands. There was enough time then. Most of the damage could be repaired. Some species of plant, some kind of animal, was able to move back and recolonize the lands devastated and laid bare.

Today, however, in the United States and throughout much of the world, a large and rapidly increasing population is exerting an enormous pressure upon the land and upon nature. Can the damage be halted? Can the situation be repaired? There is still diversity in the world. We still have marshes, thickets, quiet beaches, primitive forests. Perhaps we will fight to preserve them. This is the great challenge to Americans and to the international community in the remaining decades of the 20th century. The survival of all humanity may well depend upon the answers we find.

Lightning illuminates Arizona's Kitt Peak National Observatory in a dramatic time-exposure photograph. The 19-story domed building houses the 158-inch Mayall Telescope, which can view objects ten billion light-years away.

THE AMAZING UNIVERSE (1975)

by Herbert Friedman

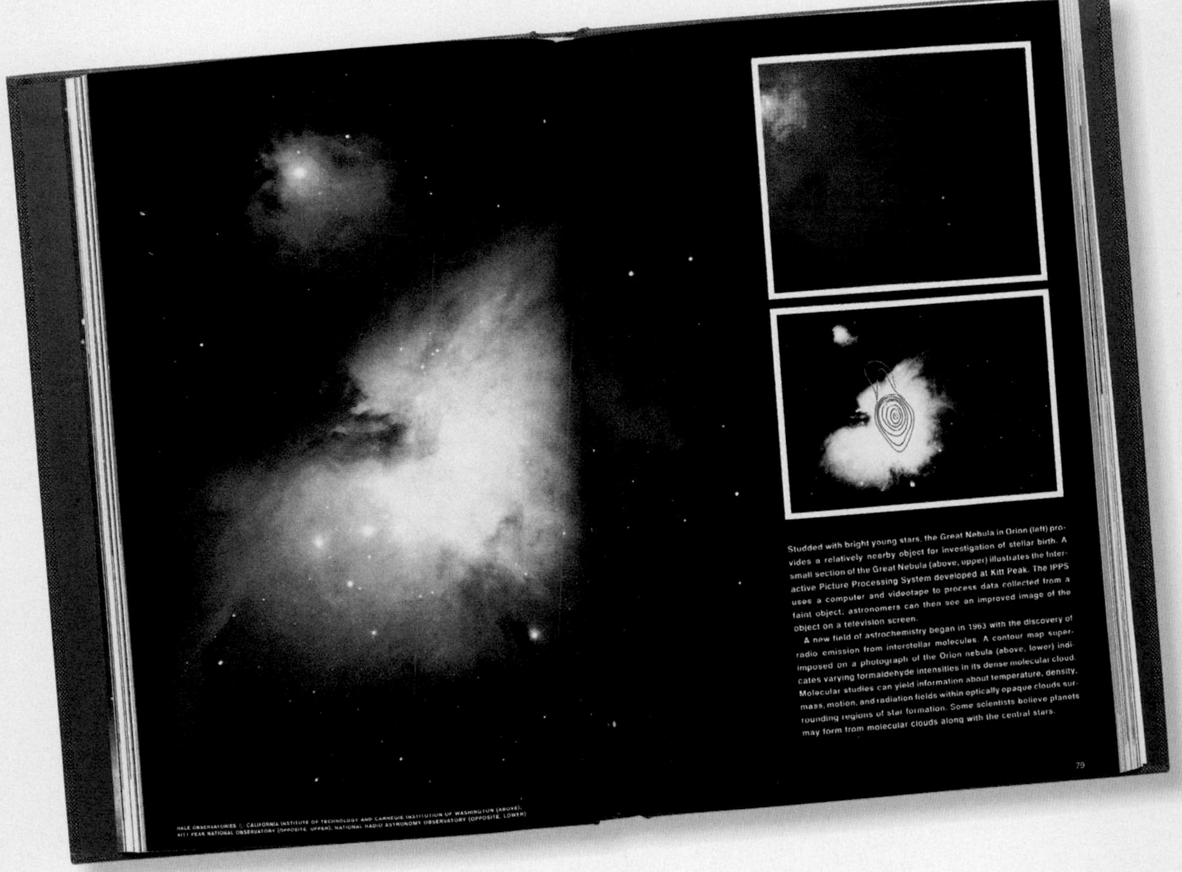

Studded with bright young stars, the Great Nebula in Orion (left) provides a relatively nearby object for investigation of stellar birth. A
small section of the Great Nebula (above, upper) illustrates the Interactive Picture Processing System developed at Kitt Peak. The IPPS
uses a computer and videotape to process data collected from a
faint object; astronomers can then see an improved image of the
object on a television screen.
A new field of astrochemistry began in 1963 with the discovery of
radio emission from interstellar molecules. A contour map super-
imposed on a photograph of the Orion nebula (above, lower) indicates varying formaldehyde intensities in its dense molecular cloud.
Molecular studies can yield information about temperature, density,
mass, motion, and radiation fields within optically opaque clouds surrounding regions of star formation. Some scientists believe planets
may form from molecular clouds along with the central stars.
79

Galaxies galore and more: Cutting-edge astronomy takes readers to the edges of the known cosmos.

Published in 1975, *The Amazing Universe* challenged readers to think and learn, as well as to gaze up wide-eyed with wonder, reckoning with the subject of our place among the stars. At the same time it introduced the great astronomers of past and present who have devoted their lives and considerable brainpower to figuring out so much about the heavens. The author was Herbert Friedman, chief scientist for the U.S. Naval Research Laboratory's E. O. Hulburt Center for Space Research. Friedman himself was one of those astronomers: In the mid-1960s he shot up a rocket borne x-ray detector during an eclipse of the Crab Nebula to see if it could sense the presence of a neutron star.

Friedman writes for the educated layman, never talking down to his readership. In this excerpt from the chapter "To the Edge of the Universe," he guides us through history as astronomers seek to determine Earth's position in the universe. From the 18th to the 20th century—from William Herschel to Harlow Shapley, Missouri farm boy, and Henrietta Leavitt, star photographer at Harvard—we travel intellectually to the edge of the Milky Way, gaining the knowledge that periods of variable stars are related to their true brightness. Even if we don't fully grasp that concept, we land safely with Maj. Edwin Hubble, who, with his study of extragalactic nebulae, once and for all places the Milky Way in the firmament of galaxies.

Reenvisioning the Universe

Making sense of the changing theories of our galaxy

Four hundred years after Copernicus removed the earth from the central position in the solar system and put the planets in orbit about the sun, a Missourian named Harlow Shapley accomplished a parallel feat: He disproved the popular concept that the sun was at the center of the Milky Way.

Interest in the distribution of stars had begun to grow by the mid-18th century. In 1755, philosopher Immanuel Kant recognized the flattened form of the galaxy—that it stretched out over a great length but was relatively thin. He also made the remarkable guess that such cloudy patches of visible nebulosity as Andromeda were themselves separate entities, or "universes," comparable to the Milky Way.

About 1780 William Herschel, a former German military bandsman whose life in England had been devoted to performing and composing music, turned to studies of the sky. Positional astronomy at the time seemed to be working out to perfection. Commenting on Newtonian mechanics and the precision with which the motions of planets

An astronomer in the Kitt Peak control room positions the 300-ton Mayall Telescope. Computers keep the scope aimed at an object while Earth rotates; low lighting helps astronomers maintain night vision.

ASTRONOMY DEALS STILL IN THE ETERNITIES,
BUT NOWADAYS IT CANNOT NEGLECT THE SPLIT-SECOND.

and stars could be calculated, Frederick the Great of Prussia reportedly remarked that everything of importance in science had been discovered.

But Herschel was not particularly concerned with positional accuracy; his interest was exploratory in the broadest sense. For that purpose he constructed a 20-foot telescope of 19-inch aperture and undertook a systematic counting of the stars. From this he tried to gauge the distance to the edge of the Milky Way. In the direction where the numbers were relatively few, he concluded we were close to the edge; where the counts were greatest, he assumed he was looking down the longest dimension to the rim. Herschel estimated that the Milky Way contained many millions of stars—not a bad guess, given the circumstances of his work.

The versatile Herschel characteristically applied his talents in a big way. The festival orchestras and choruses he conducted at Bath were among the largest assembled in England. When it came to telescopes, he was as fascinated by the challenge of building the largest instrument as by its eventual use. With a grant of £4,000 from King George III, he designed and constructed a telescope of 40-foot focal length and 48-inch aperture, comparable in size to a 48-inch Schmidt instrument of the 1950s.

Herschel was an extraordinarily prolific worker. He presented his first catalogue of a thousand nebulae and star clusters to the Royal Society in 1786 and followed it with two extensive additions. John Herschel continued his father's work, and he catalogued 5,079 objects, of which 4,630 were discovered by father or son.

AFTER WILLIAM HERSCHEL'S DEATH IN 1822, little progress was made in establishing the true position of the sun in our galaxy until Harlow Shapley, a farm boy with a doctorate from Princeton, arrived at Mount Wilson in 1914. Shapley had grown up at the edge of the Ozark country, and went to work at 15 as a crime reporter on the Chanute, Kansas, *Daily Sun*. Two years later he was refused admission to high school in Carthage, Missouri. One of his early enthusiasms was poetry—"poetry you could recite while milking a cow and keep the rhythm going." An essay on Elizabethan verse helped gain him admission to the University of Missouri, where he discovered astronomy.

The constellation Cepheus the King lies opposite the Big Dipper on the other side of Polaris, the North Star. It does not appear especially interesting except for the marked variations in the light of one of its members, Delta Cephei. Over a period of five days and nine hours, with clocklike regularity, that star passes from bright to relatively faint and back to bright again with a contrast so pronounced that it is evident to the unaided eye. Its light variations are caused by fluctuations in size: increasing in brilliance as the star swells, dimming as it shrinks. Delta Cephei was first observed in 1784; and in due course astronomers found many more such stars, some with longer periods, some shorter, and labeled them Cepheid variables.

In 1905 Henrietta S. Leavitt, an astronomer and head of photographic stellar photometry at Harvard College Observatory, received photographs from Harvard's southern observatory in Peru—repeated

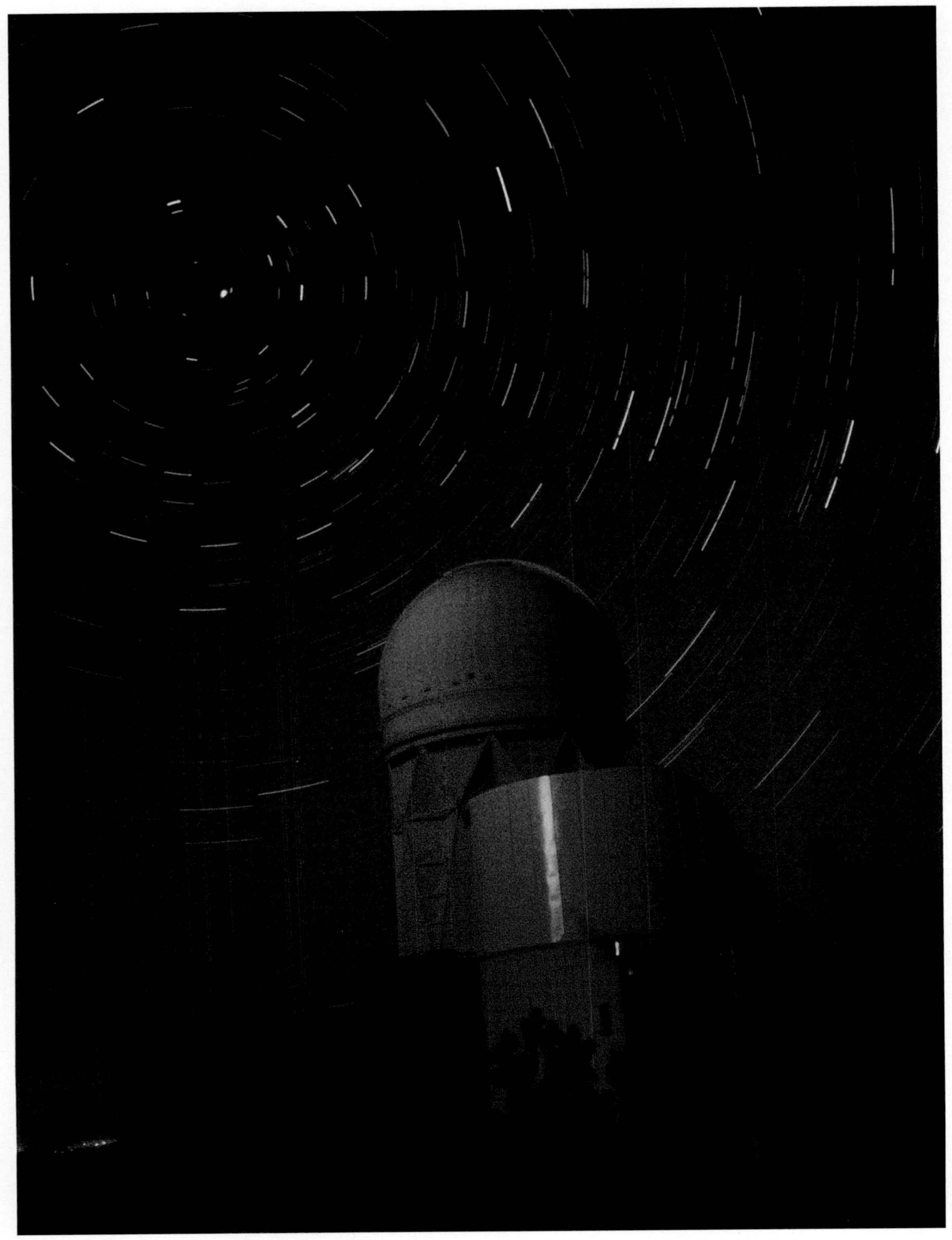

With Kitt Peak's Mayall Telescope fixed on Polaris, the North Star—which is positioned above Earth's axis—other stars leave concentric streaks in this 30-minute exposure.

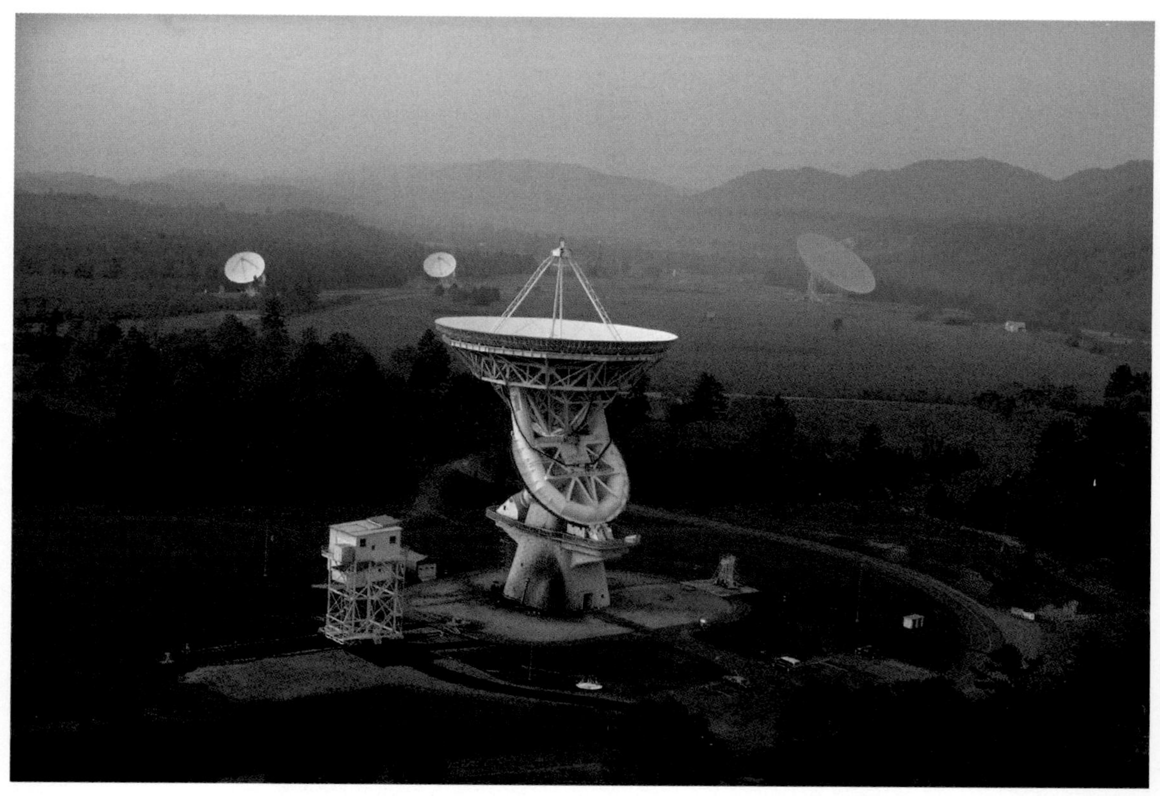

A cluster of tremendous radio telescopes in West Virginia listen out for quasars, exploding galaxies, and other celestial phenomena. Signals are converted into electrical impulses and analyzed by computers.

nightly exposures of the Magellanic Clouds. From them she was able to detect numerous variable stars with periods ranging from 1½ to 127 days. The longer the period, the brighter the star.

The relationship of apparent brightness to distance was well understood. Watch a man carry a lamp away from you, and its apparent brightness will decrease fourfold with each doubling of distance. Thus you can calculate his distance as far as the lamp's brightness can be measured.

In the case of Miss Leavitt's variable stars, since all were in the Small Magellanic Cloud, it could be assumed that all were about the same distance from earth. It followed that their fluctuation periods could be taken as measures of absolute brightness. Then, by independently establishing the distance to one nearby Cepheid in the Milky Way, and relating this distance to the star's apparent brightness and fluctuation period, astronomers had a standard candle. Miss Leavitt's work had resulted in a new astronomical yardstick.

With the Cepheid variables as his standards, Harlow Shapley began to establish the true dimensions of the Milky Way.... He derived distances for 69 clusters and found that they were distributed about a common point which, he reasoned, must be the center of the Milky Way. The sun was near the edge, two-thirds out to the outer edge of the galaxy. Thus, singlehandedly, Shapley removed the sun and earth from a central position in the Milky Way and placed us close to its outskirts—an almost Copernican accomplishment. In the Missouri native's words, it was "a rather nice idea because it means that man is not such a big chicken."

EVEN BEFORE SHAPLEY, ASTRONOMERS WERE taking interest in cloudlike objects, or nebulae. Technology improved, allowing these objects to be grouped in two broad categories. The Great Nebula in Orion, the Ring Nebula in Lyra, and the Crab Nebula were diffuse clouds of glowing gas. Many others, such as Andromeda, were spiral-shaped.

Shapley believed that all the visible universe was in or on the edge of one great system, the Milky Way galaxy. Opposition came from Heber D. Curtis, classical scholar turned astronomer. The stage for Curtis's work had been set by George Ritchey of Mount Wilson Observatory in 1917, when he photographed the nebula called NGC 6946 and found a starlike object not visible in earlier photographs. Ritchey recognized it as a nova—a brilliantly erupting star—inside the white nebula. He then searched the files of plates at Mount Wilson and discovered that two similar novae had appeared in Andromeda in 1909. Curtis found three more such examples in the plates at Lick Observatory. Their brightness suggested they must be well outside the Milky Way.

Maj. Edwin Hubble, mustered out of the U.S. Army, set to work studying nebulae in 1919. In 1923 he discovered some new Cepheid variables, and decided to try to determine the distance to Andromeda. By 1924 he was able to prove that it was far beyond the Milky Way (his estimate, though short of the actual 2.3 million light-years, was almost a million)—and, therefore, a galaxy comparable to our own. Hubble, at last, had discovered the universe.

Deep in a South Dakota gold mine, a scientist hunts for the elusive neutrino. These subatomic particles penetrate the Earth; some may react with chlorine in the tank to form a detectable gas.

A Berkeley, California, biochemical engineer checks gauges during the manufacture of interferon, an antiviral protein made naturally by genetically altering the DNA of E. coli.

Frontiers of Science (1982)

IN SEARCH OF LIFE'S BEGINNINGS

When bacteria ruled the world—for more than half of earth's nearly 4.6-billion-year history—they left behind evidence that may point to the origins of life. At a site in Western Australia, scientists discuss a well-preserved stromatolite—the inorganic debris built up by an ancient bacterial community. At right, top, wavy layers formed between sheets of bacteria pattern a stromatolite from the site. A microfossil found in rocks nearby (right, center)—dated at 3.5 billion years—may prove one of the oldest examples of organisms yet found. Earlier work at Gunflint in Ontario uncovered bacterial microfossils about two billion years old (bottom)—sparking new quests for traces of first life.

129

Noted experts contributed chapters in their fields of expertise; on-the-spot photos showed scientists at work.

This ambitious book project brought together contributions from several renowned scientists. Chapters covered the Earth, the solar system, the history of the universe, cutting-edge biology, advances in medical research, and the human brain. Tempered by the authority of experts, a gee-whiz look at the latest research provided readers a uniquely privileged guided tour of current developments in several scientific disciplines. In this excerpt from the chapter "Our Changing Planet Earth," Dr. J. Tuzo Wilson, director of the Ontario Science Centre, lays out the background of plate tectonics.

When he wrote this piece, Wilson had already retired from more than three decades of teaching at the University of Toronto. He had thus gained a long perspective on the subjects of geology and geophysics. He had taken risks during the 1960s by articulating his own theory of transform faults—rifts in the ocean floor—which was a piece of the puzzle leading to the theory of continental drift.

Wilson's career spanned the years before and after the theory of continental drift was accepted by the scientific community. In fact, as he points out, he did his fieldwork when geologists were not far removed from natural historians, content to collect rocks and fossils. Wilson's thinking moves us forward into modern theory, just as advancing technology pushed the Earth sciences into exciting new realms of discovery.

Sensing Continental Drift

J. Tuzo Wilson's firsthand story of a how a new idea developed

The following year I took up the study of geology and geophysics. I attended three major universities—Toronto, Cambridge in England, and Princeton—and if the professors mentioned continental drift at all, they scorned it as a bad joke. In those days, geology concerned itself with labeling rocks, collecting fossils, studying bits and pieces of our planet. One famous physicist compared the subject to stamp collecting.

Yet I had no regrets. I performed my doctoral work not in some cramped laboratory but in the wilderness of Montana's Beartooth Mountains, sleeping under the stars, warmed by a campfire. In the Canadian bush I came to know wild waters and the burdens of portage. I supped on seal meat as a guest of Eskimos, and on fresh moose that I had slaughtered myself. When airplanes came into use, we were resupplied by air and aerial photographs began to guide our explorations. Geologists who had known earlier times thought life was getting soft. But for all our fieldwork, geology was still virtually ignoring the three-fourths of the globe covered by water and ice. The ocean floors? Earth's interior? How would we study them?

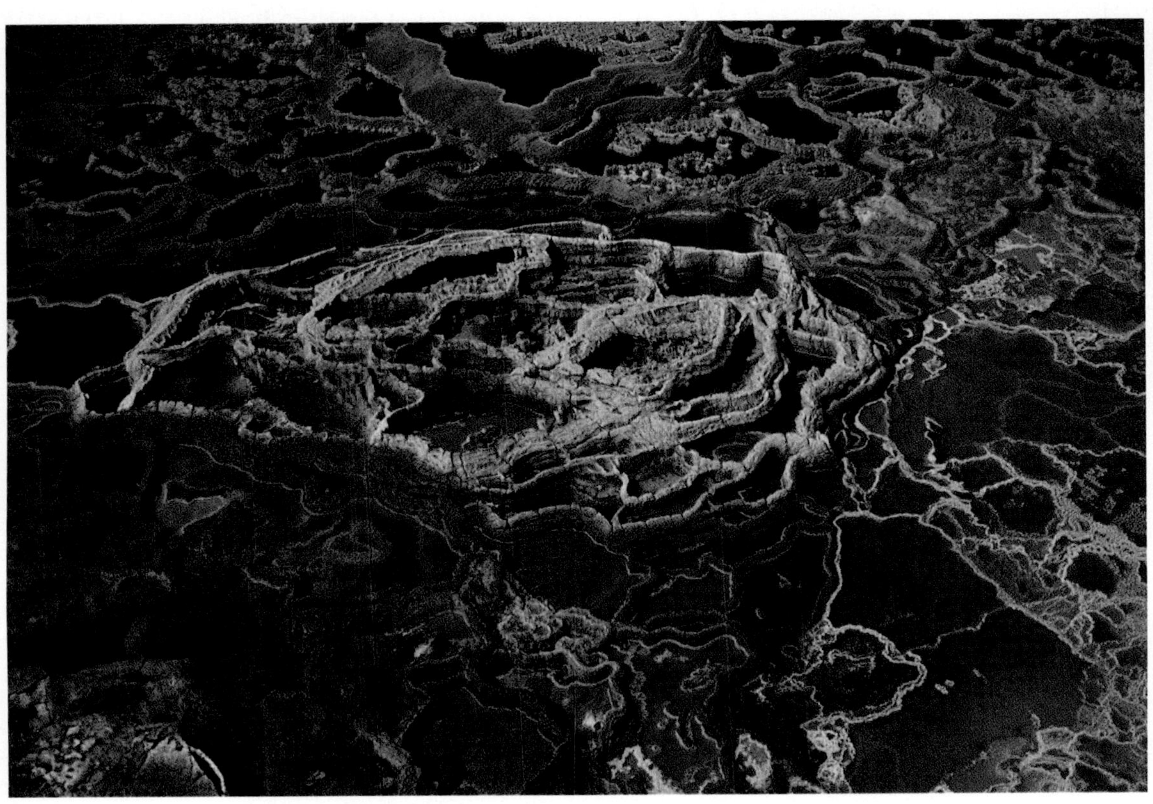

An aerial view of Ethiopia's Danakil Depression shows mineral-rich deposits encrusting the edges of pools. The area is one of the few places on Earth where seafloor spreading takes place on land.

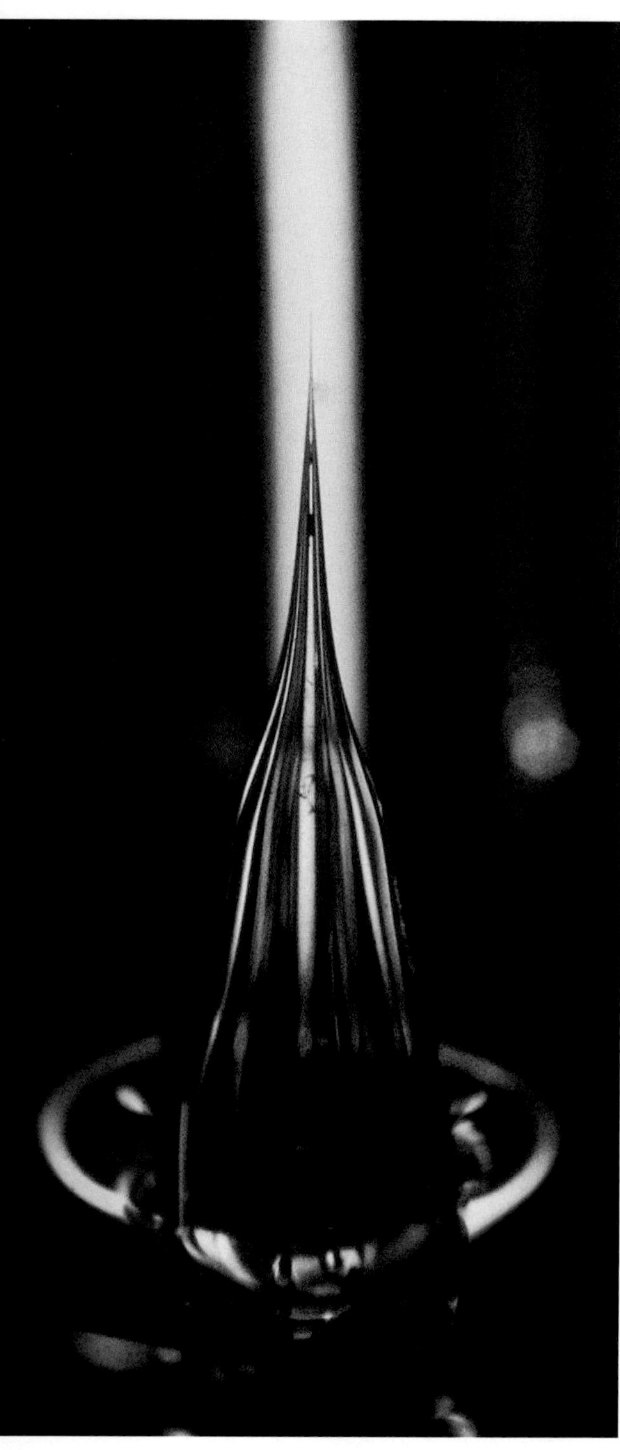

Tapering to microscopic size, a five-chambered glass pipette can deliver a minuscule amount of neurotransmitter to a single brain cell in a dish. As in a human neuron, electrical impulses push the chemical out.

Many of us sensed that we would never be able to develop a theory of how the Earth's crust behaved until we could study the globe as a whole. To do so, we would have to range the continents and seas to compile mountains of data.

At the end of World War II the tools were at hand, and revolutionary research began. There were new or improved instruments to measure magnetic and gravitational fields, to trace the flow of heat through the earth, to probe for marine sediments. Radiometric techniques—measuring the decay of radioactive materials—brought new precision to geologic dating. Seismology advanced, and its sound-wave data revealed vast new detail of the architecture of Earth's crust.

For the geologist who sought a whole-earth perspective, not the least of the marvels of the early postwar days were the patterns of air travel. Propeller planes flew low and slow; their short range forced them to call at places few of us visit in the jet age. Thus I came to know Iceland and the Azores, Wake Island, the Cocos, and the Seychelles, and I learned firsthand from leading scientists the fruits of their researches in the field. To me, those years were the most exciting the earth sciences have ever known.

ONE GREAT SOURCE OF EXCITEMENT WAS the confirmation by echo sounding of a globe-girdling mountain range—on the ocean floor! Part of it, the Mid-Atlantic Ridge, was already known; but it now became evident that this greatest of all mountain systems winds more than 40,000 miles around Africa to cross the Indian and Pacific Oceans and end at the Gulf of California. It forms one of two earthquake belts about the Earth. The other is the ring of fire around the Pacific rim, with a branch from the Himalayas through the Alps.

From the cage of Palomar Observatory's 200-inch telescope in California, an astronomer displays a CCD (charge-coupled device) that improves images of distant objects by gathering light more effectively.

Not long after the discovery of the Mid-Ocean Ridge system, the late Harry Hess of Princeton offered a proposal he diffidently called "geopoetry" that synthesized the recent evidence. At the ocean ridges the Earth's outer shell, or lithosphere, is split and spread apart by rising currents in the underlying mantle. Lava wells up from the mantle, fills the gap, and becomes welded to the crust on either side. As more lava comes up, adding to the crust, the older rock moves away from the ridge. Confirmation of Hess's theory soon came with the discovery that the pattern of ancient magnetism in the ocean floor can be read, tree-ring fashion, to roughly date the rock. And the dating sequence fits: The age of the rock that forms the ocean floor increases with distance from the ridge crests.

By 1965 many of us were convinced that the continents were moving, but not independently adrift on the oceans. Today's theory of plate tectonics holds that the continents are embedded like frozen rafts in much larger plates of moving lithosphere. The basaltic ocean plates are younger than the continents, and denser. The continents are much more ancient, more complex aggregations of rock, weatherbeaten and eroded. One scientist has called the continents the "scum of the earth"—with no derogation intended.

Skeptics have wondered how these plates can move, since the Earth behaves as a solid to a depth of nearly 2,000 miles. The answer seems to lie in the fact that just under the cold, brittle shell, the earth is very hot, and the heat creates a mobile layer. It is like having a layer of soft butter under the top crust of a loaf of bread. The crust can move.

The movement between the plates can be of three kinds. The plates can move apart, they can converge, or they can slide past one another. The three motions are connected. I can easily visualize them when I open my desk drawer. Inside the desk, as the back of the drawer moves forward, a gap forms. This corresponds to the opening of a fresh ocean floor. The front of the drawer comes toward me, perhaps colliding with the chair or my body. With earth's plates, there is always something in the way, because there is good reason to believe that the planet's size does not change materially. If an ocean is spreading by the creation of new crust, then equal areas of old crust must be absorbed into the interior.

On the floor of the Pacific the Mid-Ocean Ridge is opening at the rate of several inches a year. To the west of the ridge the Pacific plate, one of six large crustal plates, is being pushed northwestward toward the great ocean trenches and the island arcs of the Aleutians, Japan, and eastern Asia.

The evidence suggests that along the trenches and beneath the islands, the rigid surface shell of the earth is being destroyed. The oceanic plate, subjected to intense heat, is evidently bent and forced down into the mantle. These are zones of abundant earthquakes and volcanoes.

Let's go back to my desk drawer for the third kind of plate movement. Along the sides of the drawer, sliding motions occur, without collisions or opening gaps. This does not mean the sliding must be smooth. Think of a very tight drawer.

You may tug and tug without effect, until force overcomes resistance and the drawer slips loose. When a similar slippage happens between plates of the earth's crust, the result is an earthquake.

A generator at Los Alamos, New Mexico, gives protons a high-energy jolt; the protons then rocket through a linear accelerator and smash into target atoms. Subatomic pions set loose form part of experimental cancer treatments.

One area of such shearing begins at the mouth of the Gulf of California. There the spreading motion of the plate boundaries becomes more complicated. The boundaries begin to shear as well as separate, and the Pacific plate slides northwestward relative to the American plate. Because of this shearing, a fragment of western Mexico and California—once attached to the American plate—has broken off and now slides with the Pacific plate. Where the plate boundary runs aground at the San Andreas Fault, the transformation is complete. The shearing action takes over, and the plates scrape past each other.

Off Oregon, the process is reversed. Sliding reverts to a spreading motion from ocean ridges. Farther north, the sliding resumes along a fault that extends nearly to Anchorage, Alaska. Such cracks, where the plate motion is changed or transformed, I have called transform faults. In plate tectonics theory, they are seen as essential parts of the network of plate boundaries. But the concept that great motions can occur at such cracks is comparatively new.

In 1953 two geologists proposed that the part of California west of the San Andreas Fault system had slid northward several hundred miles over the last tens of millions of years. Few believed them. In 1965, when these ideas were still new, I was invited to California to lecture about them. Many were still skeptical. But when I went again in 1982, not only had the idea of large sliding motions in California been accepted, but many in the audience also held that most of Alaska and much of British Columbia consist of fragments carried north by faults that were predecessors of the San Andreas.

CHAPTER SIX

GREAT MOMENTS

Introduction by William R. Gray

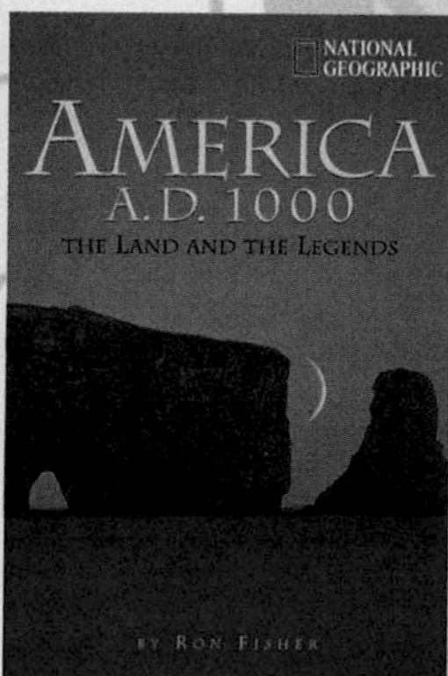

Some titles in the Special Collection transcend the categories.
These four selections represent great moments in the series's 42-year history
and epitomize the intelligence, excitement, and splendor found in every volume.

William R. Gray was a writer, editor, and publisher with the National Geographic Society for 33 years. He traveled the globe on assignments ranging from Alaska to Africa and authored books including The Pacific Crest Trail *and* Voyages to Paradise, *both titles in the Special Collection. He worked in the Book Division for more than ten years. He now lives near Durango, Colorado, and teaches at San Juan College in Farmington, New Mexico.*

On the farthest horizon, an indistinct smudge materialized from the verdigris waters of the South Pacific. Slowly, inexorably, as we approached in a small sailboat, that smudge resolved into an island of cloud-hung highlands, crenellated lava cliffs, and deeply eroded valleys lush with palm trees. Fatu Hiva: one of the most far-flung islands in the Marquesas Islands; but, even more, one of the most farflung islands in the entire Pacific. I had come to this remote realm in pursuit of the wraith of legendary English explorer Capt. James Cook, as part of the assignment for *Voyages to Paradise: Exploring in the Wake of Captain Cook.*

Stepping onto the verdant soil of Fatu Hiva and exploring a small village alive with welcoming Polynesians, I experienced the amazing feeling shared by so many other writers of Special Publications: the awareness that hundreds of thousands of people would eventually come along on this adventure of discovery.

Indeed, one of the most powerful aspects of the books in the Special Publications series—dating back to the first books in the 1960s—has been that special personal bond that developed between the creators of the books and the legions of loyal readers. Our writers felt it; our editors instilled it; and those who managed the Book Division, of which the Special Publications series was an integral part, ensured that the connection with our readers was paramount in everyone's minds. In 1993, on the publication of the 100th Special Pub, we sent out a letter to all of the members who had purchased both the first book in the series and the hundredth. I thought there might be a few score of such people. When we did the research, though, it turned out there were well over *10,000* people who had bought both—and assumedly many of the volumes in between. Clearly, readers appreciated what the National Geographic Society was providing: intriguing, enlightening, fulfilling, and intellectually stimulating books.

ONE OF THE OTHER HALLMARKS OF THE long series of Special Publications—in addition to the high quality of writing, photography, cartography, design, and printing—has been the truly unique ideas for the subjects of the books. Several signal volumes shoulder their way to the front of the line, and all because of the significance of their subjects—the ideas upon which they are based.

Vanishing Peoples of the Earth, published in 1968, was a landmark volume that took a penetrating and reflective look at cultures around the world that were still clinging to traditional ways but were poised on the final brink of assimilation into the 20th century. By the 1960s, virtually all corners of the globe had been explored and even the most remote tribes discovered. This book revealed the incredible diversity and complexity of some of the most traditional peoples—the fierce head-hunting Asmat of New Guinea;

READERS APPRECIATED WHAT THE NATIONAL GEOGRAPHIC SOCIETY WAS PROVIDING: INTRIGUING, ENLIGHTENING, FULFILLING, AND INTELLECTUALLY STIMULATING BOOKS.

the gentle Bushmen of Africa's Kalahari Desert; the remote Kraho, Waurá, and Suyá tribes of central Brazil; the nomadic Lapps of northernmost Scandinavia; and others. Many chapters were written by noted anthropologists and ethnologists—Frederick A. Milan, Sister Mary Inez Hilger, Catherine H. and Ronald M. Berndt, Vilma Chiara Schultz, among others—who had lived with and studied the peoples they portrayed. Their incisive portraits of the deep traditions of these cultures as they confronted the realities of encroaching civilization still make for compelling reading. And the photographs preserve a record of worlds now vanished. Indeed, if the idea for this remarkable book had been developed even five years later it would have been too late.

Another timely book—in fact one that was almost before its time—was *Nature's Healing Arts: From Folk Medicine to Modern Drugs,* published in 1977. One of the many outgrowths of the dramatic social and political changes in the decade of the 1970s was a focus on the healing power of natural plants and herbs, and more broadly on the importance of living a more healthy lifestyle fueled by natural foods—a lifestyle that had served humankind for millennia before. Author Lonnelle Aikman and photographers Nathan Benn and Ira Block traveled the globe in search of the story—and the history—of natural plants and herbs. And a rich story it is, reaching back some 4,000 years to Sumerian clay tablets that listed prescriptions of natural products. Through the centuries—from ancient China, Egypt, and India—the legacy of natural healing developed and contributed to important treatments for a variety of ailments and diseases, from malaria to smallpox to leprosy to congestive heart failure to childhood leukemia. The book also takes a close look at folk remedies, the use of herbs and plants to alleviate everyday complaints—aloe vera for poison ivy; the herb digitalis for heart problems; sassafras root for swelling in legs and feet; garlic for high blood pressure; wild ginseng for energy and general well-being. A comprehensive volume, it ends with scientists who are attempting to regulate disease with botanical drugs. Although it was released more than 30 years ago, I still see copies of this book in the offices of physicians who practice holistic medicine. The publication of *Nature's Healing Arts* was truly an idea whose time had come.

THE MISSION OF THE NATIONAL GEOGRAPHIC Society has been expressed as "the increase and diffusion of geographic knowledge." The Special Publications series truly succeeded in fulfilling that mission, especially in relation to the United States and North America. Many books focused on the rivers, canyons, mountains, national parks, and wilderness areas of our continent.

A unique book, *Nature's World of Wonders,* published in 1983, expanded the Society's mission to a global scale and brought the geographic and geologic wonders of the entire Earth to the doorsteps of our readers. Barry C. Bishop, Ph.D. Society staff member and conqueror of Mount Everest as part of the first American expedition in 1963, was impressed with the idea for this book. In his foreword, he wrote, "Indeed, the book brings the realization that nature is complex and simple, powerful and delicate, fleeting and enduring." The writers and photographers of this book journeyed to every continent seeking always the natural treasures that distinguished each region: from the sprawling and majestic—the Great Rift Valley of Africa, the Great Barrier Reef of Australia—to the more delicate and ethereal—Angel Falls in Venezuela, Bora Bora in French Polynesia. The photography, of course, is exquisite and inspirational.

But this volume also showcases the work of a cadre of excellent writers from the staff of Special Publications—Ron Fisher, Cynthia Russ Ramsay, and Tom O'Neill. Augmenting this group on other books were other superb staff writers—Tom Melham, Toni Eugene, Gene Stuart, Christine Eckstrom, and Jennifer Urquhart, among others. In their perceptive and creative writing, these authors helped fulfill the mission of the Society.

"Perceptive and creative" are words absolutely appropriate for another book in the series, *America A.D. 1000: The Land and the Legacy*, and they are appropriate in a couple of ways. First, the very idea for this book was ingenious. Like many publishers at the end of the last century, the Book Division was developing concepts that reflected on the past century and on the past millennium. And we published a wonderful large-format volume entitled *Eyewitness to the 20th Century*. But our creative thinkers came up with a concept that simply could not *not* be published. Instead of looking at the world at the end of the second millennium, we decided instead to evoke what North America was like at the end of the *first* millennium, painting a portrait of a continent—its natural splendor and its diverse peoples.

And the second reason that this book is "perceptive and creative" is that we assigned Ron Fisher to write it. I had made Ron's acquaintance on my first day as a writing intern for Special Publications in the summer of 1967, while I was still in college. He is to this day still one of my dearest friends, and he truly epitomizes the high quality of writing at the National Geographic Society. His first words in this book—"Imagine a time when time itself was a mystery"—set a literary tone, propelling us to the final page and inviting us on a journey to discover the world of a thousand years before.

THE SPECIAL COLLECTION TITLES HAVE ALL been about ideas. When Bob Breeden founded the division in the late 1960s, he astutely realized that ideas for new and ever better books would be the lifeblood of the future. For decades, the Society invested time, money, and intellectual creativity into developing powerful concepts for the Special Collection. Book Division staff partnered with the Society membership, our loyal readers, in selecting which ideas to develop into books to publish. Through surveys, readers told division editors which concepts most interested them and, in turn, which books they would most want to have in their home libraries.

Just as the authors of all Special Publications delighted in partnerships developed with the subjects that they wrote about—a feeling I enjoyed as I stepped onto the remote shores of Fatu Hiva—so we, as the creators of the National Geographic's Special Publications through the years, shared a partnership of ideas with our readers.

Reenacting a migration from an earlier time, Netsilik Eskimos (now called Inuit) and their huskies trek across the bleak tundra toward their autumn fishing camp on Canada's Kellett River.

Vanishing Peoples of the Earth (1968)

Autumn-hued hills of southern Hokkaido rise above traditional Ainu dwellings of wood and thatch, re-created to exemplify and preserve a disappearing way of life. Broiling fish over a sunken hearth, an Ainu woman prepares dinner for her husband, Ichitaro Nitani. A sacred prayer stick, or inau, made of a peeled willow stem with curled shavings, brings blessings to the fire pit. Below, a mother nurses her child in a shinta—a wooden cradle suspended from the ceiling.

100

Written by a team of anthropologists, this book catalogs traditional cultures giving way to modern influences.

Published four decades ago, *Vanishing Peoples of the Earth* highlights a number of tribes and ethnic groups that were on the verge of extinction. A few of them, such as the headhunters of New Guinea and the Indians of central Brazil, had only recently experienced their first contact with the outside world. Others, like the Lapps or the Hopi Indians, had managed to continue into the modern world through intermarriage with outsiders. Also cataloged were the Kalahari Bushmen, Japan's Ainu, the Nilgiri of India, the Eskimo, and the Australian Aborigines—all groups that had adapted to modern civilization to some extent while still preserving large parts of their ancient ways.

Matthew Stirling's opening essay, from which this excerpt is taken, makes the point that adaptation helped these vanishing peoples survive. The people who could not adapt—the Yahgans of South America, for example—have perished.

Stirling tells the moving story of the last survivor of California's Yahi, who, though his people had all died out, saved himself by joining a white community. "Some peoples surrender and submit to change," writes the author. "Others resist. Some are shattered and overwhelmed by change; others find strength to build a new future."

Through clear-sighted cultural reporting, this volume reflects the urgent need to preserve endangered cultures, languages, and folklore.

What We Have Lost

From Matthew W. Stirling's overview of cultures facing extinction

Chill Antarctic gusts whipped the flames on the tiny sand hearth in the center of the frail bark canoe. Cowilij, his yellow-brown body sleek with seal oil, speared a large salmon. His wife, as naked as he, wearing only a tiny otter-skin apron, then turned the canoe toward their campground, paddling steadily in the rough waters around Cape Horn. With her infant daughter straddling her back, she maneuvered close enough to the rocky coast for her husband and son to clamber ashore with the day's catch and embers from the hearth for the campfire. Mooring the canoe was woman's work. Men hunted otter, seal, and guanaco, and snared birds. Women fished with a sinew line and gathered mussels. Cowilij's wife steered to a thick kelp patch nearby, and tied rope-like branches of the seaweed to the canoe's mooring lines. A film of frost covered the leathery leaves. She slid into the waters of Tierra del Fuego and swam ashore, her baby still clinging to her.

Once there was a family like this, fearless sailors at home among bleak islands and storm-tossed seas.

In the Xingu region of Brazil, Waurá tribesmen perform ritual dances after practicing for javari, *or war games. Body-paint designs symbolize hawks, jaguars, armadillos, and other jungle creatures.*

SOME PEOPLES SURRENDER AND SUBMIT TO CHANGE. OTHERS RESIST.
SOME ARE SHATTERED AND OVERWHELMED BY CHANGE;
OTHERS FIND STRENGTH TO BUILD A NEW FUTURE.

Once there was a hardy people, the Yahgans. They lived on the islands off the southern tip of South America. Fortunately, a few of my fellow anthropologists studied and worked among the tribe, so we know something of their life. Today possibly two full-blooded Yahgans survive, but nothing of their old culture remains except vague memories, a love for the sea, and their language, spoken by a few Indians of mixed blood.

Col. Charles W. Furlong, who studied the Yahgans, captured in somber paintings the rigorous life of these people. Simply seeing his portrait of a medicine man, now part of a collection in the Smithsonian Institution in Washington, D.C., made me want to study the tribe myself. But it was too late; by the time I saw the picture, only a few of the people remained, living near the settlement of Puerto Williams, Chile, their old life gone.

WHEN CHARLES DARWIN SAILED AROUND Cape Horn in 1832, he could have counted some 3,000 Yahgans. By 1884 they numbered fewer than 1,000; in 1933 there were about 40. What happened to wipe out an entire tribe? Why did a people who could endure the raw Fuegian climate more than half naked, who lived in rude shelters of branches, grass, and skins, and who bathed their newborn in icy seas, vanish from the face of the earth?

About a hundred years ago the Yahgans felt the impact of new diseases and new ways of life. Since the 16th century, Western civilization has swept across the globe, challenging traditions. I have seen the effect of civilization on mud-walled villages, jungle-girt settlements, and desert oases.... Sometimes circumstances make the crisis so acute that, as in the case of the Yahgans, it destroys the population.

Respiratory diseases, measles, and typhoid brought to the Yahgans by white intruders caused a rapid decline of the population in the 1880's. Then clothing from well-meaning Europeans compounded the disaster. Reading Darwin's accounts of how the Yahgans lived, I can imagine the pity many of his contemporaries must have felt for the Indians. He described a woman "suckling a recently born child ... whilst the sleet fell and thawed on her naked bosom, and on the skin of her naked baby!" Before long, boxes of cast-off clothes arrived at missionary posts in the area.

Dressed, the Yahgan returned to his damp canoe. Water continued to seep in through its seams; waves continued to break over it. The canoe fire gave too little heat to dry his wet clothes, and he soon became an easy victim of pneumonia, influenza, and tuberculosis.

Darwin related a whaling captain's description of cannibalism among the Yahgans, and the stigma persisted for decades; but careful study proved the story false. Confronted with unfamiliar patterns of conduct, European travelers often misinterpreted the simplest actions and motives of the peoples they encountered in new lands.

For example, when Capt. James Cook visited Tasmania, off the southeast coast of Australia, in 1777, one of his crewmen described the aborigines there as "mild and chearfull" but rather slow-witted because they showed less interest and surprise than

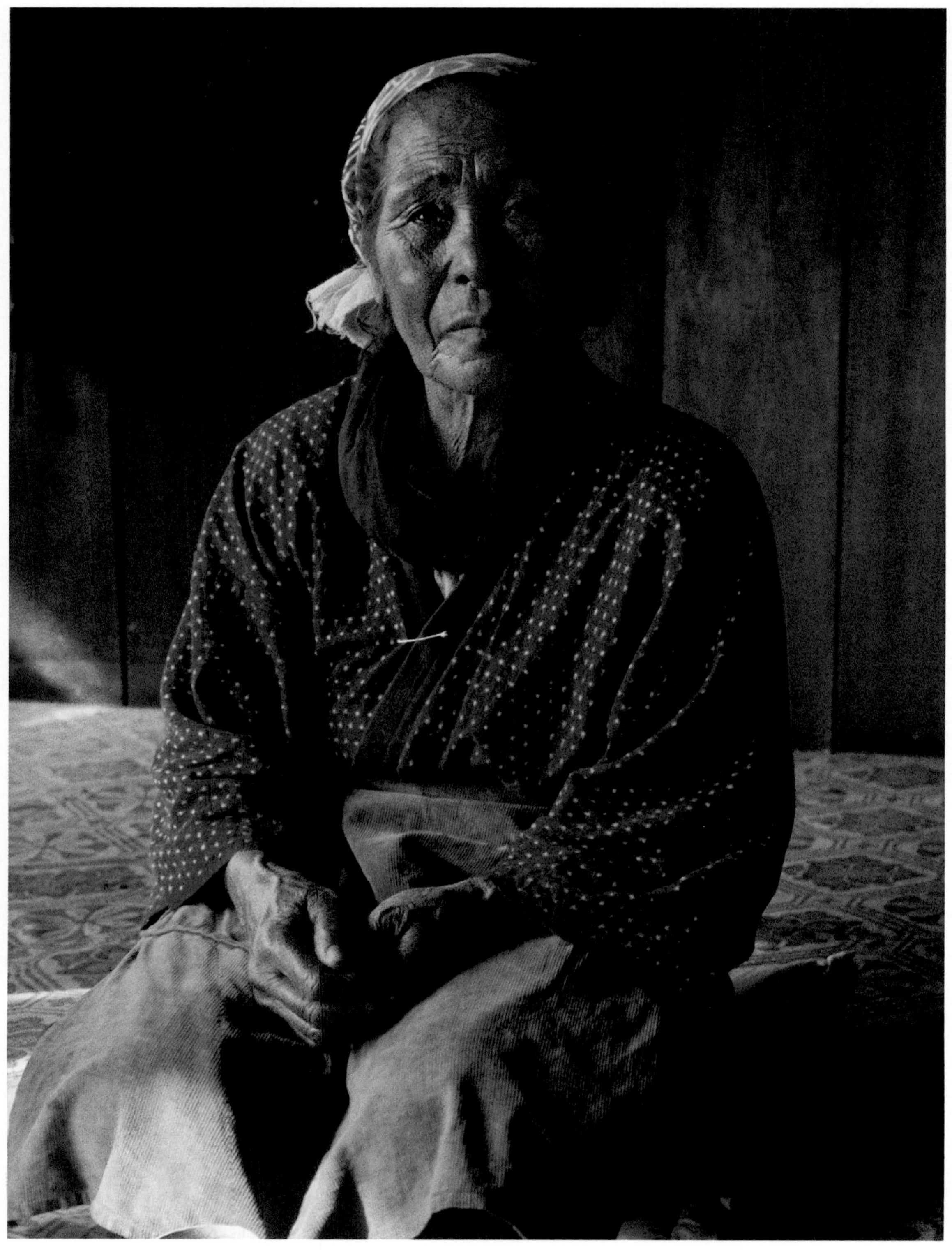

The Ainu people of Japan originated on the island of Hokkaido around 5000 B.C. Distinctive customs such as lip tattooing slowly died out among them as youngsters embraced mainstream Japanese culture.

Kalahari Bushmen of southern Africa celebrated a girl's entry into adulthood with a ceremonial dance. Two out of three Bushmen, this book noted in 1968, had abandoned nomadic life to work on farms and cattle posts and in households.

he expected when he put beads around their necks. He failed to consider that the etiquette of the people may have required a show of indifference.

We will never know with certainty why the Tasmanians failed to show interest. The entire population died out less than a century after the first sealers set up camp on the island in 1798. We have only the accounts of travelers, settlers, and government officials to give us clues to the Tasmanians' life. Records of Cook's voyage tell us: "They daub their Faces, Hair, Beards & their Bodies with red Earth, and their Bodies are ornamented in several Places, all on the forepart with large Scars." We also know that the men wore their hair in corkscrew ringlets two to three inches long, and the women shaved their heads, leaving only a patch of hair at the crown. The men hunted kangaroo and wallaby with simple spears—a lance with its point hardened in fire, and a large stick called a waddy.

According to some reports, Tasmanian women abducted by sealers killed their half-caste children. In the Black Wars from 1804 to 1830, shepherds, outlaws, soldiers, and convicts hunted down and killed most of the estimated 1,200 aborigines. In

1835, missionary George Robinson persuaded the nearly 200 survivors to settle on Flinders Island, off the north coast of Tasmania.

Massacred, degraded, bewildered, wrenched from their homeland, the refugees lost the will to live. Mourning the tribal life shattered by the Europeans, afflicted by disease and malnutrition, the Tasmanians literally pined and died, finding the white man's civilization as fatal as his musket. Within seven years after their voluntary exile, their numbers had declined to 50; the last full-blooded native Tasmanian died in 1888.

ALTHOUGH ANTHROPOLOGISTS NEVER HAD a chance to study the Tasmanians, they had a unique opportunity to observe the very last of the Yahi Indians of California, for in August 1911, the lone survivor of the tribe stumbled into the modern world from the Stone Age.

The Yahis, a branch of the Yana Indians, had lived in the northern California foothills until the gold rush brought settlers to their hunting grounds and salmon runs. The Indians treated the ranchers' sheep and cattle as game to replace deer, elk, bear, and rabbit that had grown scarce. Soldiers and vigilante bands hunted and massacred the Yahis, who numbered about 3,000, until all but 12 had died. In 1872 the tiny group found sanctuary in the caves, gorges, and chaparral around Deer Creek. Old age and illness reduced them even more. Finally one man remained.

Starved, his hair singed close to his head in mourning, he wandered into the small town of Oroville not far from Sacramento to await his fate. He expected death, but instead he acquired friends, a home, a job, a bank account, and a new name.

An anthropologist who had quickly identified the man as a Yahi arranged for him to stay at the Museum of Anthropology in San Francisco. I first met him there when I was a high-school student and watched as he demonstrated how to flake arrowheads, shape bows, and make fire with a fire drill. He patiently taught anthropologists how to pronounce Yahi words, but he could never bring himself to violate custom and speak his own name. Dr. Alfred Kroeber, under whom I later studied at the University of California, decided to call him Ishi, the Yahi word for "man."

At about age 50, Ishi had entered the 20th century abruptly and alone. I saw him face with courage the complexity of life in San Francisco—window shades and trolley cars, traffic signs and safety pins. One afternoon I joined Ishi for a ride on a streetcar. After he settled into a seat, he calmly began to pluck his whiskers with wooden tweezers, to the astonishment of the other passengers and me.

Ishi saw the *saltu*—the white man—as fortunate, inventive, and clever, but lacking in restraint and in an understanding of nature. Glue he rated next to matches as the most useful invention. He believed that the long hours spent indoors—in offices, autos, and houses—accounted for the white man's ills. An anthropologist observed, ... "he took very kindly to civilization." But Ishi viewed the world through Yahi eyes, just as all of us see through the lens shaped by our own culture.

A web of culture binds us to a style of life, to a moral order, and a definition of human nature. We see, understand, and make judgments based on the codes and values we grow up with. Knowledge of the diverse ways of mankind can give us a new perspective on man—who he is, what he can hope to become.... When myths fade from a people's memory, when their traditions lose importance, when old values no longer serve a need—the world loses something unique and precious.

An herb dealer in Christiansburg, Virginia, displays dried ginseng root. Valued as an aphrodisiac by the Chinese for thousands of years, ginseng tea was also used by Native Americans to alleviate fatigue and treat illness.

Nature's Healing Arts (1977)

by Lonnelle Aikman

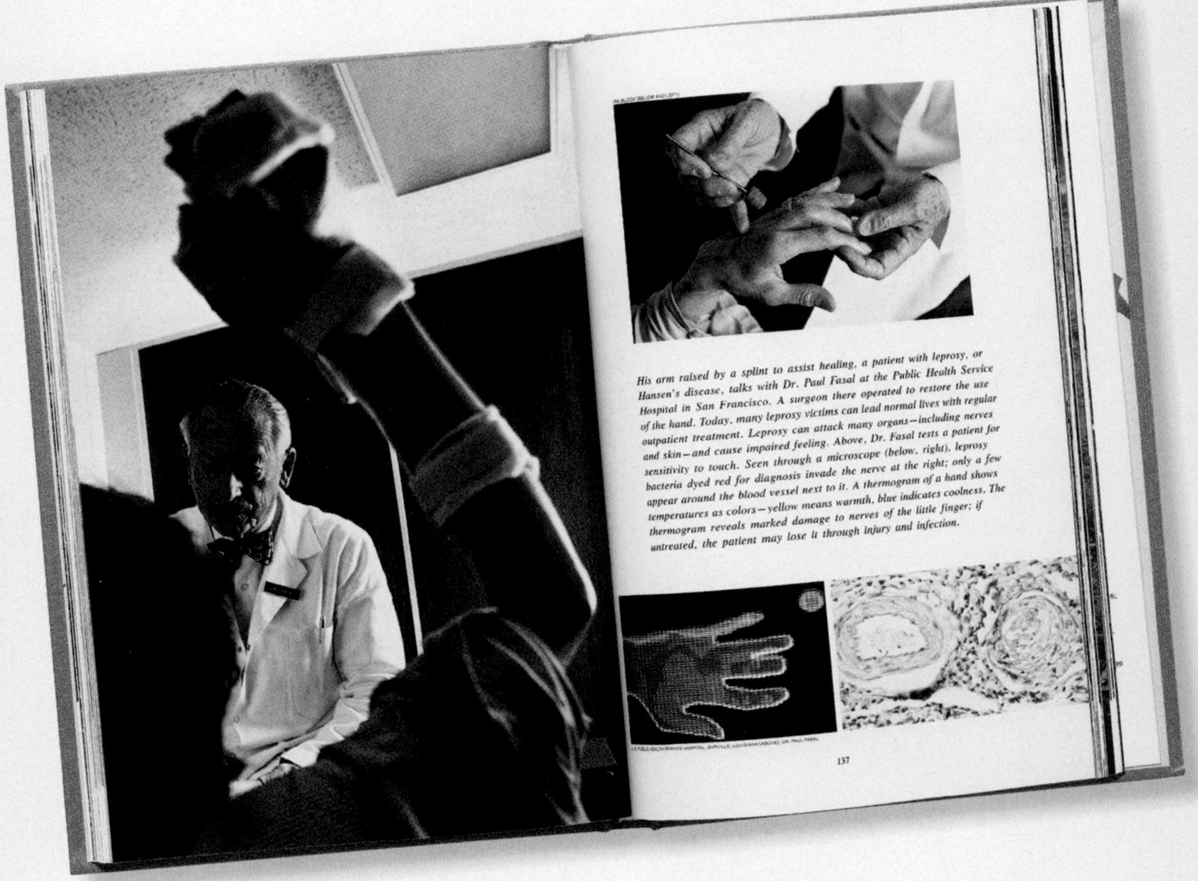

His arm raised by a splint to assist healing, a patient with leprosy, or Hansen's disease, talks with Dr. Paul Fasal at the Public Health Service Hospital in San Francisco. A surgeon there operated to restore the use of the hand. Today, many leprosy victims can lead normal lives with regular outpatient treatment. Leprosy can attack many organs—including nerves and skin—and cause impaired feeling. Above, Dr. Fasal tests a patient for sensitivity to touch. Seen through a microscope (below, right), leprosy bacteria dyed red for diagnosis invade the nerve at the right; only a few appear around the blood vessel next to it. A thermogram of a hand shows temperatures as colors—yellow means warmth, blue indicates coolness. The thermogram reveals marked damage to nerves of the little finger; if untreated, the patient may lose it through injury and infection.
137

From field and forest to lab and hospital, Nature's Healing Arts *lays out concerted efforts to find cures.*

Staff member Lonnelle Aikman wrote a number of books and articles for the National Geographic Society, including a magazine piece on natural medicine, which inspired this Special Collection title.

Written more than 30 years ago, *Nature's Healing Arts: From Folk Medicine to Modern Drugs* proves that everything old is new again. The medicinal use of roots, leaves, bark, blossoms, seeds, and other parts of herbs, shrubs, and trees "is almost as old as mankind," Aikman writes. "In fact, the botanical kingdom was by far the main source of all drugs until synthetics came of age during the present century." But, instead of dying out, many folk remedies led directly to modern medicines. As we now are turning back to such remedies to treat any number of ailments, it's interesting to note that people in the 1970s were already doing the same.

Aikman's book explores the history of natural pharmaceuticals in the United States and other countries around the world. The author explains how scientists in the '70s were continuing to open nature's medicine cabinet, where "long hidden mysteries" often show the way to new drug compounds.

The excerpt here, which closes the chapter "Legacies From the Past," traces the use of willow from 4,000 years ago in Sumeria up to the 1890s in Germany, where a chemist helped develop acetylsalicylic acid, also known as aspirin.

From Willow to Aspirin

One of many stories of herbal remedies turned modern medicine

Sir William Osler, a Canadian-American physician and historian, observed, "The desire to take medicine is perhaps the greatest feature which distinguishes man from animals." Certainly the quest for the right prescription in the right amount has never been easy. In the beginning, most primitive peoples explained the mysteries of illness and injury as punishment for their sins or as the malevolence of some angry god. Thus the herbal and animal products in ancient remedies were often mixed by priests or temple physicians and given to patients with ceremonial incantations and prayers to divinities believed to control the destinies of ordinary mortals.

As experiments continued century by century, shrewd laymen as well as professional healers learned the hard way which plants were usually harmless and which innocent-looking ones carried death in their fruits and roots. So, gradually, each developing civilization accumulated its own science of cures, which was often fanciful or dangerous, but sometimes surprisingly effective.

Tucked away in a mountain fastness in southern Virginia, an herbalist concocts a beverage of slippery elm bark. Early pioneers drank the soothing medicine as an aid to digestion.

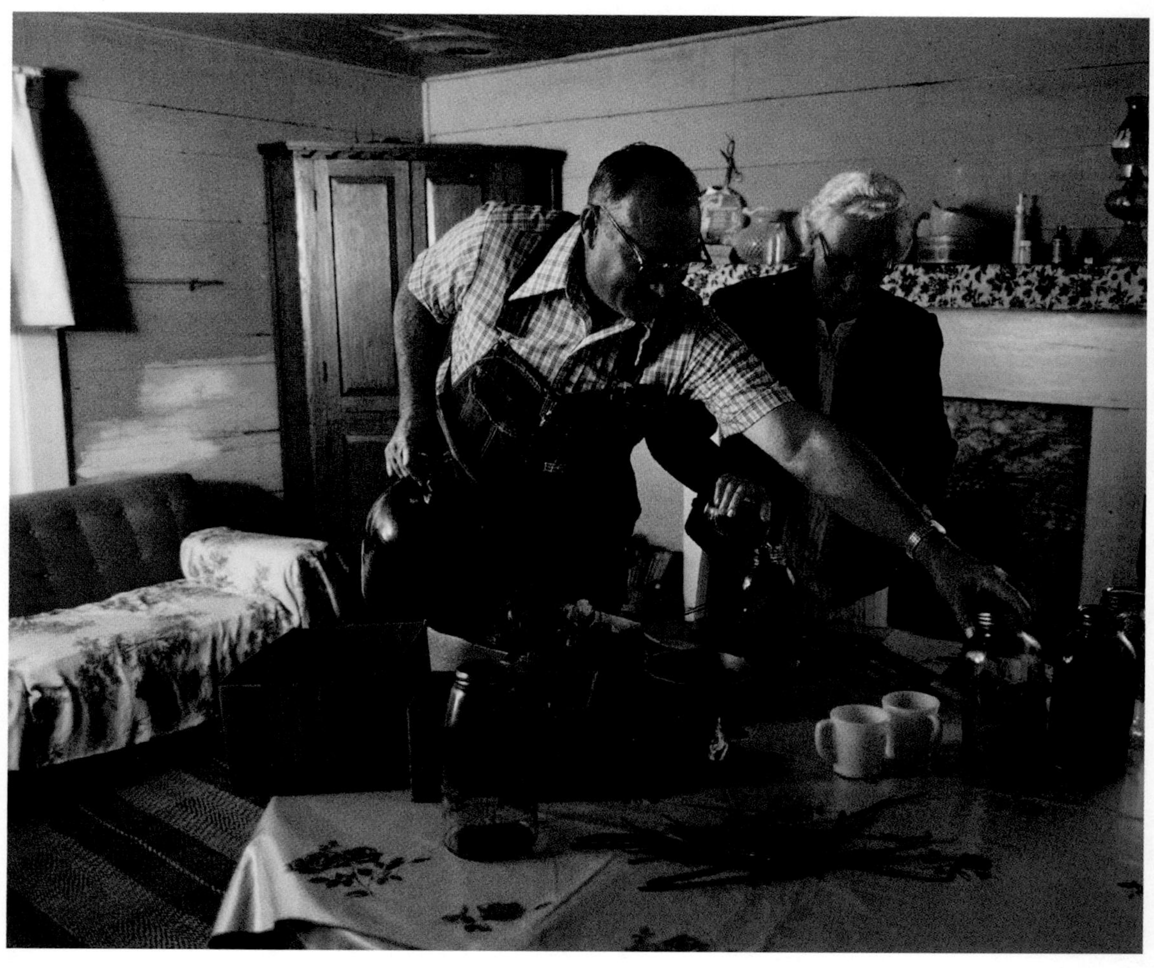

Mother and son herbalists of southeastern Virginia mix roots and barks into "good-for-what-ails-you" tonics. Bloodroot enhances the appetite; cherry bark makes one sweat; honey and sassafras add flavor; grain liquor gives a "charge."

How do we know this? The most direct and accurate knowledge that medical historians cite comes from a dozen or so original documents and other artifacts that still exist in tangible form....

HIPPOCRATES, WHO LIVED FROM ABOUT 460 to 377 B.C., is best remembered for his oath outlining the moral responsibilities of all who enter the medical profession. But even more important as a signpost to the future was his system of clinical observation of patients. As a physician at the Temple of Aesculapius, a kind of health spa dedicated to the God of Medicine on the island of Kos, Hippocrates prescribed diet, baths, and exercise, as well as hundreds of medicinal plants: then he carefully noted their effect on his patients.

Among the plants he used was the white willow, a large drooping tree that is one of the most common and salubrious of nature's gifts. The cuneiform sign for the willow appears frequently in prescriptions on the 4,000-year-old Sumerian tablet from Nippur. The Ebers Papyrus lists a liquid from the tree—probably from its bark or twigs—which was mixed with figs, frankincense, beer, and other things, and

Turkish officials measure fields of opium poppies, used in such narcotics as morphine, codeine, and heroin. Turkey banned poppy production in 1971 but reversed course four years later, after the ban proved ineffective.

"boiled, strained, and taken for four days to cause the stomach to receive bread."

Again, willow appears in [R. Campbell] Thompson's [1923] translation of the Assyrian tablets. And the Bible makes many references to these trees as a source of comforting shade and water. Remembering Zion by the rivers of Babylon, writes the author of Psalm 137, "we wept … [and] hanged our harps upon the willow…."

But the most pertinent observations on willow medication in classical times were made by Pedanius Dioscorides, a surgeon and pioneer botanist hired by the Roman Emperor Nero in the first century A.D. to travel with his troops.

Moving with the Roman army along the shore of the Mediterranean Sea, Dioscorides studied and collected thousands of plants and samples of mineral and animal products. From these he assembled his five-volume *De Universa Medicina;* this massive work was the authoritative source for physicians for the next 1,500 years.

Describing willow, he used its Latin name *Salix,* and pointed out the astringent qualities that have made it popular for so long: "the juice out of ye

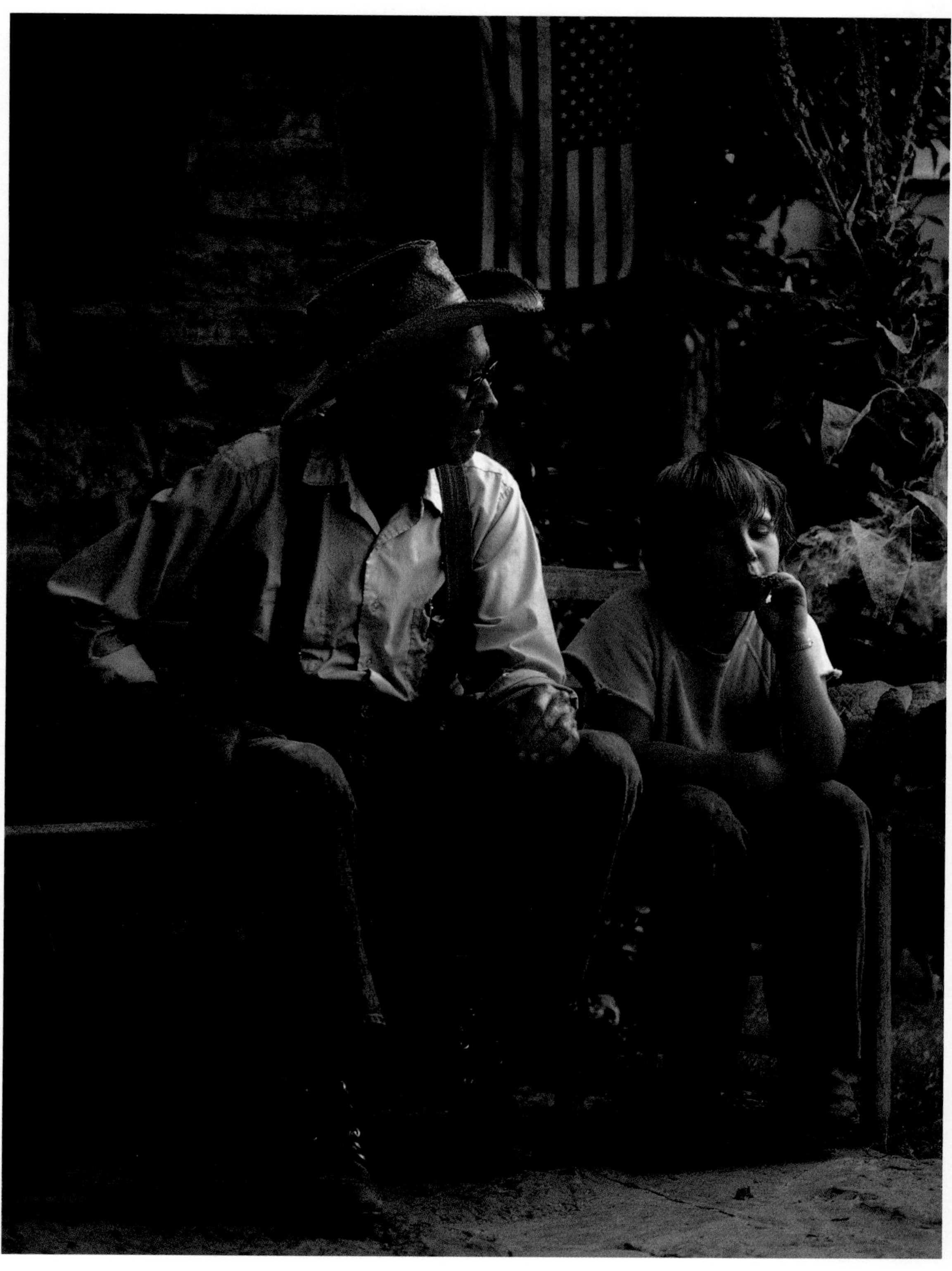

The old ways pass from one generation to the next: On the porch of his Arkansas home, Waco Johnson teaches his grandson to smoke mullein, a time-tested decongestant.

THIS YEARNING FOR WHAT IS NATURAL MAY BE A REACTION AGAINST POLLUTION, MECHANIZATION, AND THE CHEMICALS IN SYNTHETIC DRUGS. OR MAYBE IT'S JUST THE PERENNIAL NOSTALGIA THAT CHARMS US ALL.

leaues & barck ... doth help ye griefs of the eares," goes one prescription in a 17th-century English translation, "and the decoction of them is an excellent fomentation for ye Gout."

For good measure, Dioscorides added that the bark "being burnt to ashes and steeped in vinegar takes away cornes and other risings in the feet...."

THE WILLOW SAGA WAS JUST STARTING with Dioscorides. Claudius Galen, another noted Greek physician of the following century—whose name lives on in the term "galenicals" for plant preparations—regarded willow-bark extract as helpful in cleansing and healing eyes that were inflamed or infected.

Other authorities continued to stress willow's value against ailments ranging from colds to asthma. In *The Herball* of John Gerard, a monumental compilation of Elizabethan plants first published in London in 1597, the "vertues" of its leaves and bark included the power "to stay the spitting of Bloud [when] boiled in wine and drunke."

So widespread, indeed, have been the uses of the willow tree that Dr. Wayland Hand, folk medicine specialist at the Center for the Study of Comparative Folklore and Mythology at the University of California at Los Angeles, has recorded nearly a hundred accounts of magical and medical customs involving the use of parts of the willow tree. Dr. Hand keeps such references in a unique card index that he started 30 years ago.

One card on Louisiana folklore in the early 18th century tells of treating a fever by lying down on a heap of cool willow leaves. When the leaves became warm, it was believed, the fever had miraculously been transferred to them.

The modern era of willow can be dated from the late 1700's, when many doctors substituted a bitter decoction from its bark for the less available and more expensive cinchona bark, which was then the chief remedy offered to those suffering from malarial fevers.

But the final acceptance of willow products in scientific circles took place not in the woods and fields, but in the laboratory. In 1827, a French chemist named Leroux extracted the active substance in its bark that gave relief from pain. He named it "salicin," for the willow genus *Salix*.

Other scientists developed related compounds, but it was not until the 1890's that Felix Hofmann, a chemist with Friedrich Bayer and Company near Cologne, Germany, launched a successful career for one of them—acetylsalicylic acid—with the hope of finding a drug to help his arthritic father.

AS FINALLY MARKETED IN 1899, THE NEW product was baptized with the more pronounceable name of aspirin. Later, the drug was moved completely into the laboratory, when its makers shifted from natural to synthetic sources. Eventually, aspirin would become the world's best-known medication. Willow remains one of the historic drug plants whose example has inspired medical scientists to uncover the secrets of nature that form the basis of all modern remedies—a process that began nearly a century before aspirin came on the market.

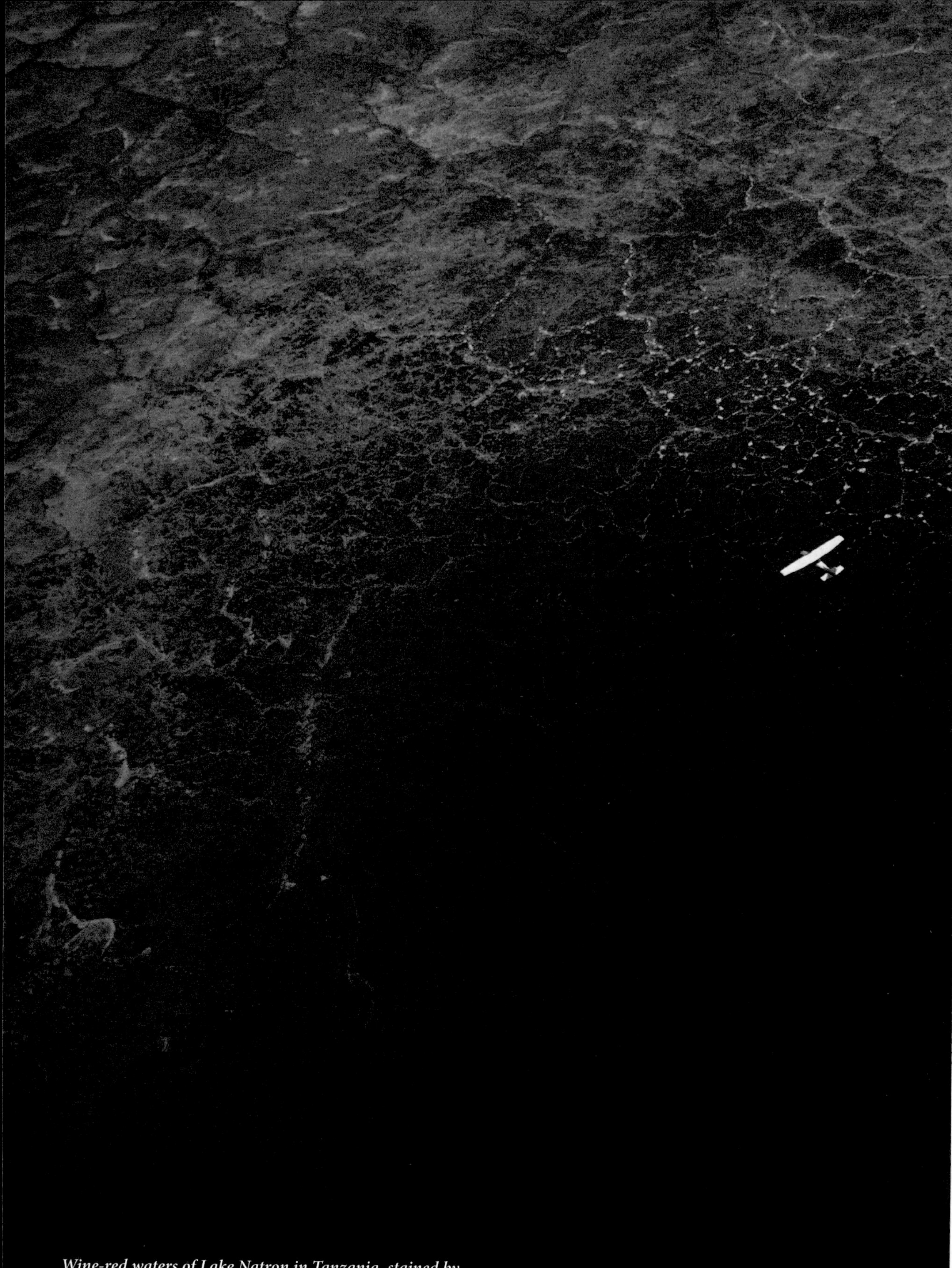

Wine-red waters of Lake Natron in Tanzania, stained by a seasonal bloom of algae, spread beneath a low-flying Cessna; a crust of soda turns pink as it dries.

Nature's World of Wonders

(1983)

Wonders of the natural world parade across the pages of this postcards-from-paradise volume.

A journey to each of the seven continents was the framework for this comprehensive book, which sought to immerse readers in the natural marvels—both well-trodden and nearly inaccessible—of the entire world. From the early 1980s era of the Special Collection, the book was a lavish seven-course meal, no expenses spared. Seasoned writers and photographers traveled to some of the remotest corners of the Earth, bringing back stories and images abounding.

The excerpt here is from the final pages of Cynthia Russ Ramsay's chapter on Australia and the Pacific Islands. A longtime member of the Special Publications staff, Ramsay traveled far and wide, writing as she traveled. On this particular Book Division assignment, she visited the tropical island of Bora Bora; swam in the warm, silky waters of the Great Barrier Reef; and hiked on Hawaii's volcanic Mount Kilauea.

Here we find Ramsay witnessing the magnificence of Ayers Rock in the heart of the Australian outback and then trekking among New Zealand's rugged Southern Alps. Accompanying her well-observed landscape description, she works in some interesting cultural background on the Aborigines, who were once nearly as much a part of the land as Ayers Rock. Likewise she smoothly brings in the Maoris of New Zealand, side by side with the explorations of Capt. James Cook.

From Ayers Rock to Mount Cook

Cynthia Russ Ramsay explores down under

Life is much less prolific in the outback, the harsh interior of Australia. In the dusty heart of the outback, where desert oaks and stunted mulga trees provide occasional shade, the solitary mass of Ayers Rock dramatically interrupts the monotony of red sand and prickly spinifex grasses.

Arriving at Ayers Rock on a short flight from Alice Springs, I first saw the rounded hump of sandstone, with its sheer, undulating walls and flattened top, from the air. A stark, enigmatic survivor of long-vanished mountains, Ayers Rock has an impact, an effect on the emotions, beyond that of its immense size and great age. It rises 1,143 feet above the surrounding desert, and covers 1,200 acres; its origin lies 500 million years in the past, when sand was deposited here in an inland sea. This sediment became sandstone, which was uplifted into a mountain range and then worn down to a flat plain. But Ayers Rock endured.

Statistics and geologic facts cannot convey the massive dignity of the place. It seems to smolder with a mysterious energy, an illusion that comes, perhaps, from its changing colors. It picks up the rose of dawn; at midday, when the sun beats down and heat radiates from the rock, it glows like a giant orange ember; and sunset kindles it into a blood-red fire that cools to lavender at twilight.

Aboriginals once roamed this region, stalking kangaroos, wallabies, and emus and gathering figs and grass seeds. For them, the springs at Ayers Rock assured a water supply in the long season of drought. The caves at the base of the rock gave shelter in the shorter season of rains. Ayers Rock, or Uluru as the Aboriginals call it, was long a ceremonial center for the Yankuntjatjara and Pitjantjatara tribes.

"To understand the significance of Ayers Rock to the Aboriginals, you have to understand their intimate relationship with the land," said Derek Roff, chief ranger in charge of Uluru National Park since 1968.

Over the years Derek has won the confidence of the Ayers Rock Aboriginals. "But," he will hasten to say, "there's a great deal that has not been revealed to me, and questioning the Aboriginals before they are ready to tell you will only bring the wrong answers."

Meltwater cascades like a beam of light into a cave in Kverkjökull, a glacier in southeastern Iceland. Writes contributing author Ron Fisher, "Iceland is nature's way of showing off."

SOME OF THE WONDERS VISITED IN THIS BOOK ARE ACCESSIBLE; OTHERS ARE IN REMOTE FASTNESSES.... BUT WE CAN ALL INDULGE OUR WANDERLUST AND CURIOSITY VICARIOUSLY.

Talking with Derek as we walked around the rock in the stifling heat of afternoon, I learned something about the Aboriginals' ties to their tribal land. The Aboriginals believe that their ancestors, part human and part animal, created the landscape as they traveled across the countryside during Dreamtime, when the world began. An ancestor's campfire became a rock hole; the place where an ancestor had bled in battle became a watercourse. All the deeds and events are chronicled in myths that form the sacred lore of the tribe. These stories of Dreamtime, passed on for untold generations, are a major force in the Aboriginals' life, and give them a special kinship with the land.

"The Aboriginals dazzle me with their knowledge of the land," said Derek. "They seem to know every blade of grass. Imagine, an old man can recognize the spot in the sandhills where his people killed a kangaroo when he was a boy!"

MY SOJOURN AT AYERS ROCK GAVE ME ONLY a brief glimpse into the spirit-filled world of the Australian Aboriginal. My excursion into the wild, precipitous mountains of New Zealand's Southern Alps gave me endless vistas of soaring, snowy peaks and pinnacled ridges, lovely shapes that would vanish in snow or sleet or mist within an hour or two.

In the catalog of Earth's mountain ranges, the Southern Alps are nowhere near the loftiest, but few are so steep or so formidable. These are, after all, the mountains where Sir Edmund Hillary trained for his conquest of Everest in 1953. "Few places in the world have such vicious, variable weather," said professional alpine guide Shaun Norman, who leads expeditions into the high country of Mount Cook National Park.

"What makes these mountains different and dangerous is their proximity to the sea. In a scant 16 miles, they rise from a lush coastal rain forest to a barrens of sandstone, snow, and ice. Winds heavy with moisture-laden air shriek in from the turbulent Tasman Sea, bringing savage storms that can strand and kill."

But Mount Cook, at 12,349 feet the highest peak in New Zealand, was basking in the sun the day I set out with Shaun. Our journey began with a flight to the small, snowbound Annette Plateau—a perch high on Mount Sealy that brought many peaks into closer view. We took off in a ski plane over the Tasman Valley. Below us, the runoff from the Tasman Glacier poured into a web of streams, gray with finely ground glacial debris. Small ponds dimpled the toe of the glacier with circles of pale jade, where the sun had melted sinkholes in the ice. Silvery rivulets trickled from snowfields down impossibly steep scree slopes and disappeared into the gravelly moraine. Ahead, the 18-mile-long glacier smothered the valley of its own making, dragging fragments of mountain in its flow.

The plane banked sharply to turn up into Mueller Valley. Above its main glacier, smaller tributary ones tumbled down slopes so steep the ice fractured into the awesome chaos of an icefall, riddled with crevasses. Finally, the plane swooped to a landing on what seemed too small a spot, sliding into a turn and a timely halt in the soft snow.

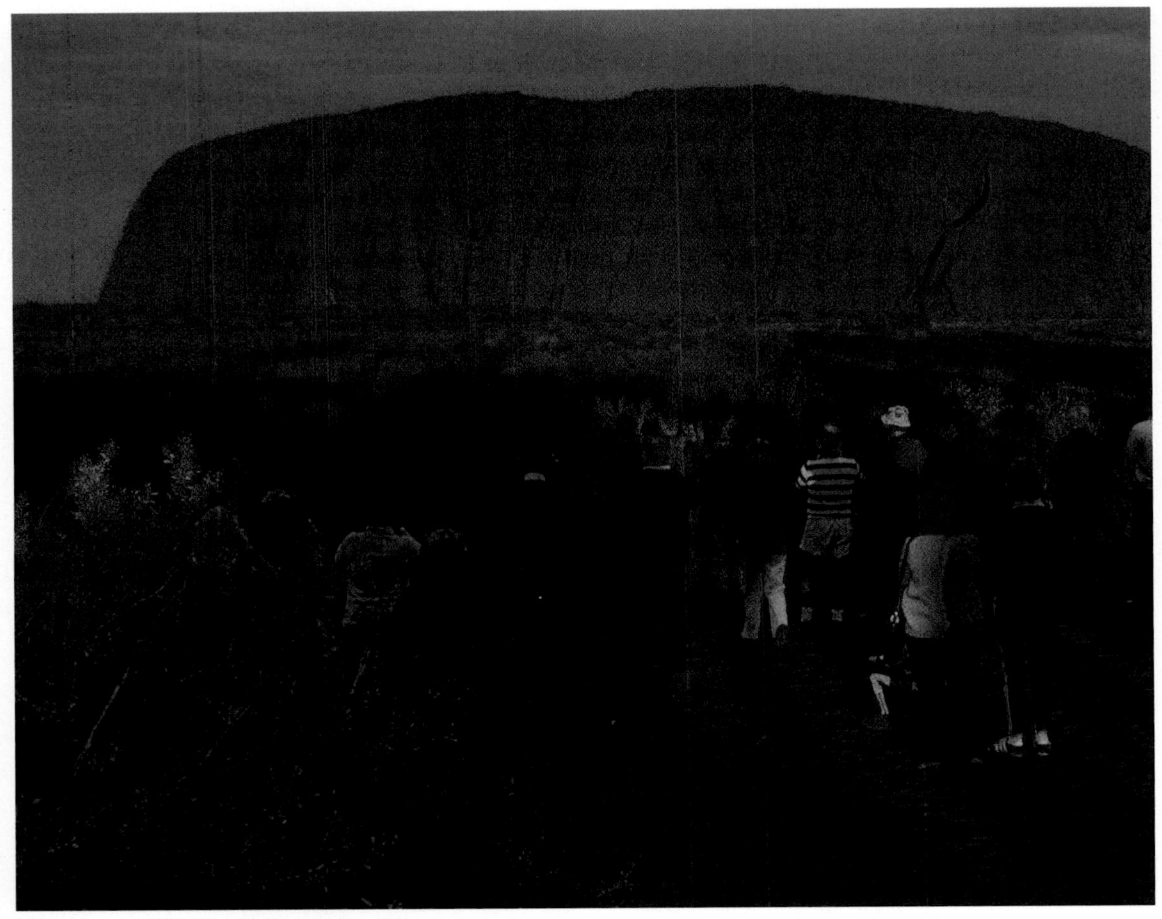

Basking in late afternoon light, Ayers Rock rises 1,143 feet from the desert floor. The sandstone monolith in the heart of Australia has long been sacred to the Aborigines.

Alert for hidden crevasses, Shaun led the way across a snowfield. "Sometimes the only indication you have is a small crack in the surface of the snow. Sometimes a narrow ridge of snow is a warning. Unless you watch out for these telltale signs, you'll be right into it—a total commitment to falling."

As we descended, snow gave way to boulder fields, and before each step I wondered where to place my foot. With each small leap from boulder to boulder, my backpack bounced, and I barely maintained my balance by using an ice ax as a walking stick; my teetering progress was heralded by the sharp clink of metal against rock.

A far nobler sound was the deep rumble of avalanches thundering down adjacent slopes in great billows of powdery snow. And any time my eyes left my feet, there was the serene beauty of the mountains. I stopped to watch clouds spilling over Mount Sefton's snowy crest. The clouds curled down the leeward side only briefly before vanishing over the valley on a continuous journey into oblivion....

The Mount Cook region is a nascent land, and much of it remains imprisoned in ice. At the southern end of the Alps, however, in New Zealand's Fiordland National Park, nearly all the glaciers retreated 14,000 years ago, leaving behind rugged,

Clinging to the hills, a town on the Greek island of Thera bathes in golden sunlight on the Aegean Sea (top); the bay was created by a collapsed volcano. A resident of Hveragerdi, Iceland (bottom left), grows roses in hothouses warmed by geothermal energy. From the air, Grand Prismatic Spring in Yellowstone National Park (center right) flares in brilliant color. Morning mist rises from the Li River in Guilin, China (bottom right), where limestone pinnacles inspire artists.

knife-edged ridges and steep-walled, U-shaped valleys. Some valleys were so deep they were drowned by the Tasman Sea as the ice melted. Fourteen of these long, narrow arms of ocean indent 200 miles of the southwest coast, thrusting inland into primeval forests thick with beeches, mosses, and ferns. The plant-choked landscape, with its lavish rains and scant sunlight, runs from mountain heights right down to the water's edge.

IN DAYS GONE BY, A VARIETY OF PEOPLE had come to the wooded fiord country—the native Polynesian population of Maoris, the great European navigators, the sealers and whalers, explorers, and gold seekers. Little remains of the stations where sealers and whalers caroused—and then went out to slaughter their quarry almost to extinction. The gold towns on Preservation Inlet crumbled and decayed after the ore ran out at the end of the 19th century. Even the band of Maoris that had sought refuge there from another tribe dwindled and passed away.

Except for the people who operate the tourist facilities on Milford Sound and Doubtful Sound, no one now inhabits the land. But fishermen challenge the rough, capricious waters to haul up their lobster pots. "Bait is anything you can catch—mackerel, blue cod. It's the lobster tails that bring in the money," say the fishermen. But the lobsters grow scarce, and so the men maneuver their boats closer and closer to the rocky shores, where the catch is best and the work most dangerous.

Aboard *Shaylene*, a sleek 50-foot cutter, we would occasionally see one of these brave little boats bobbing in the swells as it hovered close to shore. On our journey from Doubtful Sound to Dusky Sound, we were cruising along a coast as rugged and wild as it was when Capt. James Cook first found his way to the fiords in the 1770s.

Shaylene was dwarfed by the towering, jagged scarps that hem in Doubtful Sound. I felt the impassive presence of the wilderness all around me. The sea was a black mirror whose rippling surface reflected the trackless forests. The rumble of *Shaylene*'s engine seemed jarringly out of place.

"The wind is on the nose. It's coming right down the sound, and this is too confined an area to sail into the wind," said skipper Les Hutchins, as disappointed as I that he could not unfurl the sails. Captain Cook, after all, had named the sound but had never entered here because he was "doubtful" that the winds would let his bark, the *Endeavour*, sail out.

Cook, however, did spend almost six weeks in Dusky Sound, finding "rest and sustenance" after four months in the South Pacific. We arrived at Cook's safe anchorage after pitching and yawing for hours in the four-foot swells and irregular waves of the Tasman Sea. A short walk took us to the site where Cook's astronomer had cleared trees for an observatory. The moss-smothered stumps with their adz marks stood like tombstones marking man's passage through this unspoiled, enchanted corner of New Zealand. And this enclave of primitive beauty rivaled all the other wonders I had seen on my journey across the Pacific.

A sun-bleached bison skull in a wide and lonesome Dakota prairie evokes the American Plains of a thousand years ago. Herds thundered across such landscapes, followed by nomadic hunters; then the land returned to stillness.

AMERICA A.D. 1000 (1999)

by Ron Fisher

PEOPLE OF THE BUFFALO

SHE WAKES WITH A HEADACHE, dreading the day before her. There are fields to be weeded, corn and squash, and at her age the bending and stooping are tiring. She is a grandmother several times over and sometimes senses, in the lonely depths of the night, that her time is drawing to an end. When she does die, she knows, her body will be wrapped in a bison robe and placed, exposed to the elements, high on a wooden scaffold, her feet pointing toward the east, there to return to her Maker. Then her bones will be scattered. The prospect of this troubles her not at all.

She lives on the banks of the small, brown Knife River, a few hundred yards

Storm clouds darken the horizon beyond a bison skull in South Dakota. Farther north, along the banks of the Missouri, Plains Indians such as the agrarian Hidatsa had flourishing societies a thousand years ago.

93

Highlighting four indigenous cultures, this title chronicled life tuned to the cycle of sun and seasons.

Written just before the turn of the millennium, *America* A.D. *1000* casts a look backward to life on the American continents at the beginning of the previous millennium, long before any Europeans settled in. Ron Fisher's text is a beautiful feat of sustained imagination, both poetic and informative.

To write the book, Fisher sifted through hundreds of archaeological reports and other written sources, amplifying that study with knowledge from his travels and decades of writing experiences. Each chapter details a day in the life of one person—an Inuit seal hunter, a Hidatsa grandmother, a Mississippian girl, a Makah shaman—to illustrate how that tribe lived in those times. Along the way we see the rich bounty of the continent, "an Eden-like expanse of virgin forests and grasslands, seacoasts and canyons," as Fisher puts it.

The excerpt is from the final chapter, "People of the Canyon," in which the author takes the point of view of an Anasazi wiseman with special knowledge of astronomy. As in all the book's chapters, the day is June 21, the summer solstice, the longest day of the year.

"Imagine a time when time itself was a mystery," Fisher writes in his introduction. "The movement of the heavens was the only calendar, and time was another of the sacred forces of nature... Imagine the sun making its steady way across the continent... Imagine dawn..."

The Astronomer's Day

A chapter in the life of the Anasazi of the American Southwest

As he wakes, the blackness is just turning a faint gray. Edges appear. He sees the ghostly shapes of rocks and ridges. Dawn is nearly here. His back aches from leaning against a boulder. He had not intended to go to sleep. Just rest his eyes for a second.

When the sky in the east turns a delicate pink, distant buttes stand in dark silhouette. The astronomer murmurs a prayer of thanksgiving to the sun, for once again appearing, for so reliably playing its crucial role in the cosmos. He settles himself to meditate.

Another dawn. A very special dawn.

He sings, "This was a House Made of Dawn.

"It was made of pollen and of rain. The land was old and everlasting.

"There were many colors on the hills and on the plain, and there was a dark wilderness on the mountains beyond.

"The land was tilled and strong and it was beautiful all around."

The astronomer had made the long hot walk and the difficult climb to this spot high on the flank of stump-like Fajada Butte, which rises at the southern

In Alaska's brief but vigorous summer growing season, cotton grass blooms on a pond's boggy shores. The Alaska Range in Denali National Park creases the horizon.

An eastern woodlands girl cradles a handmade doll (top). A dead Blackfeet warrior (bottom) wrapped in buffalo robes lies atop a burial platform—closer to the gods—while relatives keep vigil.

end of Chaco Canyon, the previous afternoon. Rattlesnakes slithered out of his way, and roadrunners dashed to and fro, their heads and tails stretched out, bushy crowns of perky feathers atop their heads.

The astronomer is a solar priest. He needed to be in place for the sunrise, for today is the summer solstice, June 21, the longest day of the year, and he will spend it studying the movement of the sun and the shadows it casts. The sun will seem to pause here for a few days before reversing itself and turning once more toward the south.

To the astronomer's people—the Anasazi of the high desert—this is an important day. Corn, if it is to be given a chance to ripen, cannot be planted much later than today. Any later and frost will likely kill it, for winters are long, growing seasons are short, and corn takes about a hundred days to mature. And weather and rainfall can vary widely from year to year. So usually the people plant early, middle, and late crops and hope at least one will survive.

The Chacoan planting calendars—as well as religious observances—are set by close surveillance of solar and lunar cycles. Movement of the sun tells the people when animals will migrate, when to plant crops, when the sustaining rains can be expected to fall. They use the astronomer's observations to schedule ritual events and to make preparations for them—to get in the right frame of mind, for instance, or practice songs and dances, or assemble offerings and ceremonial dress....

THE ASTRONOMER WORKS THROUGH THE afternoon, with the temperature climbing and the sky filling with puffy white clouds. The wind has died down and the air is very still. From his perch high above the canyon floor, he can see, stretching into the distance, arrow-straight roads. About

Mule deer make their cautious way through tall prairie grass at dawn.
These Great Plains deer wear gray-brown winter coats; in summer they climb to higher pastures.

400 miles of the roads cross 20,000 square miles of Anasazi land, an area slightly smaller than Ireland. They are laboriously built to connect Chaco Canyon with 75 or so separate towns that depend on one another for goods and services.

The roads average 30 feet in width and disregard terrain: Since there are no wheeled vehicles or pack animals, they run up and over hills and valleys, with steps carved into the rock in the steepest parts.

On sloping ground, the roadbed is leveled and a rock berm built to retain fill. Some features will puzzle later archaeologists: Most of the roads are seemingly much wider than necessary for foot traffic, the only kind of traffic they will ever know. Further, some roads are exactly half the width of others. Some of the roads are parallel. Some are doubly parallel.

On them, Chacoans trade with groups as far south as Mexico for copper bells and macaw feathers. They acquire turquoise from mines a hundred miles to the southwest and shells for necklaces from the Pacific coast. Probably only 20 percent of the pottery used in Chaco Canyon is made here; the rest is acquired through trade, often with villages with better clay or more wood for firing the pottery.

Turquoise is the Chacoans' money. Craftsmen transform it into necklaces, bracelets, and pendants. The astronomer's wife owns a small frog carved in jet, with eyes of turquoise.

IMAGINE A DAY IN EARLY SUMMER, WHEN THE DAYS ARE LONGEST AND THE SUN IS APPROACHING ITS FARTHEST NORTH.... IMAGINE DAWN....

Chacoans communicate with distant towns via signal towers. Several structures built atop mesas are scattered around the San Juan Basin. Each tower is visible to at least one of the other towers, if not to half a dozen or more. From them, Chacoans send messages with fire at night and smoke or mica mirrors in the daytime.

BY LATE AFTERNOON THE ASTRONOMER IS hungry and thinking about his supper. His wife will have made griddle cakes or piki, a crisp corn bread. She fries food for the family on a stone griddle, or cooks meat stews, cornmeal mush, and vegetables in water in pottery vessels.

Some food she stores in fired clay pots and stone-lined cisterns, safe from rodents and moisture: Corn, beans, squash, wild plant products and dried meat see them through lean times or emergencies. Some rooms in Pueblo Bonito are reserved just for storing food. Sometimes the astronomer barters with a hunter for a jackrabbit or grouse to supplement his family's meals.

The Anasazi pottery his wife uses will be famous one day, not only for its utility but also for its beauty. It began crudely. The culture that preceded the Anasazi was known as the Basketmakers—some of their baskets were so finely woven they could hold water—and early Anasazi craftsmen merely lined a basket with clay, then burned away the basket.

Now a chalky white, the bowls and pots are decorated with mineral-based paint. Narrow-necked jars, called *ollas,* hold liquids; tall cylindrical shapes are used as ceremonial vessels. This classic Anasazi pottery will evolve over the next few decades, producing various styles, each more exquisite than the last. Nowhere else in the United States will be found earthenware vessels dating from this time that will be more beautiful in their form and in their decoration.

Potters work with neither wheel nor kiln, making paints from minerals and brushes from chewed yucca leaves. Decorative motifs will evolve from running hachuring to paneled, wide-lined designs—checkerboards, opposed contiguous triangles, interlocked key figures, and dot groups used as space fillers. The vessels will be highly polished and glow with an inner fire.

THE ASTRONOMER WILL PROBABLY HAVE a drink with his supper. Brewers ferment liquors from maguey, which is an agave; also from the nopal cactus, mesquite beans, native grapes, and other fruits. There may be music. A neighbor entertains in the evenings by playing a flute made from the wing bone of a golden eagle.

The astronomer finishes his day reassured. The stars in their heaven are running true. The seasons will continue to come and go.

Though he doesn't know it, Native Americans all over the continent, in harmony with their world, share his confidence. They take what they need from nature, give thanks for it, and count on tomorrow to be a repeat of today.

Unaware of the wider world, they have the wondrous continent to themselves.

But not for much longer.

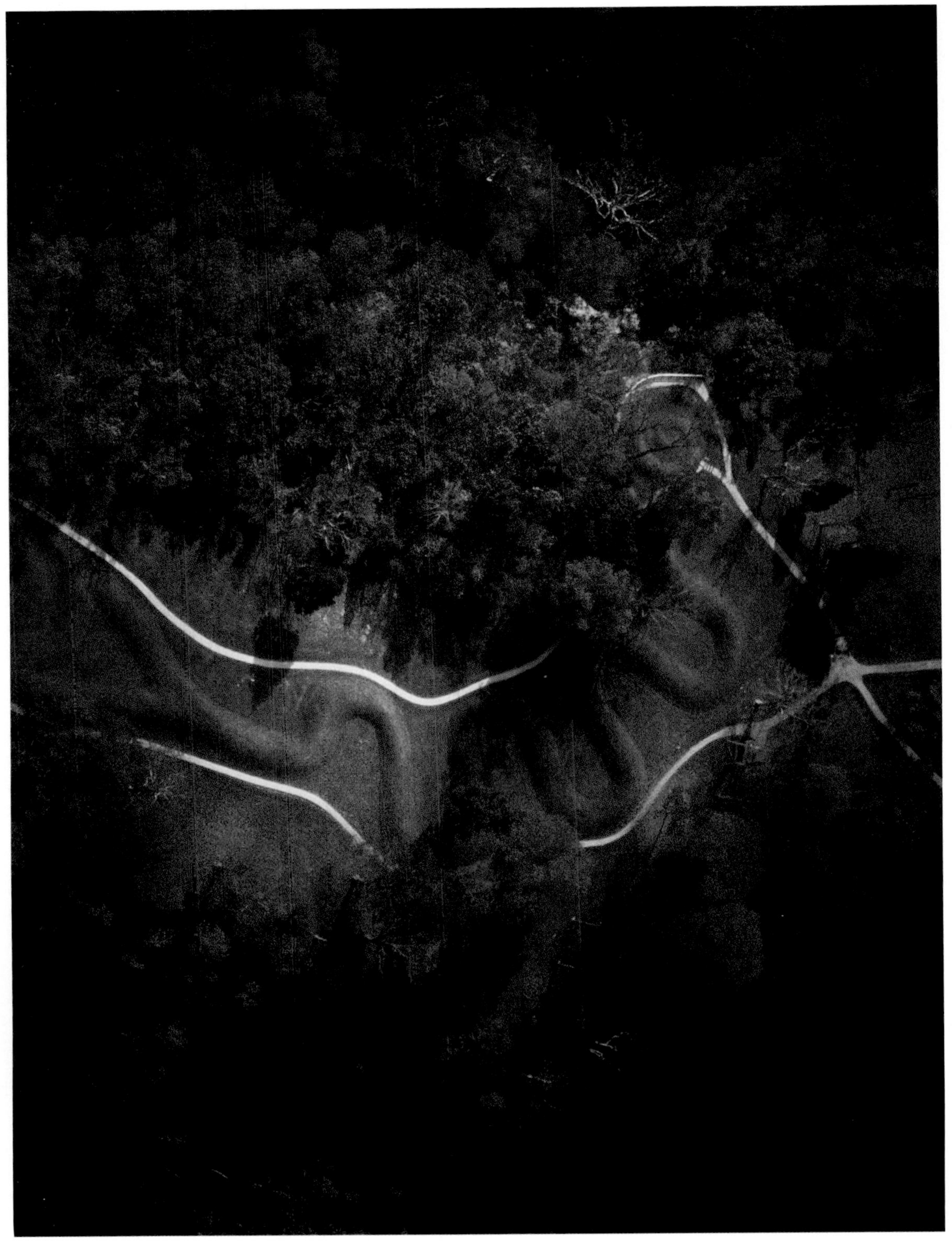

The Great Serpent Mound wriggles for a quarter mile across a southern Ohio cliff. Built by Woodland Indians some 2,000 years ago, its purpose remains unknown.

INDEX

Boldface indicates illustrations

N

O

P

Q

R

S

T

ILLUSTRATION CREDITS

5, Frank & Helen Schreider; 8, Marshall Kalahari Expeditions; 14-15, Engraving by H. S. Sadd from a painting by T. H. Matteson; 17, Kermit Roosevelt/Library of Congress; 19 (UP), Library of Congress; 19 (CTR), AP/Wide World Photos; 19 (LO), AP/Wide World Photos/Cecil Stoughton; 20-21, Frank & Helen Schreider; 23, Eliot Elisofon; 24-25, Tor Eigeland/Black Star; 26, AP/Wide World Photos; 27, W. Robert Moore; 28-29, Winfield I. Parks, Jr.; 31, Ted Spiegel; 33, Winfield I. Parks, Jr.; 34 (UP), Ted Spiegel; 34 (LO LE), Ted Spiegel; 34 (CTR RT), Dean Conger; 34 (LO RT), Ted Spiegel; 36-37, Michael Nichols, NGS; 39, Hugo Van Lawick; 40, Jay Matternes; 41, Hugo Van Lawick; 42-43, Jay Matternes; 45, Michael Nichols, NGS; 50-51, Colonial Williamsburg Foundation, Painting by James Peale; 53, United States Capitol Rotunda, Painting by John Trumbull; 54-55, National Center for the American Revolution, Painting by William B. T. Trego; 58-59, William L. Allen; 61, National Air and Space Museum, Smithsonian Institution; 63, Library of Congress, LC-USZ62-44602; 65, Victor R. Boswell, Jr.; 66-67, Gordon Gahan; 69-73, George F. Mobley; 74-75, Mark R. Godfrey; 77, Charles Deas, Indian Group, 1845, Oil on canvas, 14 1/8 x 16 1/2 inches, Amon Carter Museum, Fort Worth, Texas, 1980.42; 78, National Museum of American History, Smithsonian Institution; 79, Library of Congress, LC-USZ62-66856; 84-85, George F. Mobley; 87, Tor Eigeland/Black Star; 88-89, Thomas J. Abercrombie; 91, Victor Englebert; 92-93, Ted Spiegel; 95, Louis S. Glanzman; 97, Ted Spiegel; 98-99, Dixson Library, State Library of New South Wales; 101, Luis Marden; 103-104, Gordon Gahan; 106-107, David Alan Harvey; 109, David Alan Harvey; 110 (UP), Otis Imboden; 110 (LO)-113, David Alan Harvey; 118-123 (UP), George F. Mobley; 123 (LO), James P. Blair; 124-125, Sam Abell; 127, Sam Abell; 128-129, David Doubilet; 131, Sam Abell; 132-133, Joel Sartore; 135, Paul Chesley/NationalGeographicStock.com; 136-137, Chris Johns, NGS; 139 (UP), Carr Clifton/Minden Pictures; 139 (LO), Dennis Flaherty; 140-141, Tom Bean/CORBIS; 143, G. Brad Lewis/Getty Images; 144, Carr Clifton/Minden Pictures; 145, Bruce Dale; 147, Carr Clifton/Minden Pictures; 152-153, Bates Littlehales; 155, Bruce Dale; 157 (UP), The Mariners' Museum, Newport News, Virginia; 157 (LO), David Knudsen; 158-159, James P. Blair; 161, Linda Bartlett; 162, James P. Blair; 165, Jonathan Blair; 166-167, Gary Ladd; 169, William L. Allen and Warren Hill, Kitt Peak National Observatory/NOAO/AURA/NSF; 171, David L. Moore, Kitt Peak National Observatory/NOAO/AURA/NSF; 172, George F. Mobley; 173, James P. Blair; 174-175, Mark R. Godfrey; 177, Georg Gerster; 178-181, Mark R. Godfrey; 186-187, Guy Mary-Rousseliere, OMI, Educational Development Center; 189, Harald Schultz; 191, Eiji Miyazawa/Black Star; 192, Marshall Kalahari Expeditions; 194-198, Ira Block; 199, Gordon Gahan; 200, Nick Kelsh; 202-203, George F. Mobley; 205, Paul Chesley; 207, Georg Gerster; 208 (UP), Gordon Gahan; 208 (LO LE), Paul Chesley; 208 (CTR RT), Georg Gerster; 208 (LO RT), James P. Blair; 210-211, Annie Griffiths Belt; 213, Carr Clifton; 214 (UP), Nebraska State Historical Society; 214 (LO), Library of Congress, LC-USZ62-48427; 215, Frans Lanting; 217, Tom Till Photography.

THE WORLD & ALL THAT IS IN IT

Published by the National Geographic Society
John M. Fahey, Jr., President and Chief Executive Officer
Gilbert M. Grosvenor, Chairman of the Board
Tim T. Kelly, President, Global Media Group
John Q. Griffin, Executive Vice President; President, Publishing
Nina D. Hoffman, Executive Vice President; President, Book Publishing Group

Prepared by the Book Division
Barbara Brownell Grogan, Vice President and Editor in Chief
Marianne R. Koszorus, Director of Design
Carl Mehler, Director of Maps
R. Gary Colbert, Production Director
Jennifer A. Thornton, Managing Editor
Meredith C. Wilcox, Administrative Director, Illustrations

Staff for This Book
Susan Tyler Hitchcock, Editor
Vickie Donovan, Illustrations Editor
Peggy Archambault, Art Director
Linda Johansson, Designer
Suzanne Poole, Researcher
John M. Thompson, Contributing Writer
Richard S. Wain, Production Project Manager
Marshall Kiker, Illustrations Specialist

Manufacturing and Quality Management
Christopher A. Liedel, Chief Financial Officer
Phillip L. Schlosser, Vice President
Chris Brown, Technical Director
Nicole Elliott, Manager
Rachel Faulise, Manager

ISBN: 978-1-4262-0352-7
ISBN: 978-1-4262-0353-4 (deluxe ed.)

The National Geographic Society is one of the world's largest nonprofit scientific and educational organizations. Founded in 1888 to "increase and diffuse geographic knowledge," the Society works to inspire people to care about the planet. It reaches more than 325 million people worldwide each month through its official journal, *National Geographic*, and other magazines; National Geographic Channel; television documentaries; music; radio; films; books; DVDs; maps; exhibitions; school publishing programs; interactive media; and merchandise. National Geographic has funded more than 9,000 scientific research, conservation and exploration projects and supports an education program combating geographic illiteracy. For more information, visit nationalgeographic.com.

For more information, please call 1-800-NGS LINE (647-5463) or write to the following address:

National Geographic Society
1145 17th Street N.W.
Washington, D.C. 20036-4688 U.S.A.

Visit us online at www.nationalgeographic.com

For information about special discounts for bulk purchases, please contact National Geographic Books Special Sales: ngspecsales@ngs.org

For rights or permissions inquiries, please contact National Geographic Books Subsidiary Rights: ngbookrights@ngs.org

Library of Congress Cataloging-in-Publication Data
The world & all that is in it : four decades of the National Geographic special collection / National Geographic Society.
p. cm.
Includes index.
ISBN 978-1-4262-0352-7 -- ISBN 978-1-4262-0353-4 (deluxe ed.)
1. Historical geography. I. National Geographic Society (U.S.) II. Title: World and all that is in it.
G141.W67 2008
910--dc22
2008023140

Printed in U.S.A.

09/RRDW/1